D0205254

CHILDREN AND THEIR CARETAKERS

transaction/**Society** Book Series

CHILDREN AND THEIR CARETAKERS

edited by
Norman K. Denzin

Transaction Books
New Brunswick, New Jersey
Distributed by E.P. Dutton & Company

Mitchell Memorial Library
Mississippi State University

478531

Unless otherwise indicated, the essays in this book originally appeared in *trans*action/**Society** magazine

Copyright © 1973
Transaction, Inc.

All rights reserved. No part of this publication may be reproduced or transmitted in any form or by any means, electronic or mechanical, including photocopy, recording or any information storage and retrieval system, without prior permission in writing from the publisher.

Transaction Books
Rutgers University
New Brunswick, New Jersey 08903

Library of Congress Catalog Card Number: 72-91470
ISBN: 0-87855-062-3 (cloth); 0-87855-559-5 (paper)

Printed in the United States of America

Contents

Preface

For the past decade, *trans*action, and now Society, has dedicated itself to the task of reporting the strains and conflicts within the American system. But the magazine has done more than this. It has pioneered in social programs for changing the social order, offered the kind of analysis that has permanently restructured the terms of the "dialogue" between peoples and publics, and offered the sort of prognosis that makes for real alterations in economic and political policies directly affecting our lives.

The work done in the magazine has crossed disciplinary boundaries. This represents much more than simple cross-disciplinary "team efforts." It embodies rather a recognition that the social world cannot be easily carved into neat academic disciplines; that, indeed, the study of the experience of blacks in American ghettos, or the manifold uses and abuses of agencies of law enforcement, or the sorts of overseas policies that lead to the celebration of some dictatorships and the condemnation of others, can best be examined from many viewpoints and from the vantage points of many disciplines.

The editors of Society magazine are now making available in permanent form the most important work done in the magazine, supplemented in some cases by additional materials edited to reflect the tone and style developed over the years by *trans*action. Like the magazine, this series of books demonstrates the superiority of starting with real world problems and searching out practical solutions, over the zealous guardianship of professional boundaries. Indeed, it is precisely this approach that has elicited enthusiastic support from leading American social scientists, many of whom are represented among the editors of these volumes.

The subject matter of these books concerns social changes and social policies that have aroused the long-standing needs and present-day anxieties of us all. These changes are in organizational lifestyles, concepts of human ability and intelligence, changing patterns of norms and morals, the relationship of social conditions to physical and biological environments, and in the status of social science with respect to national policy making. The editors feel that many of these articles have withstood the test of time, and match in durable interest the best of available social science literature. This collection of essays, then, attempts to address itself to immediate issues without violating the basic insights derived from the classical literature in the various fields of social science.

As the political crises of the sixties have given way to the economic crunch of the seventies, the social scientists involved as editors and authors of this series have gone beyond observation of critical areas, and have entered into the vital and difficult tasks of explanation and interpretation. They have defined issues in a way that makes solutions possible. They have provided answers as well as asked the right questions. These books, based as they are upon the best materials from *trans*-action/Society magazine, are dedicated to highlighting social problems alone, and beyond that, to establishing guidelines for social solutions based on the social sciences.

The remarkable success of the book series to date is indicative of the need for such "fastbacks" in college course work and, no less, in the everyday needs of busy people who have not surrendered the need to know, nor the lively sense required to satisfy such knowledge needs. It is also plain that what superficially appeared as a random selection of articles on the basis of subject alone, in fact, represented a careful concern for materials that are addressed to issues at the shank and marrow of society. It is the distillation of the best of these, systematically arranged, that appears in these volumes.

THE EDITORS
*trans*action/Society

The Politics of Childhood

NORMAN K. DENZIN

Every society creates a period between birth and maturity and consigns to that period persons who have yet to acquire the attributes of adulthood. Such persons may be called small adults, infants, children, adolescents, little people, troublemakers or simply incompetents. The United States, like other industrialized societies, has constructed and politically institutionalized a series of age-graded phases through which its young pass. Associated with each of these phases are socially approved institutions which are directed to transform the young into more competent individuals: preschools, day care centers, head start programs, elementary and secondary schools, colleges, trade schools, finishing schools, summer church camps and institutions for the delinquent and wayward adolescent. These institutions are inextricably interwoven with the society's political system. Most if not all are legitimated

—accredited—by the political system, and federal funds support their long-range programs. Thus, the politics of childhood quickly translate into the politics of education and socialization—for to be a child or the caretaker of a child is to be a political creature, to be a person who acts in a number of ways that complement or challenge broader political ideologies and beliefs. Children, then, are political products—they are created and defined and acted upon in political terms.

Americans, in their sometimes confused attempts to produce better children, have relegated their responsibilities of child care and education to the political system; and these responsibilities, in turn, have generally been acted out in the schools. But politicians often undertake to legislate their conceptions of what a proper child should or should not be with little if any attention to the interests of children. Educators translate political and legal directives into educational programs, often in ways that serve their best interests, not the child's. Parents, lacking a solid political base, are seldom able to consensually organize themselves as a counterpower block; they act in ways that reflect their own self-interest, or in ways that will potentially benefit their children, instead of the children of other parents. Caught between these competing forces, without a clear spokesman for their collective position, children find themselves talked about, legislated over, tested and scrutinized by society's experts: by its social workers, educational psychologists, probation officials, judges, courts, teachers, sociologists, anthropologists, politicians and psychiatrists.

It is time to call into question America's theories of children and child development. It is my intention in this introduction to discuss how a society's theories of childhood and adulthood become entrenched in the ways it educates its children. But first it will be necessary to define what a child is and to show how the perspective of the caretaker is embodied in our definition of the child.

Producing a Child

Children are *social objects*—objects without intrinsic meaning. To be defined as a child is to be a child. All social objects, whether ephemeral like democracy and belief in God, or concrete like chairs, typewriters or people, are social products. Their specific meaning arises out of the behaviors people direct toward them. Children are like other social objects in this respect. There are as many different types of children as there are people defining what a child is. The readings in this volume describe battered children, good children, delinquent children, hyperactive children, slow learners, white children, black children, Indian children, poor and rich children. But, while diverse definitions are to be encouraged, American parents, educators and politicians have blithely assumed that if only the right set of experts could be located and trained, right and proper children would be produced. Thus, without malice they legitimate day care centers for the urban poor, support separate and unequal educational programs in their high schools, discourage interracial dating, and encourage the destruction of distinct ethnic and racial identities.

If children are social products, they are *cultural products* as well. Every social group with a distinct cultural awareness attempts to legislate what to them is a proper concept of children and adulthood. The Amish, for example, eschew dominant American values, balk at compulsory education, and encourage their children to go only as far as the eighth grade in schools managed by the Amish. By the age of two, the Amish young cease to be children: they are treated like small adults and are encouraged to assume an adult's responsibilities. Similar support for the cultural product assumption can be drawn from the practices of other ethnic groups. Traditional orthodox Jewish families, for instance, attempt to instill in their children a set of values different from those found in Italian, German, Moravian, French, Polish, Spanish-American or Japanese-American families.

As we have already indicated, children are *political* products, but in a special sense. If politics is broadly construed as a battle over scarce resources and over the allocation of power and authority, then children can be seen as pawns in a larger political arena, which extends beyond the closed havens of the family to the preschool, the grade school and the high school. Their caretakers argue and debate over who the child shall be and what he or she shall become. In these political debates children are collectively bargained over, priced and sold to the lowest bidder. For example, some metropolitan high schools let contracts to educational resource corporations in exchange for a promise that the corporation can raise the IQ, reading and mathematics test scores of each child 15 to 20 points over a year's time. Social workers, teachers and politicians often use children and their welfare as an excuse for gaining more personal and institutional power.

President Nixon recognized this fact in his most recent veto of the national day care program. He pandered to the silent majority's fears that their traditional family systems would be destroyed if national day care centers were instituted. To Nixon this program represented a challenge to the American nuclear family and as such constituted a radical departure from traditional child-rearing. It signaled, he feared, a movement to communal modes of child care. That Americans have had some form of extended, extrafamilial child care for at least 150 years went unnoticed in his public statement. Nixon and other critics have overlooked such diverse forms of child care as hired babysitters, summer church camps for children, and expensive boarding and finishing schools for the economic and political elite. And of course they have ignored nineteenth-century forms of child care such as orphanages, reformatories and the "putting out system" in England. Had they not, they might have noticed that some nineteenth-century forms have twentieth-century parallels: *crèches* in Russia and England functioned much like contemporary day care centers for the urban poor.

Children are *historical products*. This fact was recognized by Phillipe Ariès in *Centuries of Childhood* where he argued that children as they are known in the contemporary western world did not come into existence until the mid-sixteenth century. Peter Lasslet and Richard Sennett have criticized certain aspects of Ariès's research, but certainly prior to this time, particularly in France, children were considered small adults.

Every social group asserts through its actions toward children what a child is, and this assertion reflects the group's particular place in history. Thus, French peasants view children differently than do their middle-class and aristocratic counterparts. And ghetto blacks of a Muslim persuasion hold views of their children which are quite unlike those held by upper-class blacks or middle-class Italians. Furthermore, each group attempts to mold the school setting to fit its concepts of child and adult. Recent challenges to the present school system from "free-school" proponents display an inclination to redefine currently held concepts. John Holt and Paul Goodman, for example, argue that today's child will not be like children of the past. To challenge the idea that what a child is today is what children have always been and will always be is to challenge long-standing institutional arrangements.

If children are social, cultural, political and historical products it can also be argued that they are *economic products*. For Americans, membership in the extended developmental period called childhood is an economic luxury, a luxury that is denied the urban poor, and nearly all nonwhite racial and ethnic groups. (Ariés's research also supports this proposition: aristocratic or elitist concepts of childhood emerge in societies before lower-class or ethnic minority views.)

Groups which lack regular access to a stable set of economic resources simply cannot afford to send their children to expensive preschools, to hire babysitters, and to give their sons and daughters large allowances. In the typical pattern of child caretaking in the black lower class, for example, a daughter ceases to be a child at the approximate age of seven and becomes a woman at the onset of menstruation. Joyce Ladner, in her sensitive study of the black adolescent female (*Tomorrow's Tomorrow: The Black Woman*), reveals that the eldest daughter in the black family automatically becomes the chief caretaker for the younger brother or sister. Similarly the young black male, as David Schultz and Lee Rainwater have shown, is expected at the onset of adolescence to make his own money and earn his keep in the family. Thus, for many black males living in the ghetto, schools are dysfunctional in the attainment of manhood.

Members of the white middle class, on the other

hand, have exploited their economic advantages. They encourage education at an early age, systematically deny their young access to adult rights and obligations, and prolong childhood through the period of high school and usually college. For them a child becomes a man or a woman only after regular entry into the economic workplace and only after marriage. For the woman, adulthood may not be gained until the birth of a legitimate child.

It can be argued, finally, that children are *scientific products*. Here we have only to compare the children studied by Pavlov and Watson with the offspring examined by Freud, Hull, Skinner, Piaget, Bruner, Gessell, Spock and the modern behaviorists. Each of these scientists views children differently. Each proposes different developmental sequences; each shortens or prolongs the period of childhood; each offers a different explanation for good and bad children. Their theories have been debated in political arenas, differentially incorporated into textbooks for grade school and high school teachers, and each has found its way into preschool and day care centers. Fads and fashions in the social and psychological sciences quickly appear in schools, in popular magazines, and eventually find their place on the bookshelves of concerned parents.

If there is one quality shared by all of these theories of children and human behavior, it is that they fail to see the human being in active, interactionist terms. They pay little attention to the fact that humans are symbol manipulating organisms and as such are capable of engaging in *mindful, self-conscious activity*. By proposing that the child is responsive to fixed innate needs or drives, or by suggesting that the personality is firmly established in the first five years of life, these theories fail to grasp the shifting, unfolding, creative aspects of all human behavior, from birth to death. These theories of learning which view the child in passive terms have been systematically translated into theories of education. Teachers, not children, are seen as experts on all matters. Children are thought to be unreliable objects, who must be actively controlled, tested repeatedly, never given a say in what they are taught, and rewarded for passive acceptance of the teacher's and the school's point of view. These theories of learning, then, complement and support the broader position that children are incompetent social beings.

Alternative views, such as the progressive education movement led by Dewey, James, Mead and others, have seldom been given a chance to prove themselves. More often than not the central thesis of the progressive education movement—that children can engage in self-conscious behaviors if stimulated to do so—has been exploited to the educator's advantage. Consequently, while experimental laboratories for children from preschool on were established at many nationally prominent universities, these settings were quickly transformed into laboratories where the psychologist and social psychologist could exploit his or her captive audience for research purposes. Their original intent—to present the child with a stimulating learning environment—was subverted for "scientific" purposes.

A Brief Digression on Theories of Child Development

In general it can be said that theories of child development fall into one of three broad categories: structural, psychological or interactional. Psychosocial developmental schemes (Piaget's is the most well elaborated) propose that age per se is associated with and calls out certain fixed responses on the part of children. Thus, children pass through a variety of age-graded developmental phases: autistic, egocentric, sociocentric. Children may not act like accountable social interactants until after the age of seven. Until that age Piaget suggests they engage in egocentric conversations and parallel, not conjoint, play; in short, they do not take account of one another in reciprocal terms. Evidence presented later in this volume (Denzin, Joffe, Hamblin) calls these psychosocial schemes into doubt. It is proposed, instead, that by the age of three children are able systematically to take one another's roles, present definitions of self, construct elaborate games and manipulate adults into desired directions. The interactionist view of child development, which is my position, argues that neither age nor sociostructural variables such as race, religion and ethnicity, will directly call out fixed responses or developmental skills in childhood. Rather it is the nature of the interactive experiences children are exposed to that shapes their behavioral styles and abilities. Children, then, must be approached seriously and taken seriously. Translating this proposition into research and into the educational arena suggests that schools should be constructed so as to allow children to actively construct and take part in their own learning experiences. It demands that the researcher actively attempt to enter the child's world of behavior and thought. Experimental paradigms, fixed interview questions and standardized IQ tests do not enter that world. Schools as presently constructed reflect mixes between the structural and the psychosocial view of childhood. The readings in this volume call for a new perspective, here labeled interactionist.

Clarifying the Status of Children and Youth

In general the view one holds of any object reflects the relationship one has with that object. Politicians view children politically. Parents see them in moral dimensions. Social scientists value children as sources of data for their theories of human behavior. Children are thus confronted with competing definitions of who they are. The fact that there are no consistent definitions of children and childhood accounts, in part, for the enormous variations in "childlike" behavior among children. And it can be argued, as Lemert and Lerman suggest, that bad children—delinquents—are simply acting out their rejections of the usual concepts of who they are.

Children are complex beings. They are continually confronted with competing and conflicting definitions which span cultural, historical, political, economic, social and scientific dimensions. The sheer complexity of these definitions increases the probability that *no* clear-cut image of children and childhood will emerge. While Americans make social and legal distinctions between infants and children (birth to five years), children and adults (five years to 16, 18 or 21) and adults (married and stably employed), they have no clear image of what kind of person one should be at six, eight, ten, 15, 18 or 21. Nor do they make any systematic sexual and racial differentiations. Accordingly, the child's self-definition directly reflects the definitions of childhood he or she confronts on a daily basis, from conversations with peers, siblings, parents and teachers. Images of youth, children and childish behavior presented in the press and mass media, on records, in movies or television programs to a considerable degree also shape his self-definition. To be a child in America today is to be in an ambiguously defined status category. In some respects, however, these diverse definitions of children and childhood are functional and useful. Those who occupy positions that are ill-defined have greater latitude in defining who they are and who they wish to be. The problem is that the current situation neither systematically rewards nor sanctions children for selecting one set of definitions over any other.

Despite their attempts to give massive attention to their young, American adults have only complicated the growing up of their children. Adults quarrel and debate over which scientific theory of childhood is correct. They challenge and disparage the social organization of schools. They ridicule the fads and fashions of the young, yet incorporate into their own wardrobes long hair, bell bottom and flare pants, miniskirts and see-through blouses. They mock the symbolic leaders of youth, yet buy the records of Dylan, the Beatles and the Stones. They recoil at the thought of their children smoking marijuana, yet drink to excess themselves, and perhaps on occasion smoke a joint if it is passed to them. They deplore sexual intercourse before marriage and forget their own sexual experiences as youths, and perhaps overlook their own sexual promiscuity after marriage. Adults ridicule the position of children and youth, yet take from children that which pleases and withhold from youth those prizes which would confer the sacred status and rights of adulthood—the right of self-control, the right to give and take at will, the right to make contracts and so forth.

The status of children could be clarified legally, and has been in some instances, as when the state defines what a child is. But legal definitions alone will not resolve the meaning of children and childhood because these meanings must be established and reestablished every time children confront adults. Legal definitions must be acted on by individuals in their daily encounters and confrontations with one another, encounters that will be different for each participant. The meaning of any object, then, must be established every time one confronts it, and modifications of the legal code alone will not solve the problem.

Economic solutions are often sought: "If we only had more money for our schools the problem would be cleared up." But economic measures work only insofar as people commit themselves to such measures. New schools, more teachers, higher salaries and better buses will not in themselves clarify the status of children, nor will these expenditures give children new role models or better educations. They only cost money and obfuscate the real issue, which is: *What stance do Americans want to take towards their children and their schools?*

Recently a romantic solution has been proposed. Like most romantic solutions it is quite simple: return to a less complex, more rural society—take our children out of the urban rat race. Like the economic proposals, this solution ignores what adults want children to be and simply states a new definition of what an adult is.

Some Proposals

It appears that some headway might be gained in the educational arena if those persons most central to education—children and youth—were given more of a say in their daily programs. Legal and economic proposals represent attempts to legislate and act on behalf of children but give no credence to the child's position and point of view. We are conducting a crusade *against*, not for, children.

If Americans are to successfully change the status of the young, if they are to improve the character of mass education, they must systematically seek out the thoughts of youth, take them seriously, and give youth an active hand in the determination of their own fate.

They must recognize that current definitions of youth and childhood are largely derogatory and contradictory in nature. Good children have always known this and have usually exploited it to their best advantage.

Massive federal expenditures for new and better schools might better be used in the economic workplace so that children could be given economically respectable jobs, not makework during summer vacations. The Philadelphia Plan, for example, attempts to place high school students in work organizations during the academic year so that they may gain on-the-spot experience in a variety of occupational pursuits. Here students serve in a capacity similar to the traditional apprentice role in labor unions and are paid for their work commensurate with their output.

Regular electoral procedures should be developed for hearing the opinions of children and youth. Here schools and local communities could hold regular elections for youth in which a fixed number of persons would be elected as minority and majority representatives of the under-18 constituency.

Conventions at the local, state and national level (similar to the annual White House Conference on Children) could be held and would be attended by elected political figures and perhaps representatives from parent groups, educators and the social sciences. This proposal would bring together on a regular, face-to-face basis the chief actors in the educational arena: children, parents, educators, politicians, social scientists and social workers. It would have the main function of at least publicly airing the perspectives of those most intimately involved in the politics of childhood.

Proposals such as these presume that social change starts and ends in the immediate world of everyday social experience: in the worlds of childhood and adulthood; in schools, on playgrounds and street corners; in homes, families and neighborhoods. But alteration in the relative situations of children and their caretakers must begin in the closed interactive worlds of the family—in the home. Here parents directly confront, reward and sanction their children for approved and disapproved behaviors. Here, initially at least, children try out alternative views of themselves, their peers and their parents. Here children report back on their experiences with teachers, principals, social workers and counselors.

Each family can be viewed as a distinct social unit that values things not valued by other families and sanctions behaviors not rewarded elsewhere. Each family is a distinct political, cultural and historical entity, whose distinctiveness should be respected, encouraged and cultivated in schools and neighborhoods. Parents, as the most immediate caretakers of children, must assert their obligations in this regard, and not give up easily those values and definitions they cherish and reward. The immediate world of the family must be taken seriously by those in education and politics.

More direct lines of accountability between families and schools must be established such as direct parental observation of classroom activities, parental consultation in program revisions, and student evaluations of teachers and curricula. Regular forums for involving students and PTA in the operation of schools must be developed.

Ways of expanding and confirming the competence of children and youth must be developed. While most theories of education rest on the assumption that children are incompetent (as indicated above and in several essays in this collection), this proposal assumes that any person will be as competent as he or she is permitted to be. Barring massive mental retardation or physical disabilities, most persons can function at highly complex levels—if they are motivated, encouraged and permitted to do so. I am not calling here for a lionization of children (a stance which is romantically movitated and only encourages more childlike behaviors on the part of children). Rather I am proposing that children be accorded the rights to act like adults, be given the responsibility that comes with those rights, and be given access to the resources to organize and act out such rights. This suggests a need to reevaluate the current age-IQ structure of schools. If, as some suggest, preschools are now functioning as kindergartens, then perhaps children who attend preschool should be moved directly to the first grade. Furthermore, children should be encouraged to struggle against the age-structured basis of classroom learning. The assumption that fourth graders know more than third graders works only as long as teachers, parents and third and fourth graders believe it works. There is nothing about the age of a child, again barring mental deficiency, that prohibits that child learning at a higher level. Society, not age per se, requires such distinction.

Perhaps the entire educational process could be defined as a creative, exciting experience rather than obligatory drudgery. Smaller, decentralized schools and classrooms would encourage more open interaction between students and teachers, and would permit teachers to break out of their formal role. Competition in classrooms over grades might be replaced with a more open appreciation for the learning experience with awareness that an emphasis on grades leads, as Howard Becker has observed, to a commitment to *making the grade* rather than learning. The progressive education movement, for example, encouraged students to set their own pace, to pursue their own special interests and abilities, and to join together in a sociable fashion in the pursuit of learning. More recent movements toward the so-called "open classroom" represent other modest steps in this direction.

The last proposal assumes that schools might best be viewed as complex organizations with multiple paths or tracks to the top. Classes could be organized with children from diverse age-groups where presence in the class is based on special interest or competence, not IQ score or grade average. The usual model of tracking, as Walter Schafer and his associates indicate in this volume, rests on a two-track model: bright white kids in the best track, dull nonwhite kids in the worst track. The tracking system thus mirrors and perpetuates broader lines of stratification in the outside society. The form of tracking proposed here would disregard age, sex and racial attributes and simply place children of whatever age or sex in classes which most interest them and in which they have special skills. Student skills in this regard could be assessed through several procedures. Students could be asked to designate those study topics they find most stimulating. Classroom instructors and counselors could be encouraged to develop alternative measures of study ability (e.g. self-report, scores on new types of objective tests, teacher reports, parental input and so forth). In general I am proposing a more open and flexible system of placing students in those courses and settings where they would be most stimulated. Schools, among other institutions in our society, teach children to fail and to accept their place in society. The readings in this volume reinforce the perspective advanced in this essay; I have organized them into four categories.

Part 1. Learning and Getting it Right at an Early Age

Rolando Juarez has argued that schools and day care centers teach children how to be children. To get it right at an early age is to learn the role of child as soon as possible. The caretaker's job is greatly eased once children know what behaviors are expected of them. To get it right is to know, as Jules Henry argues, that one is expected to be docile and accepting of the teacher's position, playful when play is demanded, sleepy when it is time to go to bed, hungry when meals are served, interested in reading when reading time rolls around. *Not to get it right* at an early age is to place oneself in an untenable position—in a position where whether you want to or not, you must get it right. Thus, if necessary, schools will, as Charles Witter shows, administer amphetamines and stimulants to "hyperactive" children —those who have balked at getting it right.

Estelle Fuchs, in the first chapter in this section, supports Juarez's argument. Teachers develop ideologies which keep children in their place. When confronted with students who score badly on reading tests, the teacher must reconcile these failures with her own abilities. She does not blame herself, but instead claims that she simply has a bad batch of students; if they were good, their test scores would be good. The rhetoric of student failure is communicated to young teachers by old hands. Children from the inner-city ghetto areas are defined as failures before they have a chance to prove themselves. Blame is placed on the home environment— on the parents—and teachers successfully (in their own minds and in the minds of politicians) absolve themselves of any responsibility. Teachers expect certain students to fail and thereby set in motion a self-fulfilling prophecy that insures failure.

Robert Hamblin and associates provide an important and provocative challenge to the situation observed by

Fuchs. The school experience for many hyperactive, autistic and nonwhite ghetto children is one of "getting the teacher," not "learning." Getting the teacher involves taunting her, refusing to read, throwing objects across the classroom, fighting and shouting. These activities, Hamblin argues, are reinforced by the teacher. She shouts and yells at these students, and claims that they are unteachable. Thus, teachers produce and reinforce negative schoolroom behaviors on the part of "bad" students. Through a simple, yet ingenious application of modern learning and exchange theories, Hamblin was able to raise the reading and IQ scores of autistic, hyperactive and Afro-American ghetto children. They instructed teachers not to reward the aggressive "get the teacher" behaviors of students and to reward behaviors which expanded the child's reading and talking abilities. And they succeeded.

We have here an important alternative to the situations described by Fuchs, Witter and the Silberbergs. For while Witter reports large-scale use of Ritalin in American schools to control hyperactivity, Hamblin was able to modify the behaviors of hyperactive children through a simple stimulus-response, reward-punishment program. The Silberbergs extend Hamblin's position that bad children can learn in schools. They argue that schools are presently organized so as to take any excitement out of learning. The persistent emphasis on reading rituals, tests and examinations effectively takes learning out of the classroom. Reading should be taught like any other skill—not made a fetish of. John Dewey's position, "that books be thrown out of the classroom so we can get down to the business of educating children," bears repeating, especially in light of Hamblin's research.

Part 2. Preschools and Day Care Centers

Schools are organized so as not to take young children seriously. They are to be taught to read, write and count; if they do not behave like teachers want them to they will either be drugged or placed in second-class educational settings. Joffe reverses the usual view of young children. Building on observations in one preschool she shows that by as early as three years of age the young child is able to establish and communicate sophisticated definitions of his situation. Through games, battles, costumes, songs and rituals, children produce in the preschool a social organization that cries out to be taken seriously. They make territorial designations, develop friendships, compliment and put one another down. In short, like any other interactor, the young child develops a social world, a social organization of self and others which reflects his or her stance toward that world.

My own essay, "The Work of Little Children," also argues that young children need to be taken seriously. While adults typically see young children in nonserious, playful terms, my preschool observations indicate that small children *work at* constructing reality. They are involved in such important problems as friendship and language construction. Their games, better seen as focused worklike behaviors, reveal attempts to order their social experiences.

Steiner shows how welfare mothers and their children have become the favorite tinker toys of the political system. Their wishes, hopes and aspirations have seldom been solicited, let alone taken seriously. He argues that before the national government legislates new proposals for day care centers the interests of the involved public should be sought out.

Corey and Cohen's findings are perhaps the most distressing. Without public consultation the Department of Defense has instituted a series of military summer programs for young ghetto males. The enemy within ceases to be Communism. It reappears in the form of poverty, delinquency and broken homes in the urban slums. To battle the enemy, the Army, the Navy, the Air Force and the Marines each summer now ship to their bases around the country large numbers of black youths, and during intensive drilling programs instruct them in the ways of war and armed defense. The Department of Defense thus adds yet another form of schooling to the American scene. Not only do we have preschools for the rich and the poor, headstart programs for the dull, Montessori schools for the elite, day care centers for the nonwhite, but now we have public military academies for the recalcitrant, delinquent, male adolescent.

Part 3. Schools and Finding Your Place

Children find their caretakers everywhere—in schools, on playgrounds and street corners, at home and in the neighborhood. All children, regardless of sex, race, class or income find themselves abused by society's educational systems. Schools are organized to keep students in their place and to socialize those who refuse to accept their failure. Until the child-caretaker relationship is reexamined and systematically restructured, the conditions described earlier will continue.

This fact is clearly established by Schafer, Olexa and Polk. Contrary to the common belief that the American educational system is the most democratic in the world, their data show systematic efforts to institute two educational programs in high schools: one for the college-bound student, one for the dropout and the failure. Students in the college-bound program seldom receive grades below B, while students in the second track seldom receive As or Bs. Like Fuchs, Schafer, Olexa and Polk document the fact that schools are organized on the basis of a self-fulfilling prophecy. Good students will always do well, bad students will always do badly. As a consequence, students thrown into the second track find themselves in a situation where "getting the teacher," not "learning" is encouraged and rewarded.

A.D. Fisher shifts our focus from American schools and the plight of the dropout, to the educational plight of North American Indians in the Canadian school system. Canadian schools, he notes, have largely adopted American philosophies of education, as indicated by their efforts to employ standardized tests (California Achievement Test, etc.) and to develop separate programs for the good and the bad student, in this case the Anglo student and the Indian student. Schools and schooling, he argues, function as a rite of passage; if one successfully passes through school the doors of opportunity are thrown open. Failure to achieve in schools is typically explained through recourse to one of three theories. First, the dropout is said to be a juvenile delinquent who has been inadequately socialized. Second, the dropout comes from a bad family situation. The family and its culture are at fault. Third, the dropout is alienated because he or she lacks access to legitimate channels of opportunity. This alienation is funneled into illegitimate activities—into deviant behavior.

Fisher calls all of these theories into question and proposes an alternative. Students are not at fault, but the schools and their rites of passage which systematically derogate and punish students who do not "get it right." This accounts for the fate of Canadian Indians who start out ahead of their white peers on all tests, but by the age of adolescence fall far behind. The schools, Fisher proposes, are encouraging Indian students to become white men. In so doing they alienate the student from both white and Indian cultures. Schools, then, promote and produce the very deviance they so vehemently cry out against. The federal government, in turn, responds to the schools' ideological position by allocating more funds for better tracking programs for the second-class student.

Frank Petroni reveals the penetration of larger societal values regarding interactions between blacks and whites into the subcultures of the American high school. Interracial dating and marriage are thought inevitable by many integrationalists, but Petroni's data indicate that such behavior is now judged deviant and of questionable morality by high school students. Interracial dating occurred only between high status black athletes and white females; in no case did a white man date a black girl. The morality of the white woman was called into question in all cases and she and her partner found themselves without support from family, school or peer groups. It appears extremely unlikely that an *infused racial system* based on intermarriage between blacks and whites will soon appear in the United States. (The infused racial system, as defined by Sidney J. Kronus and Mauricio Solaun, is based on sanctioned inter-marriage between the races such that racial boundaries are so blurred as to be nearly nonexistent.) American values combined with the behavior of youth will not permit its development. Schools are admirably filling their functions as moral and political agencies of socialization.

Part 4. Bad Kids or Bad Parents?

The essays in this section shift our focus from schools, teachers and students to parents, children and the courts. Yet the problem remains. Who produces bad children? Earlier we showed that schools claim no fault in this process. Now we find that other systems of caretaking—the courts and social welfare agencies—similarly seek absolution. With impunity juvenile courts claim that their procedures in no way make criminals out of wayward adolescents. Lemert argues that the courts seek to succeed where parents have failed, by trying to replace the family and the peer group as a socializing agency. Their dubious success, at best, is documented by Lerman and Lemert. Working with a disease theory of deviance, the juvenile courts propose to remove the deviant child from a diseased environment (the culture of poverty, the disorganized home) and place him or her in a setting where positive mental health and socially sanctioned behaviors can grow and be nurtured.

Justice Abe Fortas (also quoted by Lemert) described the situation of the incarcerated delinquent, on the occasion of the *Gault* v. *Arizona* majority opinion, as follows:

> Instead of mother and father and sisters and brothers and friends and classmates, his world is peopled by guards, custodians, state employees, and "delinquents" confined with him for anything from waywardness to rape and homicide.

Only recently (*Gault* v. *Arizona*) have juveniles been accorded any of the legal rights of adults in the court system. This right, Lemert argues, is only a modest step towards the development of a humane court system for America's youth.

Paul Lerman's analysis of juvenile justice appropriately precedes Lemert's. He documents the degree to which adolescents are repeatedly defined and treated as deviant. The paradox here is that youth who engage in adult-like behaviors (such as sexual intercourse) are often regarded as delinquent (or sexually promiscuous) by the courts and welfare agencies. If their offenses are judged too serious they are incarcerated. Lerman's analysis reveals that Americans have not clearly decided what is acceptable behavior for teenagers. No clear rites of passage exist for entering adulthood and leaving childhood. Lacking any consensual direction, the courts and schools have taken over the responsibility of defining the boundaries; but they have done so without much consideration of the rights and wishes of parents and children.

Serapio Zalba documents the blight of the battered child and shows that such abuse is staggering in proportions (according to David G. Gil's research, between 6,000 and 7,000 cases annually). Beyond the scope of Zalba's work, but relevant to our thinking, is the question of who benefits from locating deviant parents. Ostensibly it is the child, but unpublished research by Reynaldo Rey Baca on the praxiology of social workers in the San Francisco Bay Area suggests that these practitioners develop a self-serving version of psychoanalysis to define who becomes (and why they become) an abusive parent. This perspective works best—if not in practice, in theory—on lower-class, nonwhite ethnic groups. Predictably, parents from these sectors of the population are most often categorized as abusive. Baca suggests that many abusive parents only do what all parents on occasion wish—that is, they physically control their child's behavior. Unfortunately, lower-class parents find that their misconduct is everyone's business. (These observations are also borne out in the research of Gil and Giovannoni and Billingsley and Kadushin, and in Leontine Young's informative *Wednesday's Children: A Study of Child Neglect and Abuse*.)

We find, then, that bad children and bad parents are moral products. We find too that our society has institutionalized a complex set of agencies and organizations to judge who are good and bad people. The readings in this volume suggest that *a good or bad child or parent is a person who has been so defined by some person, or social organization*. They have been labeled fit or unfit, college-bound, a dropout, hyperactive or autistic. Unfortunately, Americans from the middle-income sector have been too successful in securing the acceptance of their moral perspectives. They and their schools and social welfare agencies repeatedly establish the fact that bad parents and bad children do not come from "good" respectable families. That this moral perspective will change in the near future is doubtful. Too much is at stake; Wednesday's Child remains.

LEARNING AND
GETTING IT RIGHT
AT AN EARLY AGE

How Teachers Learn
to Help Children Fail

ESTELLE FUCHS

Ideally, public schools exist to educate the child. But a high percentage of pupils fail as early as the fifth or sixth grade, especially in the urban slums. For many children, the educational process bogs down at a time when it has barely begun, and educators and social scientists have proposed a number of theories to explain this high rate of failure among slum-school children. One of them is that the slum-school system's tacit belief that social conditions outside the school make such failures inevitable *does* make such failures inevitable.

How this expectation of failure affects the instruction of lower-class children and becomes a self-fulfilling prophecy is suggested in data collected by Hunter College's Project TRUE (Teacher Resources for Urban Education), a study that focused on the experiences of 14 fledgling teachers in New York's inner-city elementary schools. As part of the study, several new teachers tape-recorded accounts of their first-semester teaching experiences in "special service" schools—schools that invariably had high Negro or Puerto Rican enrollments, retarded reading levels among the students and constant discipline problems.

The following excerpts from one teacher's account show how the slum school gradually instills, in even the best-intentioned teacher, the prevailing rationale for its own failure: the idea that in the slum, it is the child and the family who fail, but never the school.

October 26. Mrs. Jones, the sixth-grade teacher, and I were discussing reading problems. I said, "I wonder about my children. They don't seem too slow; they seem average. Some of them even seem to be above average. I can't understand how they can grow up to be fifth- and sixth-graders and still be reading on the second-grade level. It seems absolutely amazing."

Mrs. Jones [an experienced teacher] explained about the environmental problems that these children have. "Some of them never see a newspaper. Some of them have never been on the subway. The parents are so busy having parties and things that they have no time for their children. They can't even take them to a museum or anything. It's very important that the teacher stress books."

Mrs. Jones tells her class, "If anyone asks you what you want for Christmas, you can say you want a book." She told me that she had a 6-1 class last year, and it was absolutely amazing how many children had never even seen a newspaper. They can't read Spanish either. So she said that the educational problem lies with the parents. They are the ones that have to be educated.

It's just a shame that the children suffer. This problem will take an awful lot to straighten it out. I guess it won't take one day or even a year; it will take time.

December 14. Here I am, a first-grade teacher. I get a great thrill out of these children being able to read but I often wonder, "Am I teaching them how to read or are they just stringing along sight words that they know?" I never had a course in college for teaching phonetics to children. In this school we have had conferences about it, but I really wish that one of the reading teachers would come in and specifically show me how to go about teaching phonetics. I have never gotten a course like this and it is a difficult thing, especially when there is a language barrier and words are quite strange to these children who can't speak English. How can they read English? We have a great responsibility on our shoulders and teachers should take these things seriously.

January 4. Something very, very important and different has happened to me in my school. It all happened the last week before the vacation on Tuesday. Mr. Frost, our principal, came over to me and asked if I would be willing to take over a second-grade class starting after the vacation. Well, I looked at him and I said, "Why?"

He told me briefly that the registers in the school have dropped and according to the board of education the school must lose a teacher. Apparently he was getting rid of a second-grade teacher and he wanted to combine two of the first-grade classes. The registers on the first grade were the lowest in the school, I believe. Anyway, he told me that he was going to all the afternoon first-grade teachers asking if any of them would be willing to change in the middle of the term. He said he thought perhaps someone would really want it and, instead of his just delegating a person, it would be better if he asked each one individually.

I was torn between many factors. I enjoyed my class very, very much and I enjoyed teaching the first grade. But because I was teaching afternoon session (our school runs on two different sessions), I was left out of many of the goings-on within the school as my hours were different and it also sort of conflicted with my home responsibilities. Well, even with these two points in mind, I really felt that I would rather stay with my class than to switch over in the middle of the term.

But he explained further that some of the classes would not remain the same because there would be many changes made. So, being the type of person that I am, I felt that, even though I did want to stay with my class and the children and the first grade, if something had to be done in the school, there was no way of stopping it and I might as well do it. I explained to Mr. Frost that even though I wouldn't want to change in the middle—after all it would be a whole new experience, two classes of children would be suffering by the change—but if it had to be done I would be willing to take on the new responsibility.

With that, Mr. Frost said, "Thank you," and said he would go around to the other teachers to see if anyone really wanted to change. Well, already I felt that it was going to be me, but I wasn't sure.

A little later on in the day I was taking my class to recess, and we were lining up in the hall. I spoke to Miss Lane, another teacher, and she said that he had also spoken to her. At that point Mr. Frost came over and told me that he was sorry but that I had been the one elected. Well, I said that I hoped that I would be able to do a good job, and that was that.

From that point on, there was an awful lot of talk in

the school. Everybody was talking about it, at least, everyone who knew something about the matter. So all the afternoon first-grade teachers and all the morning first-grade teachers knew, and many of the new teachers (those that I came into the school with), and apparently there was a lot of business going on that I can't begin to describe because I don't know how the whole thing started in the first place. However, from the office I did find out that it wasn't Mr. Frost's fault or anything that the second-grade teacher was going to be dismissed. It was a directive from higher up that stated he would lose a teacher. How he chose this particular teacher to let go I really can't say. I understand that they really didn't get along too well and neither of them were too happy in the school working together.

Everything went so quickly and everybody was talking to me. Mrs. Parsons spoke to me. She is my assistant principal. She was supervisor of the first grade and she will be in charge of the second grade also. I was told that I would have to take over the new class on January 2, the first day that we return from the vacation. I really felt terrible about my children, but it was something that had to be done and I did it.

Thursday, Mr. Frost talked to the other afternoon teachers and myself. He referred to me as the hero and he said, "Now it is your turn to be heroes also." He asked the afternoon first-grade teachers if they would be willing to have their registers become higher by having my 27 children split up among the four remaining afternoon classes, or did they think he should have them split up among all the first-grade classes, some of which met in the morning.

He was straightforward, saying that he didn't think it would be a good idea for the children to be split up among all the first-grade teachers. I agreed with him. He felt that it would be trying on the parents and on the children to have a whole new schedule worked out. After all, if you're used to going to school from 12 to 4, coming to school from 7:30 to 12 is quite a difference. It would be very, very hard on the parents. Especially in this neighborhood 'where sometimes they have a few children in the same grade, a few in different grades. So I agreed with Mr. Frost. The other teachers didn't seem too happy about the idea, but they said they would go along with it.

Mr. Frost and Mrs. Parsons worked out a plan whereby the 1-1 class register would go up to 35 which is generally what a 1-1 class has. The 1-3 class register would go up 32 or 33. And so forth down the line. 1-5 (my class) would be erased. The teachers didn't think it was so bad then, but we all did have added responsibilities.

Mr. Frost then added that if we had any children in our classes that we felt did not belong, this was our chance to have them changed, since there would be many interclass transfers in order to make more homogeneous classes. So we all had to sit down and think—"Who belongs? Who doesn't belong?" I, of course, had to decide where 27 children would belong.

Class is Divided

I went through my class and divided them into groups to the best of my ability. In the 1-1 class, I put Joseph R., who scored the highest on the reading-readiness test. As a result of his score and his work in class, I felt Joseph did belong in the 1-1 class. Lydia A., who I believe is a very smart girl and who wasn't really working as well as she could in my class, I felt belonged in the 1-1 class. Lydia scored second highest on the reading-readiness test. In the 1-1 class, I also put Anita

R. Anita is a bit older than the rest of the children but she has caught on beautifully to most phases of school work even though she just came to the United States last March. Also, she scored the same as Lydia on the reading-readiness test.

Then I decided that I would put Robert M. in the 1-1 class. I felt strongly that Robert was by far the best child in my class. Robert did every bit of the work ever assigned. He caught on very, very quickly to all phases of work besides doing his work well, quickly, efficiently and neatly. Even though on reading-readiness he only scored in the 50th percentile, I felt he really stood out and I also felt that once you're in a "1" class, unless you really don't belong, you have a better chance. The "1" class is really the only class that you would term a "good" class. So those four children I recommended for the 1-1 class.

Then I went down the line for the 1-3 class, I picked nine children, really good children who, on the whole, listened and did their work. Most of them scored in the 50th and 40th percentile on reading-readiness, and they were coping with school problems very, very well. In the 1-7 class, I put the slower children and in the 1-9 class, of course, which is Mrs. Gould's, I put all the children that really weren't doing well in school work at all. First, Alberto S. Alberto is still not able to write his name. Then I put Beatrice L., Stella S., Pedro D. and several others, who really were not working well, in the 1-9 class.

I know that the other teachers do have a big job before them because whichever class these children are placed in will not have been doing exactly the same work. The children either have much to catch up on or they might review some of the work, and the teachers will have to be patient either way. I really don't think anyone will have serious discipline problems, except perhaps in the 1-1 class where Lydia and Anita have been placed.

Telling the Children

The time came when I had to tell the children that I would not be their teacher anymore. Well, as young as they are, I think that many of them caught on immediately, and before I could say anything, faces were very, very long and the children were mumbling, "But I wanted you for a teacher."

That was all I needed! I felt even worse than I felt when I found out that I wouldn't be with them anymore. So I continued talking and I told them that it's just something that happens and that I would still be in the school and maybe next year they would get me when they go to the second grade. I told them that I would miss them all, that they would have a lot of fun in their new classes, and they would learn a lot. And, of course, I said, "You know all the other teachers. Some of you will get Mrs. Lewis. Some will get Miss Lane, some will get Miss Taylor, and some will get Mrs. Gould."

To my astonishment Anita kept saying over and over, "But I want you for a teacher. But I want you for a teacher."

I looked around the room. Most of the children were sitting there with very, very long faces. Joseph C. was sitting there with the longest face you could imagine, Robert G. said he didn't want another teacher, and all of a sudden Joseph started crying and just didn't stop. He cried all the way out into the hall when we got dressed to go home. I spoke to him softly and said, "Joseph, wouldn't you like Miss Lane for a teacher?"

She was standing right near me, and finally he stopped crying.

I said goodbye to them and that I would see them all. And that was the end of my class. . . .

Good schools. Poor schools. What is a good school? Is a good school one that is in a good neighborhood, that has middle-class children? Is a poor school one in a depressed area where you have Negro and Puerto Rican children? These are common terms that people refer to all the time. They hear your school is on Wolf Street—"Oh, you must be in a bad school."

I don't really think that that is what a good or a bad school is. I think a good school is a school that is well run, has a good administration, has people that work together well, has good discipline and where the children are able to learn and also, of course, where there are numerous facilities for the children and the teachers. In my estimation a poor or a bad school would be one in which the administration and the teachers do not work together, are not working in the best interests of the children, and where learning is not going on. Also, a poor school is one where you don't have proper facilities. I am not acquainted with many of the public schools, and I really can't say that the ones that I know are better or worse.

I believe my school is a pretty good school. It isn't in the best neighborhood. There are many, many problems in my school but on the whole I think that the teachers and the administration work together and I do believe that they are doing the best they can with the problems that are around.

You have to remember that in a school such as ours the children are not as ready and willing to learn as in schools in middle-class neighborhoods.

When a new teacher enters the classroom, she must learn the behavior, attitudes and skills required in the new situation. Much of this learning is conscious. Some of it is not. What is significant is that, while on the job, the teacher is socialized to her new role—she is integrated into the society of the school, and learns the values, beliefs and attitudes that govern its functioning.

The saga of class 1-5 shows the subtle ways in which one new teacher is socialized to her job. In just a few months, she accepts the demands of the school organization and its prevailing rationale for student failure.

The new teacher of class 1-5 in a slum school begins her career with a warm, friendly attitude toward her students. She respects and admires their abilities and is troubled by what the future holds for them: By the sixth grade in her school, educational failure is very common.

Very early in her teaching career, however, a more experienced teacher exposes this new teacher to the belief, widely held, that the children come from inferior backgrounds and that the deficits in their homes—expressed here as lack of newspapers and parental care—prevent educational achievement. That the teachers and the school as an institution contribute to the failure of the children is never even considered as a possible cause. The beginning teacher, in her description of what happens to class 1-5, then provides us with a graphic account of the ways in which this attitude can promote failure.

First, let us examine the actual instruction of the children. Early in her career, this new, very sincere teacher is painfully aware of her own deficiencies. Unsure about her teaching of so fundamental a subject as reading, she raises serious questions about her own effectiveness. As yet, she has not unconsciously accepted the notion that the failure of children stems from gaps in their backgrounds. Although no consensus exists about reading methodology, the teacher tells us that there are serious weaknesses in feedback evaluation—and that she is unable to find out what the children have been taught or what they have really learned.

By the end of the term, all this has changed. By that time, the eventual failure of most of class 1-5 has been virtually assured. And the teacher has come to rationalize this failure in terms of pupil inadequacy.

In the particular case of class 1-5, the cycle of failure begins with a drop in the number of students registered in the school. The principal loses a teacher, which in turn means dissolving a class and subsequently distributing its children among other classes. The principal and the teachers have no control over this event. In the inner-city schools, education budgets, tables of organization and directions from headquarters create conditions beyond the control of the administrators and teachers who are in closest touch with the children.

A drop in pupil registers would seemingly provide the opportunity for a higher adult-pupil ratio and, consequently, more individualized instruction and pedagogical supports for both youngsters and teachers. In a suburban school, this is probably what would have occurred. But in this slum school, the register drop leads to the loss of a teacher, larger classes, and—perhaps most important—increased time spent by the administrator and his staff on the mechanics of administration rather than on the supervision of instruction. (Why *this* particular teacher is released is unclear, though her substitute status and low rank in the staff hierarchy probably contribute to her release.) As a result many classes are disrupted, several first-grade class registers grow larger, time for instruction is lost, and concern is felt by teachers and pupils alike.

An even more significant clue to the possible eventual failure of the children is described in poignant detail— when the teacher tells how the youngsters in her class are to be distributed among the other first-grade classes. Educators now know that children mature at different rates; that they have different rates of learning readiness; and the developmental differences between boys and girls are relevant to learning. To forecast the educational outcome of youngsters at this early stage of their development, without due provision for these normal growth variations, is a travesty of the educational process. Yet here, in the first half of the first grade, a relatively inexperienced young teacher, herself keenly aware of her own deficiencies as an educator, is placed in the position of literally deciding the educational future of her charges.

A few are selected for success—"I felt that once you're in a '1' class, unless you really don't belong, you have a better chance. The '1' class is really the only class that you would term a 'good' class." Several children are placed in a class labeled "slow." And the remaining youngsters are relegated to a state of limbo, a middle range that does not carry the hope of providing a "better chance."

Early Tracking of Children's Futures

Thus, before these youngsters have completed a full four months of schooling, their educational futures have been "tracked." All through the grades, the labels of their class placement will follow them, accompanied by teacher attitudes about their abilities. Some youngsters are selected very early for success, others written off as slow. Because differential teaching occurs and helps to widen the gap between children, the opportunity to move from one category to another is limited. In addition, the children become aware of the labels placed upon them. And their pattern for achievement in later years is influenced by their feelings of success or failure in early school experiences.

The teacher, as she reflects upon what a "good" or a "bad" school is, continues to include how well the children learn as a significant criterion, together with good relations between staff and administration. But the children in her school do not achieve very well academically, so when describing her school as "good," she stresses the good relations between the administration and the teachers. The fact that the children do not learn does not seem so important now: " . . . the children are not as ready and willing to learn as in schools in middle-class neighborhoods."

How well our teacher has internalized the attitude that deficits of the children themselves explain their failure in school! How normal she now considers the administrative upheavals and their effects upon teachers and children! How perfectly ordinary she considers the "tracking" of youngsters so early in their school years!

The teacher of class 1-5 has been socialized by the school to accept its structure and values. Despite her sincerity and warmth and obvious concern for the children, this teacher is not likely to change the forecast of failure for most of these children—because she has come to accept the very structural and attitudinal factors that make failure nearly certain. In addition, with all her good intentions, she has come to operate as an agent determining the life chances of the children in her class—by distributing them among the ranked classes on the grade.

This teacher came to her job with very positive impulses. She thought highly of her youngsters and was disturbed that, with what appeared to be good potential, there was so much failure in the school in the upper grades. She looked inward for ways in which she might improve her efforts to forestall retardation. She was not repelled by the neighborhood in which she worked. There is every indication that she had the potential to become a very effective teacher of disadvantaged youngsters.

Her good impulses, however, were not enough. This young teacher, unarmed with the strength that an understanding of the social processes involved might have given her, and having little power within the school hierarchy, was socialized by the attitudes of those around her, by the administration, and by the availability of a suitable rationale to explain her and the school's failure to fulfill their ideal roles. As a result she came to accept traditional slum-school attitudes toward the children—and traditional attitudes toward school organization as the way things have to be. This teacher is a pleasant, flexible, cooperative young woman to have on one's staff. But she has learned to behave and think in a way that perpetuates a process by which disadvantaged children continue to be disadvantaged.

The organizational structure of the large inner-city school and the attitudes of the administrators and teachers within it clearly affect the development of the children attending. No theory proposed to explain the academic failure of poor and minority-group children can ignore the impact of the actual school experience and the context in which it occurs.

September 1968

Changing the Game from "Get the Teacher" to "Learn"

ROBERT L. HAMBLIN, DAVID BUCKHOLDT
DONALD BUSHELL, DESMOND ELLIS
AND DANIEL FERRITOR

Almost any experienced educator will assure you that it is next to impossible—and often actually impossible—to teach normal classroom subjects to children who have extreme behavior problems, or who are "too young." Yet at four experimental classrooms of the Central Midwestern Regional Educational Laboratories (CEMREL), we have been bringing about striking changes in the behavior and learning progress of just such children.

In the 18 months of using new exchange systems and

Note: The work reported here was done by the Central Midwestern Regional Educational Laboratory, a private, non-profit corporation supported in part as a Regional Educational Laboratory by funds from the U.S. Office of Education, Department of Health, Education and Welfare. The opinions expressed here do not necessarily reflect the position or policy of the Office of Education, and no official endorsement by the Office of Education should be inferred.

working with different types of problem children, we have seen these results:

1. Extraordinarily aggressive boys, who had not previously responded to therapy, have been tamed.
2. Two-year-olds have learned to read about as fast and as well as their five-year-old classmates.
3. Four ghetto children, too shy, too withdrawn to talk, have become better-than-average talkers.
4. Several autistic children, who were either mute or could only parrot sounds, have developed functional speech, have lost their bizarre and disruptive behavior patterns, and their relationships with parents and other children have improved. All of these children are on the road to normality.

Our system is deceptively simple. Superficially, in fact, it may not even seem new—though, in detail, it has never been tried in precisely this form in the classroom before. In essence, we simply reinforce "good" behavior and nonpunitively discourage "bad" behavior. We structure a social exchange so that as the child progresses, we reinforce this behavior—give him something that he values, something that shows our approval. Therefore, he becomes strongly motivated to continue his progress. To terminate bizarre, disruptive or explosive patterns, we stop whatever has been reinforcing that undesirable behavior—actions or attention that teachers or parents have unwittingly been giving him in exchange, often in the belief that they were punishing and thus discouraging him. Study after study has shown that whenever a child persists in behaving badly, some adult has, perhaps inadvertently, been rewarding him for it.

"Socialization" is the term that sociologists use to describe the process of transforming babies—who can do little but cry, eat and sleep—into adults who can communicate and function rather effectively in their society. Socialization varies from culture to culture, and, while it is going on all around us, we are seldom aware of it. But when normal socialization breaks down, "problems" occur—autism, nonverbal or hyperaggressive behavior, retardation, delinquency, crime and so on.

The authors, after years of often interesting but by and large frustrating research, realized that the more common theories of child development (Freudian, neo-Freudian, the developmental theories of Gesell and Piaget, and a number of others) simply do not satisfactorily explain the socialization process in children. Consequently, in desperation we began to move toward the learning theories and then toward the related exchange theories of social structure. Since then, working with problem children, our view has gradually been amplified and refined. Each experimental classroom has given us a different looking glass. In each we can see the child in different conditions, and can alter the conditions which hinder his socialization into a civilized, productive adult capable of happiness.

By the time they become students, most children love to play with one another, to do art work, to cut and paste, to play with Playdoh, to climb and swing on the playground, and so on. Most preschools also serve juice and cookie snacks, and some have television sets or movies. There is, consequently, no dearth of prizes for us to reward the children for good behavior. The problem is not in finding reinforcers, but in managing them.

The Basic System: Token Exchange

One of the simpler and most effective ways, we found, was to develop a token-exchange system. The tokens we use are plastic discs that children can earn. A child who completes his arithmetic or reading may earn a dozen tokens, given one by one as he proceeds through the lessons. And at the end of the lesson period comes the reward.

Often it is a movie. The price varies. For four tokens, a student can watch while sitting on the floor; for eight, he gets a chair; for 12, he can watch while sitting on the table. Perhaps the view is better from the table—anyway, the children almost always buy it if they have enough tokens. But if they dawdled so much that they earned fewer than four, they are "timed out" into the hall while the others see the movie. Throughout the morning, therefore, the children earn, then spend, then earn, then spend.

This token-exchange system is very powerful. It can create beneficial changes in a child's behavior, his emotional reactions and ultimately even his approach to life. But it is not easy to set up, nor simple to maintain.

At the beginning the tokens are meaningless to the children; so to make them meaningful, we pair them with M&M candies, or something similar. As the child engages in the desired behavior (or a reasonable facsimile), the teacher gives him a "Thank you," an M&M and a token. At first the children are motivated by the M&Ms and have to be urged to hold on to the tokens; but then they find that the tokens can be used to buy admission to the movie, Playdoh or other good things. The teacher tells them the price and asks them to count out the tokens. Increasingly, the teacher "forgets" the M&Ms. In two or three days the children get no candy, just the approval and the tokens. By then, they have learned.

There are problems in maintaining a token exchange. Children become disinterested in certain reinforcers if they are used too frequently, and therefore in the tokens that buy them. For instance, young children will work very hard to save up tokens to play with Playdoh once a week; if they are offered Playdoh every day, the charm quickly fades. Some activities—snacks, movies, walks outdoors—are powerful enough to be used every day.

As noted, the children we worked with had different behavior problems, reflecting various kinds of breakdowns in the socialization process. Each experiment we conducted concentrated on a particular type of maladjustment or a particular group of maladjusted children to see how a properly structured exchange system might help them. Let us look at each experiment, to see how each problem was affected.

Aggression

Unfortunately, our world reinforces and rewards aggressive behavior. Some cultures and some families are open and brazen about it—they systematically and consciously teach their young that it is desirable, and even virtuous, to attack certain other individuals or groups. The child who can beat up the other kids on the playground is sometimes respected by his peers, and perhaps by his parents; the soldier achieves glory in combat. The status, the booty or the bargaining advantages that come to the aggressor can become reinforcement to continue and escalate his aggressions.

In more civilized cultures the young are taught not to use aggression, and we try to substitute less harmful patterns. But even so, aggression is sometimes reinforced unintentionally—and the consequences, predictably, are the same as if the teaching was deliberate.

In the long run civilized cultures are not kind to hyperaggressive children. A recent survey in England, for instance, found that the great majority of teachers felt that aggressive behavior by students disturbed more classrooms than anything else and caused the most anxiety among teachers. At least partly as a result, the dropout rates for the hyperaggressives was 2½ times as great as for "normals," and disproportionate numbers of hyperaggressives turned up in mental clinics.

The traditional treatment for aggressive juveniles is punishment—often harsh punishment. This is not only of dubious moral value, but generally it does not work.

We took seriously—perhaps for the first time—the theory that aggression is a type of exchange behavior. Boys become aggressive because they get something for it; they continue to be aggressive because the rewards are continuing. To change an aggressive pattern in our experimental class at Washington University, therefore, we had to restructure appropriately the exchange system in which the boys were involved.

As subjects we (Ellis and Hamblin) found five extraordinarily aggressive four-year-old boys, all referred to us by local psychiatrists and social workers who had been able to do very little with them. Next, we hired a trained teacher. We told her about the boys and the general nature of the experiment—then gave her her head. That is, she was allowed to use her previous training during the first period—and this would provide a baseline comparison with what followed after. We hoped she would act like the "typical teacher." We suspect that she did.

Let's Play "Get the Teacher"

The teacher was, variously, a strict disciplinarian, wise counselor, clever arbitrator and sweet peacemaker. Each role failed miserably. After the eighth day, the average of the children was 150 sequences of aggression per day! Here is what a mere four minutes of those sequences were like:

Mike, John and Dan are seated together playing with pieces of Playdoh. Barry, some distance from the others, is seated and also is playing with Playdoh. The children, except Barry, are talking about what they are making. Time is 9:10 A.M. Miss Sally, the teacher, turns toward the children and says, "It's time for a lesson. Put your Playdoh away." Mike says, "Not me." John says, "Not me." Dan says, "Not me." Miss Sally moves toward Mike. Mike throws some Playdoh in Miss Sally's face. Miss Sally jerks back, then moves forward rapidly and snatches Playdoh from Mike. Puts Playdoh in her pocket. Mike screams for Playdoh, says he wants to play with it. Mike moves toward Miss Sally and attempts to snatch the Playdoh from Miss Sally's pocket. Miss Sally pushes him away. Mike kicks Miss Sally on the leg. Kicks her again, and demands the return of his Playdoh. Kicks Miss Sally again. Picks up a small steel chair and throws it at Miss Sally. Miss Sally jumps out of the way. Mike picks up another chair and throws it more violently. Miss Sally cannot move in time. Chair strikes her foot. Miss Sally pushes Mike down on the floor. Mike starts up. Pulls over one chair. Now another, another. Stops a moment. Miss Sally is picking up chairs, Mike looks at Miss Sally. Miss Sally moves toward Mike. Mike runs away.

John wants his Playdoh. Miss Sally says "No." He joins Mike in pulling over chairs and attempts to grab Playdoh from Miss Sally's pocket. Miss Sally pushes him away roughly. John is screaming that he wants to play with his Playdoh. Moves toward phonograph. Pulls it off the table; lets it crash onto the floor. Mike has his coat on. Says he is going home. Miss Sally asks Dan to bolt the door. Dan gets to the door at the same time as Mike. Mike hits Dan in the face. Dan's nose is bleeding. Miss Sally walks over to Dan, turns to the others, and says that she is taking Dan to the washroom and that while she is away, they may play with the Playdoh. Returns Playdoh from pocket to Mike and John. Time: 9:14 A.M.

Wild? Very. These were barbarous little boys who enjoyed battle. Miss Sally did her best but they were just more clever than she, and they *always* won. Whether Miss Sally wanted to or not, they could always drag her into the fray, and just go at it harder and harder until she capitulated. She was finally driven to their level, trading a kick for a kick and a spit in the face for a spit in the face.

What Miss Sally did not realize is that she had inadvertantly structured an exchange where she consistently reinforced aggression. First, as noted, whenever she fought with them, she *always lost*. Second, more subtly, she reinforced their aggressive pattern by giving it serious attention—by looking, talking, scolding, cajoling, becoming angry, even striking back. These boys were playing a teasing game called "get the teacher." The more she showed that she was bothered by their behavior, the better they liked it, and the further they went.

These interpretations may seem far-fetched, but they are borne out dramatically by what happened later. On the twelfth day we changed the conditions, beginning with B1 (see Figure 1). First, we set up the usual token exchange to reinforce cooperative behavior. This was to develop or strengthen behavior that would replace aggression. Any strong pattern of behavior serves some function for the individual, so the first step in getting rid of a strong, disruptive pattern is substituting another one that is more useful and causes fewer problems. Not only therapy, but simply humanity dictates this.

First, the teacher had to be instructed in how *not to reinforce* aggression. Contrary to all her experience, she was asked to turn her back on the aggressor, and at the same time to reinforce others' cooperation with tokens. Once we were able to coach her and give her immediate feedback over a wireless-communication system, she structured the exchanges almost perfectly. The data in

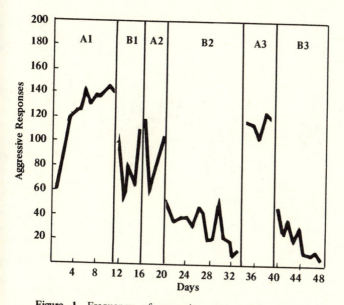

Figure 1. Frequency of aggressive sequences by days for five 4-year-old boys. In A1, A2 and A3 the teacher attempted to punish aggression but inadvertently reinforced it. In B1, B2 and B3 she turned her back or otherwise ignored aggression and thus did not reinforce it.

Figures 1 and 2 show the crucial changes: a gradual increase in cooperation—from about 56 to about 115 sequences per day, and a corresponding decrease in aggression from 150 to about 60 sequences!

These results should have been satisfactory, but we were new at this kind of experimentation, and nervous. We wanted to reduce the frequency of aggression to a "normal" level, to about 15 sequences a day. So we restructured the exchange system and thus launched A2.

In A2, we simply made sure that aggression would always be punished. The teacher was told to *charge* tokens for any aggression.

To our surprise, the frequency of cooperation re-

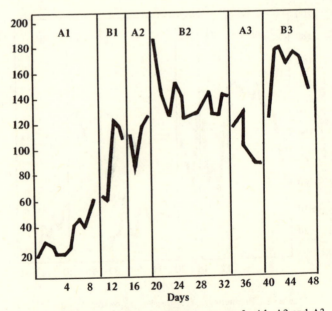

Figure 2. Frequency of cooperative sequences. In A1, A2 and A3 the teacher structured a weak approval exchange for cooperation and a disapproval exchange for noncooperation. In B1, A2, B2 and B3, she structured a token exchange for cooperation.

mained stable, about 115 sequences per day; but aggression *increased* to about 110 sequences per day! Evidently the boys were still playing "get the teacher," and the fines were enough reinforcement to increase aggression.

So, instead of fining the children, the teacher was again told to ignore aggression by turning her back and giving attention and tokens only for cooperation. The frequency of aggression went down to a near "normal" level, about 16 sequences per day (B2), and cooperation increased to about 140 sequences.

Then, as originally planned, the conditions were again reversed. The boys were given enough tokens at the beginning of the morning to buy their usual supply of movies, toys, and snacks, and these were not used as reinforcers. The teacher was told to do the best she could. She was not instructed to return to her old pattern, but without the tokens and without our coaching she did—and with the same results. Note A3 in Figures 1 and 2. Aggression increased to about 120 sequences per day, and cooperation decreased to about 90. While this was an improvement over A1, before the boys had ever been exposed to the token exchange, it was not good. The mixture of aggression and cooperation was strange, even weird, to watch.

When the token exchange was restructured (B3) and the aggression no longer reinforced, the expected changes recurred—with a bang. Aggression decreased to seven sequences on the last day, and cooperation rose to about 181 sequences. In "normal" nursery schools, our observations have shown that five boys can be expected to have 15 aggression sequences and 60 cooperation sequences per day. Thus, from extremely aggressive and uncooperative, our boys had become less aggressive and far more cooperative than "normal" boys.

Here is an example of their new behavior patterns,

taken from a rest period—precisely the time when the most aggressive acts had occurred in the past:

All of the children are sitting around the table drinking their milk; John, as usual, has finished first. Takes his plastic mug and returns it to the table. Miss Martha, the assistant teacher, gives him a token. John goes to cupboard, takes out his mat, spreads it out by the blackboard, and lies down. Miss Martha gives him a token. Meanwhile, Mike, Barry and Jack have spread their mats on the carpet. Dan is lying on the carpet itself since he hasn't a mat. Each of them gets a token. Mike asks if he can sleep by the wall. Miss Sally says "Yes." John asks if he can put out the light. Miss Sally says to wait until Barry has his mat spread

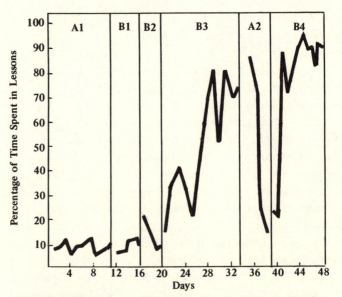

Figure 3. Percentage of scheduled time spent in lessons by days for five hyperaggressive boys. In A1 and A2, teacher structured approval exchange for attendance, disapproval for non-attendance. In B1 and B2, a token exchange for attendance was structured, but not effectively until B2 and B4.

properly. Dan asks Mike if he can share his mat with him. Mike says "No." Dan then asks Jack. Jack says, "Yes," but before he can move over, Mike says "Yes." Dan joins Mike. Both Jack and Mike get tokens. Mike and Jack get up to put their tokens in their cans. Return to their mats. Miss Sally asks John to put out the light. John does so. Miss Martha gives him a token. All quiet now. Four minutes later—all quiet. Quiet still, three minutes later. Time: 10:23 A.M. Rest period ends.

The hyperaggressive boys actually had, and were, double problems; they were not only extremely disruptive, but they were also washouts as students. Before the token system (A1), they paid attention to their teacher only about 8 percent of the lesson time (see Figure 3). The teacher's system of scolding the youngster for inattention and taking their attention for granted with faint approval, if any, did not work at all. To the pupils, the "Get the Teacher" game was much more satisfying.

After the token exchange was started, in B1, B2, B3 and B4, it took a long, long time before there was any appreciable effect. The teacher was being trained from scratch, and our methods were, then, not very good. However, after we set up a wireless-communication system that allowed us to coach the teacher from behind a one-way mirror and to give her immediate feedback, the children's attention began to increase. Toward the end of B3, it leveled off at about 75 percent—from 8 percent! After the token exchange was taken out during A2, attention went down to level off at 23 percent; put back in at B4, it shot back up to a plateau of about 93 percent. Like a roller coaster: 8 percent without, to 75 with, to 23 without, to 93 with.

Normal Children

These results occurred with chronic, apparently hope-

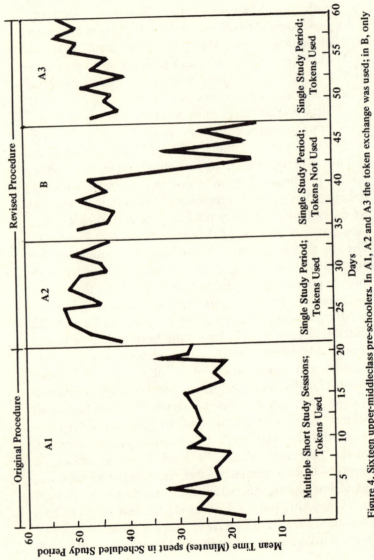

Figure 4. Sixteen upper-middleclass pre-schoolers. In A1, A2 and A3 the token exchange was used; in B, only approval.

less hyperaggressive boys. Would token exchange also help "normal," relatively bright upper-middle-class children? Sixteen youngsters of that description—nine boys and seven girls, ranging from 2 years 9 months to 4 years 9 months—were put through an experimental series by Bushell, Hamblin and Denis Stoddard in an experimental pre school at Webster College. All had about a month's earlier experience with the token-exchange system. The results are shown in Figure 4.

At first, the study hour was broken up into 15-minute periods, alternating between the work that received tokens, and the play or reward that the tokens could be used for. Probably because the children were already familiar with token exchange, no great increase in learning took place. On the 22nd day, we decided to try to increase the learning period, perhaps for the whole hour. In A2 (Figure 4), note that the time spent in studying went up rapidly and dramatically—almost doubling—from 27 to level off at 42 minutes.

During B, the token exchange was taken out completely. The teachers still gave encouragement and prepared interesting lessons as before. The rewards—the nature walks, snacks, movies and so on—were retained. But, as in a usual classroom, they were given to the children free instead of being sold. The children continued at about the same rate as before for a few days. But after a week, attention dropped off slowly, then sharply. On the last day it was down to about 15 minutes—one-third the level of the end of the token period.

In A3, the token exchange was reinstituted. In only three days, attention snapped back from an average of 15 minutes to 45 minutes. However, by the end of A3, the students paid attention an average of 50 of the available 60 minutes.

A comparison of the record of these normals with the

record of the hyperaggressive boys is interesting. The increase in attention brought by the token exchange, from about 15 minutes to 50, is approximately three-fold for the normal children; but for the hyperaggressive boys—who are disobedient and easily distracted—it is about eleven-fold, from 8 percent to 93 percent of the time. The increase was not only greater, but the absolute level achieved was higher. This indicates strongly, therefore, that the more difficult the child, the greater may be the effect of token exchange on his behavior.

The high rates of attention were not due to the fact that each teacher had fewer children to work with. Individualized lessons were not enough. Without the token exchange, even three teachers could not hold the interest of 16 children two to four years old—at least not in reading, writing and arithmetic.

Praise and approval were not enough as rewards. The teachers, throughout the experiment, used praise and approval to encourage attention; they patted heads and said things like "Good," "You're doing fine," and "Keep it up"; yet, in B, when the token exchange was removed, this attention nevertheless ultimately declined by two-thirds. Social approval is important, but not nearly so powerful as material reinforcers.

Finally, it is obvious that if the reinforcers (movies, snacks, toys or whatever) do not seem directly connected to the work, they will not sustain a high level of study. To be effective with young children, rewards must occur in a structured exchange in which they are given promptly as recompense and thus are directly connected to the work performed.

The Very Young Child

According to accepted educational theory, a child

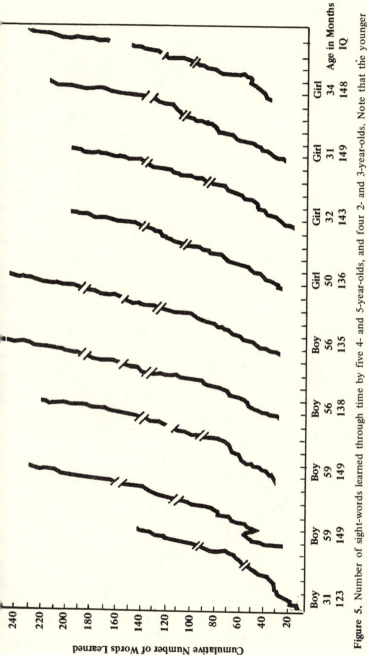

Figure 5. Number of sight-words learned through time by five 4- and 5-year-olds, and four 2- and 3-year-olds. Note that the younger children did about as well as the older ones—except for one boy whose IQ was somewhat lower than the others in the group. (Gaps indicate absences.)

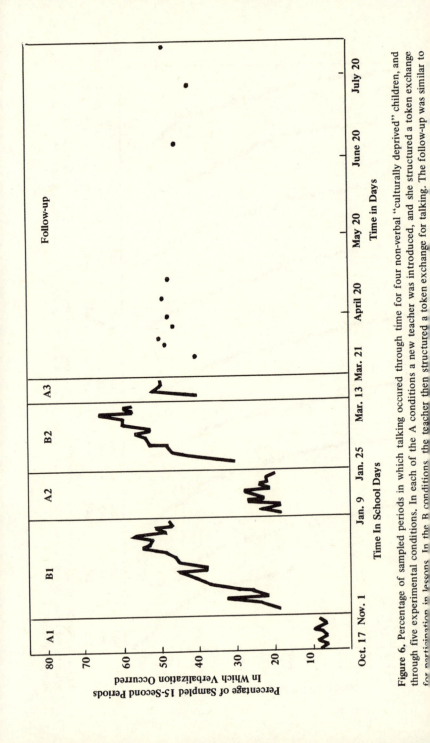

Figure 6. Percentage of sampled periods in which talking occured through time for four non-verbal "culturally deprived" children, and through five experimental conditions. In each of the A conditions a new teacher was introduced, and she structured a token exchange for participation in lessons. In the B conditions, the teacher then structured a token exchange for talking. The follow-up was similar to

must be about six and a half before he can comfortably learn to read. But is this really true, or is it merely a convenience for the traditional educational system? After all, by the time a normal child is two and a half he has learned a foreign language—the one spoken by his parents and family; and he has learned it without special instruction or coaching. He has even developed a feel for the rules of grammar, which, by and large, he uses correctly. It is a rare college student who becomes fluent in a foreign language with only two and a half years of formal training—and our college students are supposed to be the brightest of our breed. Paul Goodman has suggested that if children learn to *speak* by the same methods that they learn to *read*, there might well be as many nonspeakers now as illiterates.

What if the problem is really one of motivation? If we structured an exchange that rewarded them, in ways they could appreciate, for learning to read, couldn't they learn as readily as five-year-olds?

We decided that for beginners, the number of words a child can read is the best test of reading ability. In an experiment designed by Hamblin, Carol Pfeiffer, Dennis Shea and June Hamblin, and administered at our Washington University preschool, the token-exchange system was used to reward children for the number of words each learned. The results are given in Figure 5. Note that the two-year-olds did about as well as the five-year-olds; their sight vocabularies were almost as large.

There was an interesting side effect: at the end of the school year, all but one of these children tested at the "genius" level. On Stanford-Binet individual tests, their IQ scores increased as much as 36 points. It was impossible to compute an average gain only because three of the children "topped out"—made something in excess of 149, the maximum score possible.

In general, the lower the measured IQ at the start, the greater the gain—apparently as a result of the educational experience.

The Nonverbal Child

What happens when ghetto children are introduced into a token-exchange system? At our Mullanphy Street preschool, 22 Afro-American children—age three to five—attend regularly. All live in or near the notorious Pruitt-Igoe Housing Project, and most come from broken homes. When the school began, the teachers were unenthusiastic about a token exchange, so we let them proceed as they wished. The result was pandemonium. About half of the children chased one another around the room, engaged in violent arguments and fought. The others withdrew; some would not even communicate.

After the third day, the teachers asked for help. As in the other experimental schools, we (Buckholdt and Hamblin) instructed them to ignore aggressive-disruptive behavior and to reward attention and cooperation with social approval and the plastic tokens, later to be exchanged for such things as milk, cookies, admission to the movies and toys. The children quickly caught on, the disruptions diminished, and cooperation increased. Within three weeks of such consistent treatment, most of the children took part in the lessons, and disruptive behavior had become only an occasional problem. All of this, remember, without punishment.

Our attention was then focused upon the children with verbal problems. These children seldom started conversations with teachers or other students, but they would sometimes answer questions with a word or perhaps two. This pattern may be unusual in the middle classes, but is quite common among ghetto children.

Our research has shown that children so afflicted are usually uneducable.

As we investigated, we became convinced that their problem was not that they were unable to talk as much as that they were too shy to talk to strangers—that is, to nonfamily. In their homes we overheard most of them talking brokenly, but in sentences. Consequently, we set up a token exchange for them designed specifically to develop a pattern of talking with outsiders, especially teachers and schoolchildren.

As it happened, we were able to complete the experiment with only four children (see Figure 6). During A1, the baseline period (before the tokens were used), the four children spoke only in about 8 percent of the 15-second sampling periods. In B1, the teachers gave social approval and tokens *only* for speaking; nonverbalisms, like pointing or headshaking, would not be recognized or reinforced. Note the increase in verbalization, leveling out at approximately 48 percent.

In A2 we reversed the conditions by using a teacher new to the school. The rate of talking dropped off immediately, then increased unevenly until it occurred in about 23 percent of the sample periods.

In B2 the new teacher reintroduced the token exchange for talking, and once more there was a dramatic rise: The speaking increased much more rapidly than the first time, ending up at about 60 percent. (This more rapid increase is known as the Contrast Effect. It occurs in part, perhaps, because the children value the token exchange more after it has been taken away.)

In the final test, we again took out the token exchange, and introduced yet another new teacher. This time the drop was small, to 47 percent.

We followed the children for three months after the end of the experiment. Their speech level remained at

48 percent, with little dropoff. This compares with the 40 percent talking rate for our other ghetto children, and the 42 percent rate for upper-middle-class children at the Washington University preschool.

Frequency of speech, however, was not the only important finding. At the end of B1, the children spoke more often but still in a hesitant and broken way. By the end of B2, they spoke in sentences, used better syntax and frequently started conversations.

Mothers, teachers and neighbors all reported that the children were much more friendly and assertive. But some claimed that the children now talked too much! This could reflect individual bias; but there was little doubt that at least one child, Ben, had become an almost compulsive talker. He was given to saying hello to everyone he met and shaking his hand. So we terminated the experiment—what would have happened to Ben had we started *another* exchange?

This experiment shows that token exchange can bring on permanent behavior change, but that the culture must reinforce the new behavior. Talking is important in our culture, and so is reading; therefore they are reinforced. But other subjects—such as mathematics beyond simple arithmetic—are not for most people. For behavior to change permanently it must be reinforced at least intermittently.

Autism

The problems of autistic children usually dwarf those of all other children. To the casual observer, autistic children never sustain eye contact with others but appear to be self-contained—sealed off in a world of their own. The most severe cases never learn how to talk, though they sometimes echo or parrot. They remain dependent upon their mothers and become more and more demanding. They develop increasingly destructive and bizarre behavior problems. Finally, between five and ten years old, autistic children ordinarily become unbearable to their families and at that point they are almost invariably institutionalized. Until recently, at least, this meant a rear ward to vegetate in until they died.

The breakthrough in therapy from autism came in 1964 when Dr. Ivar Lovaas and Dr. Montrose Wolfe and a graduate student, now Dr. Todd Risley, simultaneously developed therapy systems using well-established principles of operant conditioning. They were particularly successful with those children who randomly echoed or imitated words or sentences (this is called echolalia).

The therapy systems we have designed, developed and tested, though similar in some ways to those developed by Lovaas, Wolfe and Risley, are quite different in others. First, we do not use punishment, or other negative stimuli. We simply terminate exchanges that reinforce the autistic patterns, and set up exchanges that reinforce normal patterns. Second, our children are not institutionalized; they live at home, and are brought to the laboratory for 20 minutes to three hours of therapy per day. Third, as soon as possible—usually within months—we get the children into classrooms where a therapist works with four or five at a time. Fourth, we train the mother to be an assistant therapist—mostly in the home, but also in the laboratory. These changes were introduced for several reasons, but primarily in the hope of getting a better, more permanent cure for autism.

The Etiology of Autism

Is autism hereditary, as many believe? Our studies

indicate that this is not the important question. Many mental faculties, including IQ, have some physiological base. But the real issue is how much physiologically-based potential is socially realized, for good or bad. As far as we can tell, the exchanges that intensify autism get structured inadvertently, often by accident; but once started, a vicious cycle develops that relentlessly drives the child further into autism.

When autism starts, the mother often reacts by babying the child, trying to anticipate his every need before he signals. Thus normal communication is not reinforced, and the child never learns to work his environment properly. But even if he doesn't know how to get what he wants through talking, he does learn, through association, that his oversolicitous and anxious mother will always respond if he acts up violently or bizarrely enough. And she must, if only to punish. He thus learns to play "get mother's attention"; and this soon develops into "get mother exasperated, but stop short of the point where she punishes and really hurts." Here is an example (observed by Ferritor in the first of a series of experiments by the laboratory's staff, not reported here):

> Larry is allowed to pick out his favorite book. His mother then attempts to read it to him, but he keeps turning the pages so she can't. He gets up and walks away from the table. The mother then yells at him to come back. He *smiles* (a sign of pleasure usually but not always accompanies reinforcement). Mother continues to talk to the child to try to get him back for the story. Finally, he comes over to the table and takes the book away from her. She lets him and goes back to the bookcase for another book. He then sits down and

> she begins to read. He tries to get up, but his mother pulls him back. Again. Again. She holds him there. He gets away and starts walking around the room. Goes to the toy cabinet. Mother gets up to go over and take a toy away from him. He sits on the floor. The mother comes over and sits down by him. He gets up and goes over by the door and opens it and tries to run out. She tells him he has to stay. He *smiles*. She resumes reading. He gets up and starts walking around the table. She grabs him as he comes by. He *smiles*.

A clinical psychologist who had tested Larry did not diagnose him as autistic, but as an educable mental retardate with an IQ of perhaps 30. Yet he had gaze aversion and we suspected that Larry, like other autistics, was feigning inability as a way of getting what he wanted from his mother, and then from other adults. He began to respond to the attractive exchanges that we structured for him, and as we did, he began to tip his hand. For example, at one point when his mother was being trained to be an assistant therapist, the following incident occurred:

> Mrs. C. told Larry that as soon as he strung some beads he could have gum from the gum machine that was across the room. For about ten minutes he fumbled, he whined, all the time crying, saying "I can't." Finally, he threw the beads at his mother. Eventually, the mother had the good sense to leave the room, saying, "As soon as you string those beads, you can have your gum." With his mother out of the room, according to our observers he sat right down and, in less than 30 seconds, filled a string with beads with no apparent trouble.

Just two weeks later, after the mother had been through our ten-day training program, they again had a "story time."

> The mother begins by immediately asking Larry questions about this book (the same book used a few weeks before). He responds to every question. She gives approval for every correct answer. Then she tries to get him to say, "That is a duck." He will not say it intelligibly, but wants to turn the page. Mother says, "As soon as you say 'duck,' you may turn the page." Larry says "duck" and turns the page. He *smiles*.

> After seven minutes, Larry is still sitting down. They have finished one book and are beginning a second.

Most autistic children play the game "look at me, I'm stupid," or "look at me, I'm bizarre." These are simply attention-getting games that most adults repeatedly reinforce. Man is not a simple machine; he learns, and as he develops his abilities, he develops stronger and stronger habits. Thus, once these inadvertent exchanges get established, the child becomes more and more dependent, more and more disruptive, more and more bizarre, more and more alienated from the positive exchanges that are structured in his environment. What is sad is that the parents and the others in the child's life sense that something is terribly wrong, but the more they do, the worse the situation becomes.

It seems to those of us who have been involved in these experiments from the beginning that the exchange techniques and theories we have used have without question demonstrated their effectiveness in treating and educating problem children. Watching these children as they go peacefully and productively about their lessons toward the end of each experimental series is both an exhilarating and humbling experience. It is almost impossible to believe that so many had been written off as "uneducable" by professionals, that without this therapy and training—or something similar —most would have had dark and hopeless futures.

But it is not inevitable that so many hyperaggressive or environmentally retarded ghetto children become dropouts or delinquents; it is not inevitable that so many autistic children, saddest of all, must vegetate and die mutely in the back wards of mental hospitals.

January 1969

FURTHER READING

The Analysis of Human Operant Behavior by Ellen P. Reese (Dubuque, Iowa: William C. Brown Company, 1966)

The Emotionally Disturbed Child in the Classroom by Frank Hewett (Boston: Allyn and Bacon, Inc., 1968).

Early Childhood Autism edited by J.K. Wing (London: Pergamon Press, Ltd., 1966).

Case Studies in Behavior Modification by Leonard P. Ullman and Leonard Krasner (New York: Holt, Rinehart and Winston, Inc., 1965).

Drugging and Schooling

CHARLES WITTER

Minimal brain dysfunction (MBD), one of at least 38 names attached to a subset of learning disabilities, can significantly hinder a grammar school student of average or above-average intelligence from achieving his full potential. Hyperactive, often loud and demanding and little responsive to the feelings of others (or himself), the MBD child can be seen as the very model of the uncontrollable student. Then, 30 years ago, it was discovered that amphetamines, stimulants and/or tranquilizers could calm the hyperactive child who was so often disruptive in class or at home. Amphetamines and stimulants such as Ritalin have a "paradoxical effect" in the prepubescent child: instead of being "speed," they actually slow him down, make him more tractable and teachable and permit calm to be restored for the harassed parent and overburdened teacher.

Such was the conventional wisdom on September 29,

1970 when Congressman Cornelius E. Gallagher (D-New Jersey) convened a hearing of his House Privacy Subcommittee. This chapter is a critique of the hearing and an urgent appeal for social scientists to assert humanist concern in a world increasingly reliant on biochemical manipulation.

For the child who is very carefully tested by a team of neurologists, pediatricians, psychologists and educators, the symptoms of MBD can be masked by drugs in as high as 80 percent of the cases, according to some authorities. Others say 50 percent, while dissenters state that the good results are due either to the increased personal attention received by the child or the magical properties the child ascribes to the drug. A careful reading of Department of Health, Education, and Welfare (HEW) testimony at the Gallagher hearing suggests that 200,000 children in the United States are now being given amphetamine and stimulant therapy, with probably another 100,000 receiving tranquilizers and antidepressants.

All the experts agree, however, that the use of medication to modify the behavior of grammar school children will radically increase—"zoom" was the word connected with the man most responsible for the promotion of the program at the National Institute of Mental Health (NIMH). Already specialists in this therapeutic method state that at least 30 percent of ghetto children are candidates, and this figure could run as high as four to six million of the general grammar school population. The authoritative *Journal of Learning Disabilities* puts it bluntly: "Disadvantaged children function similarly to advantaged children with learning disabilities."

Not all children with the ill-defined, perhaps indefinable, syndrome are likely to be treated with medication, but it must be recognized that drugs are a cheap alternative to the massive spending so obviously necessary to revitalize the public school system. Lest there by any doubt about whether leadership in America would be reluctant to embrace quick, inexpensive answers to social problems, consider the plan of the president's former internist, Dr. Arnold Hutschnecker, who would give all six-to-eight-year-olds in the nation a predictive psychological test for their criminal potential. Those who flunked these tests—which have been shown to provide successful individual prognosis slightly over 50 percent of the time—would be sent to rehabilitation centers "in a romantic setting with trees out West," as Hutschnecker phrased it. This late, unlamented proposal was sent on White House stationery to the secretary of HEW with a request for suggestions on how to implement it. Once again, Mr. Gallagher's was the only congressional voice raised in opposition, and he branded those camps "American Dachaus." After hearings were threatened, HEW reported unfavorably, and the White House dropped the idea. Many other plans have gone forward, but the Hutschnecker proposal is important because of its high-level endorsement and encouragement, and the distressing impact it would have had on virtually every American family.

The National Institute of Mental Health, which studied the Hutschnecker plan for some three months, has granted at least $3 million to study drug therapy. The clearest statement on the reality of minimal brain dysfunction, however, has come from Dr. Francis Crinella, a grantee of the Office of Education. He said that MBD "has become one of our most fashionable forms of consensual ignorance." No simple medical examination or even an electroencephalogram can disclose the presence of the disorder; "soft" neurological signs seem to be the only physical manifestation.

Passing the Buck

Dr. John Peters, director of the Little Rock Child Study Center of the University of Arkansas, testified that the only way to separate the active child from the hyperactive one was to have had his long experience in seeing thousands of normal and "deviant" children and then making a personal judgment. In Omaha, where the drugging was first discovered by the *Washington Post*'s Robert Maynard, the doctors are not even that confident. How else does one explain the lines, reported also by Nat Hentoff, from the *Bulletin of the Omaha Medical Society*: "The responsibility of the prescription was not that of the doctor, but rather of the parent. The parent then vests responsibility in the teacher."

Wow! One could say with equal validity that the facts in a book are not the responsibility of the author; rather, he has vested responsibility in the researcher, who in turn has relied solely on secondary sources.

The conclusion must be that it is behavior and behavior alone that creates the diagnosis of MBD, and this behavior can only be found in the classroom or at home. Mark Stewart, who received NIMH support, wrote in the July 1970 *Scientific American*: "A child who has been described by his mother as a demon may be an angel when he comes to a psychiatrist's office. Most hyperactive children tend to be subdued in a strange situation and to display their bad behavior only when they feel at home. The explanation may lie in a stress-induced release of norepinephrine in the brain cells. Thus, *a state of anxiety may produce the same effect as a dose of amphetamine—through exactly the same mechanism"* (emphasis added). With relentless logic, Stewart then discusses the behavior of lobotomized monkeys.

Two points on the physical aspects of drugs demand emphasis. First, John Oates of Vanderbilt University has found that "chronic use of amphetamine in small doses may produce symptoms which very closely resemble paranoid schizophrenia." Second, Stewart discredits the alleged "paradoxical effect" by pointing out that "it has been found that amphetamine has a somewhat similar effect on the performance of normal adults who are assigned a boring or complex task."

Would it then be unduly provocative and aggressively argumentative to phrase the question: "Does a long-term dosage of amphetamine and/or Ritalin induce stress in the bored child, producing a perfect student, whose anxiety-ridden behavior may be paranoid schizophrenic and resemble that of a lobotomized monkey?"

It was to speak to a considerably less loaded version of that question that Gallagher invited the provocative educator John Holt. Holt's contempt for orthodox teaching is well known; he compares today's schools to maximum security prisons. Gallagher had phrased his concern, "I fear there is a great temptation to diagnose the bored but bright child as hyperactive, prescribe drugs, and thus deny him full learning during his most creative years," and he introduced Holt's testimony as putting the discussion in the most important context, that of the child.

Holt's response did nothing to lower the issue's hyperbolic content:

> We take lively, curious, energetic children, eager to make contact with the world and to learn about it, stick them in barren classrooms with

teachers who on the whole neither like nor respect nor understand nor trust them, restrict their freedom of speech and movement to a degree that would be judged excessive and inhuman even in a maximum security prison, and that their teachers themselves could not and would not tolerate. Then, when the children resist this brutalizing and stupefying treatment and retreat from it in anger, bewilderment and terror, we say that they are sick with "complex and little-understood" disorders, and proceed to dose them with powerful drugs that are indeed complex and of whose long-run effects we know little or nothing, so that they may be more ready to do the asinine things the schools ask them to do.

Unfortunately, there are those of us who have either forgotten our own grammar school experiences or who think that only an in-depth, scholarly, jargonized study can yield an accurate description of reality. As a result, Holt's testimony needs reinforcement. This was made distressingly clear to me when, during the weeks prior to the hearing, I would describe our witness list and state: "John Holt, a former grammar school teacher." Invariably, the reply would be, "Yes, but what are his credentials?"

Among the abundance of supportive evidence of Holt's findings is that contained in Charles Silberman's recently published *The Crisis in the Classroom*. This study, commissioned by the prestigious Carnegie Corporation, found today's schoolrooms to be "grim" and "joyless." Could we not then wonder if the predicted "zoom" in hyperkinetic diagnosis and its concomitant drug therapy will not be used against precious childhood joy? Has Hutschnecker become institutionalized within the medical-educational complex? Have we put the

Dachaus in the pill and then put the pill in the kid?

Dr. Rada Dyson-Hudson of Johns Hopkins University begins a letter to Gallagher: "As an anthropologist with a background in genetics and biology who is also the parent of a hyperactive son," and goes on to describe how her family moved to a rural setting to avoid being mangled by urban society. Based on her own personal observations, she says, "Where there are important, tiring or responsible physical jobs to do, a hyperactive child is a joy to have around." But a hyperactive child is no joy in overcrowded city classrooms or to the modern housewife.

Dyson-Hudson's professional judgment is also fascinating. She suggests that the prevalence of MBD in the population could mean that it is an inherited trait, has a selective advantage and, therefore, should not be regarded as pathological. She says that the selective advantage must be quite large, in order to counterbalance the higher mortality rate in hyperactive children. This is confirmed in dozens of letters to Gallagher that describe the MBD child as a mass of bandages and stitches, and Mark Stewart finds that many of the children he has studied have been victims of accidental poisoning.

On the other side, a recent New Jersey report states that in 80 children studied, four times as many children who show learning disabilities are adopted than those not adopted. But Dyson-Hudson's point demands further extensive research for two reasons.

First, pediatricians, psychiatrists and educators, particularly school administrators, contend that parents of hyperactive children are excitable, have a history of alcoholism and instability and fail to provide the child with a warm and loving upbringing. (This point is directly denied by hundreds of letters disclosing a real agony in parents who must finally go to drugs as a last resort.) With that sort of finding buttressing the experts' faith in themselves, it is easy automatically to write off the complaints of a child's parents and to coerce them into acquiescing to or embracing drug therapy.

Second, it is fair to speculate that hyperactivity may well be a considerable advantage for children, especially for ghetto kids. The latter truly have no childhood; they are instantly forced to match wits with hustlers, gang leaders, police and antipolice violence and an entire milieu where the prize of physically growing up goes to the toughest and the shrewdest. Theodore Johnson, a black chemist from Omaha, testified to the problems of coming of age in the ghetto and listed causative agents that could produce MBD-like behavior. In the school, he mentioned racist attitudes among teachers and administrators, inferior and outdated textbooks, irrelevant curriculum and inadequate facilities; and for the child, he found malnutrition, broken rest patterns, unstable home environment and physical fatigue.

On a larger social plane, it is possible to speculate that the use of drugs to make children sit perfectly still and reproduce inputs may once have had some functional purpose. Schools formerly trained the vast majority of students to become effective cogs in giant factories, and they were designed so that assembly line learning would result in assembly line production during working years. Yet, it is now obvious that service-oriented businesses are rapidly replacing manufacturing as the major source of employment. It is not unreasonable to suggest that children no longer need to be preconditioned for the rigid regimentation involved in earning a livelihood; an inquiring mind in an inquiring body is now marketable.

There would be far less need for many additional McLuhanesque probes into MBD drug medication if we could rely on the testimony of the Department of Health, Education, and Welfare before the Gallagher

Privacy Subcommittee. If that testimony could stand up under informed scrutiny and if it reflected a conscientious effort to understand and to disclose all the facts, this article would also be unnecessary.

When the federal government sends officials to the Congress to defend a program of such impact, one has a right to expect that rigorous research and rigid control have gone into the decision. In my judgment, both were lacking, and several examples will illustrate my conviction that this massive technological incursion into the sanctuary of the human spirit operated on faulty intelligence.

First, with $3 million from NIMH alone, and with at least 300,000 children and 30 years' experience in the program, it could be expected that hundreds of studies could be cited to show the long-term effect on the children who have been given drugs. Yet, only in 1970 had funds been granted for this essential study, and the man selected to follow up on 67 children was Dr. C. Keith Conners. The HEW witnesses bristled when Gallagher offered the comment that Conners was engaged in evaluating "his own thing," but it is a fact that, prior to the grant for evaluation of these specific children, Conners had been given $442,794 in grants beginning in 1967 to test the effectiveness of drugs on children. Those studies were cited by HEW witnesses as confirming the validity of the treatment.

Wanted: Scientific Dedication

So, as we zoom up to and beyond six million grammar school children on drugs, we are offered a study of 67 cases that was begun in 1970, is now only in its preliminary data-gathering phase and is being carried out by a man whose professional career has been spent proving how effective the therapy is. One can scarcely imagine the cries of rage that would greet any mayor or governor proposing to evaluate road construction in this manner, but one can only assume that scientific research rises above such petty considerations as conflict of interest. In fairness to the selection of Conners, Ronald Lipman, Ph.D. (chief, Clinical Studies Section, National Institute of Mental Health), pointed out at the hearings:

> I think one of the reasons why there have been so few followup studies is that they are so very difficult to do. They involve going back into medical records that are very difficult to come by. They involve tracking down people after a period of 20 years. This is very difficult logistically. *It requires a certain kind of scientific dedication that you just don't find too many people have* (emphasis added).

Other testimony confirmed Lipman's pessimistic view of his colleagues. Dr. Dorothy Dobbs, director of the Food and Drug Administration's Division of Neuropharmacological Drug Products, and HEW's chief witness, Dr. Thomas C. Points, deputy assistant secretary for health and scientific affairs, both testified that they had conducted "cursory" investigations of the administration of these drugs in Omaha and that nothing was wrong. Later in the hearing it was disclosed that Dr. Byron Oberst, the program's primary proponent in Omaha, was unaware that the Food and Drug Administration (FDA) had listed two of the drugs he was using as "not recommended for use in children under 12." Dr. John Peters, director of the Little Rock Child Study Center, was found to be equally in the dark about FDA guidelines on one of the drugs he dispensed. (It must be mentioned that FDA has no authority to insist that drugs not be used; it has a formal mechanism that permits just about anything to be administered under a doctor's prescription.)

Two points are crucial, however: 1) the HEW witness did not volunteer the information that the department had communicated with Oberst pointing out his oversight; and 2) leading practitioners of drug therapy were unaware of FDA's recommendations.

Moreover, while the HEW witnesses cited some 40 studies conferring validity on the use of drugs to mask hyperactive behavior, they did not refer to Crinella's Office of Education study referred to earlier—"one of our most fashionable forms of consensual ignorance" is a line certainly worth repeating—nor did they mention HEW's own studies by John Oates and Mark Stewart. But perhaps most compellingly, we heard nothing of the June 1970 statement of the American Academy of Pediatrics Committee on Drugs. In light of the supposedly wide support within the medical community for the efficacy of drugs, the academy's words are particularly significant:

> An accurate assessment of the effectiveness of the chemotherapeutic approach poses enumerable difficulties. These stem from factors such as 1) the lack of uniform terminology, 2) marked variability in methodology for evaluation, 3) the absence of standardized requirements for precise diagnosis and classification of the symptomatology constituting learning impediments, and 4) the paucity of long-term, properly controlled studies. As a result, a valid evaluation of response and objective comparison of the effectiveness of drugs administered in an attempt to mitigate or lessen learning impediments becomes impossible.

Finally, the HEW testimony dismissed any possible connection between children relying on drugs during grammar school and the incredible problem of drug abuse in high schools and in the rest of society. The

hearing ran for approximately eight hours, and Gallagher hammered away all day long on this most obvious
"paradoxical effect," but it was only during the
questioning of Sally Williams, chief of the School Nurse
Division of the National Education Association, that a
glimmer appeared. She had strongly supported the use
of behavior modification drugs (controlled, naturally
enough, by the school nurse), but, almost as an
afterthought, she disclosed that ten students at her
school were now on Ritalin at their own discretion. Her
exact testimony is most revealing: "They were taken off
the medication and they still came back to the 'springs
inside,' the inability to control their behavior. So the
doctor has put it on a PRN, which means when
necessary, so because they are senior high school
students they come up to the health office and come to
me and say, 'I think I need my Ritalin now.' "

Apparently, the administration shared some of these
doubts, because two short weeks after the hearing, the
director of the Office of Child Development at HEW
announced his intention to form a "blue ribbon" panel
to consider the problem. Dr. Edward F. Zigler's statement of October 12 is very different from the tone of
the HEW testimony of September 29: he said the panel
would "inform educators that perhaps it is as much a
problem of the kind of schoolroom children have to
adjust to rather than what is wrong" with the nervous
systems of the children. On March 10, 1971 the panel
issued its report, and Gallagher commended it for
approximately one-half of his remarks in the *Congressional Record* of that day. He singled out two sentences:

> It is important to recognize the child whose
> inattention and restlessness may be caused by
> hunger, poor teaching, overcrowded classrooms,
> or lack of understanding by teachers and par-
> ents. . . . Variations in different socioeconomic

and ethnic groups must be considered in order to arrive at better definitions of behavior properly regarded as pathological.

In light of the evidence we gathered that drug company salesmen were huckstering their products' wonder-working capabilities at PTA meetings and at professional educational society gatherings, Gallagher also praised this stern warning: "These medicines should be promoted ethically and *only* through medical channels" (emphasis in original).

Unfortunately, the second half of Gallagher's statement was not reflected in media reports. He was sharply critical of the panel's failure to do any independent investigation; they had only produced a compendium, in layman's terms, of existing studies. Moreover, while the report reiterated many of the criticisms surfaced by the Privacy Subcommittee, the report made no comment on the desirability of having a mechanism within the federal establishment to encourage sensible caution at the local level. Gallagher said that "the suspicion still exists that these programs will be used to modify the behavior of black children to have them conform to white society's norms," and that "as admirable as the recommendations in the report are, they will be nothing but high-sounding platitudes unless supervision of local schools can assure that they are given the attention I think they deserve." He called for the Office of Child Development to become the mandated overseer of the increasing nationwide use of behavioral modification drugs.

Assumption of this responsibility became absolutely essential when the Privacy Subcommittee was abolished by its parent Committee on Government Operations on March 31, 1971. Along with a special panel under Congressman Benjamin Rosenthal (D-New York) that had a remarkably effective record of protecting the consumer, the new committee chairman, Chet Holifield (D-California), decreed, as was his right with subcommittees without direct jurisdiction over specific federal agencies, that these issue-oriented studies were outside the committee's ambit. (Holifield has been either chairman or vice-chairman of the Joint Committee on Atomic Energy since its inception. At the risk of being labeled hyperactive myself, it is disquieting that the man who now says there is no valid reason for concern over privacy or consumer matters in the House has consistently stated that there are no dangers from nuclear power plants.)

It would be possible to continue to discuss privacy generally and behavior modification therapy specifically at a length only slightly less than that of the collected works of Dickens, but a brief reference to the National Education Association (NEA) is essential. It has become one of the most effective lobbies in the legislative and executive circles in Washington, and its proposals often quickly turn into public policy. For that reason, it is important to find out just what it has in mind for future generations of American children. A particularly relevant example comes from the *NEA Journal* of January 1969 in an article entitled "Forecast for the 1970's." Two professors of education at Indiana University point to a radically altered school environment, but one of their statements says it all: "Biochemical and psychological mediation of learning is likely to increase. New drama will play on the educational stage as drugs are introduced experimentally to improve in the learner such qualities as personality, concentration, and memory. The application of biochemical research findings, heretofore centered on infra-human subjects, such as fish. . . ."

Fish? Fish! Gallagher has long been concerned with the privacy-invading aspects of credit bureaus, electronic surveillance, the computer and psychological testing, and he has said that the Age of Aquarius will become the Age of Aquariums, in which all our lives are lived in a fish bowl. His assumption, up until the investigation of the drugging of grammar school children, was that there would still be ordinary water in those aquariums; now the concern must be that human rights will be drowned in an exotic brew of biochemical manipulators, stirred and watched by an untouchable medical-educational complex.

The implications and ramifications to our future were well expressed in June 1970 by America's most highly placed social critic. Social scientists would do well to take action on the words of the former president of the Baltimore County Parent-Teacher Association, Spiro T. Agnew: "We as a country have hardly noticed this remarkable phenomenon of legal drug use, but it is new, it is increasing, and the individual and social costs have yet to be calculated."

July/August 1971

FURTHER READING

Federal Involvement in the Use of Behavior Modification Drugs on Grammar School Children of the Right to Privacy Inquiry (Hearings before a Subcommittee of the Committee on Government Operations, House of Representatives, Ninety-First Congress, Second Session, September 29, 1970) can be purchased from the Superintendent of Documents, U.S. Government Printing Office, Washington, D.C. 20402, 65 cents (check or money order).

The Right to Learn versus The Right to Read

NORMAN E. SILBERBERG
and MARGARET C. SILBERBERG

Back in 1969, when he was United States Commissioner of Education, James E. Allen, Jr., declared that for the quarter of our population who do not do well in reading, "education, in a very important way, has been a failure, and they [the failures] stand as a reproach to all of us who hold in our hands the shaping of the opportunity for education." In the same speech, Allen further pointed out that "one of every four students nationwide has significant reading deficiencies," and "in large city school systems, up to half of the students read below expectation." He went on about the "knowledge and inspiration available through the printed word" despite the fact, or because of it, that a Gallup poll showed that 58 percent of the American people admit that they have *never* read a book. Allen then demanded the public and political recognition of "the right to read."

With all the studies done on reading, we still don't know why some children do not read efficiently. It is difficult, when a parent asks why a child can't read well, to suggest (in professional language, of course) that "that's not his bag." Yet, that is what most such appraisals often come down to. There are thousands of diagnoses of what is "wrong" with a child who does not read efficiently, and nearly as many supposed "cures" for these problems, but no one seems to have considered the possibility that we may be barking up the wrong tree in *expecting* all children to read well. These studies have identified many correlates of inefficient reading, but in none has a causal relationship been satisfactorily demonstrated. For example, although there is high correlation between socioeconomic class and reading skills, closer inspection of the terms reveals that the same thing may be lurking under the middle classes' "learning disabilities" and the poor's "cultural depriva-tion." For the poor, home environment is blamed for inefficiency in reading. For the rich, it is brain damage, which is presumably less reversible. In neither case do we really know why some children in all socioeconomic classes read inefficiently—only that they do.

More important is the fact that, by definition, 50 percent of children must read at grade level or below, since grade level only means the median level achieved in a particular grade. Thus, it is not too surprising that Commissioner Allen finds as many as 50 percent of children who are encountering difficulties in reading. As long as grade equivalent is used as a criterion of reading skill, there has to be 50 percent who are below the median in this skill area. One could question the statistical appropriateness of labeling 50 percent of the population as "abnormal," but the real point is that we as a society are attempting to narrow the range of acceptable learning behavior to a specific point, which we have predetermined as appropriate conformity. This seems, at least, a self-defeating task.

Up Against the Curve

We have found seven longitudinal studies of remedial reading. Not one shows any long-term beneficial effect. The current administration is also rather skeptical of these efforts. In a speech given early in 1970, President Richard Nixon described the results after almost $1 billion had been spent yearly on reading programs under Title I of the Elementary and Secondary Education Act of 1965: "Before-and-after tests suggest that only 19 percent of the children in such programs improve their reading significantly; 15 percent appear to fall behind more than expected, and more than two-thirds of the children remain unaffected—that is, they continue to fall behind." There is currently no evidence that one can "remediate" reading as long as reading is measured in relative rather than absolute terms. We can strive to move the whole reading curve up, but we cannot possibly eliminate its bottom half. Research on the cost effectiveness of such efforts, however, indicates, as they would say at the Pentagon, there is not much bang obtained for the remedial buck.

The better we get at measuring school learning skills, the better able we are to describe them. As the social sciences amass more and better measurements of behavior, we can define with good accuracy what percent of children will have difficulty in reading, what percent of children will have behavior problems and so forth. The only thing that we cannot do is to predict into which family such a child will fall. When parents come to us and ask why their child does not achieve or adjust properly in school, we are often tempted to tell the parents it's just their tough luck. What else can we tell them?

The only other response, it seems to us, is the reminder that bearing or adopting children guarantees parents nothing. We—as a society—have not communicated to parents the probabilities of their having children who do not conform to our predetermined narrow range of achievement. Someone should tell parents that they stand at least a 50 percent chance of having a child who will not be successful in school. This is not as difficult for most people to take as one might expect. Parents, for example, are not particularly shocked if it is suggested to them that their children are likely to resemble them in school learning abilities. (In speeches to upwardly mobile suburban parent groups, our suggestion that the parents pull their old report cards out of the attic to hang on the refrigerator as an inspiration to their children is always met with embarrassed laughter.) Unfortunately, however, parents and teachers take personal responsibility for altering a child's behavior so that he conforms to the standards set forth by the media, industry, the whole striving ethos of our culture. We have had parents of children accept the diagnosis of poor school achievement but fall to pieces when told the child should *not* attend college.

Marking Time

American society is moving more and more toward establishment of academic skill as the *sine qua non* of acceptance within that society. Even though we are, for all intents and purposes, attempting to provide some form of academic education to the total society, our demands become less and less realistic. In 1941, the median educational level in this country was ninth grade. Now we keep almost all of our children through tenth grade. Thus, those children who, in our parents' days, were not learning in school and left in sixth grade to work in mines or on farms are now forced *by law* to sit in school for three or four years longer. While they sit in school, they are usually offered either watered-down versions of the same reading-based curriculum the more talented children receive, or woodworking and shop courses which, it is realized by both teachers and students, provide no entry to a meaningful occupation. Even much of the curriculum research for educable retarded children is aimed not at the experience unit, but rather at ways of improving literacy in this group of persons whose tested language skills are in the bottom 5 percent of the population.

Credentialism

Despite the fact that academic potential (IQ) and intelligence (ability to survive in the environment) are very poorly related in many individuals, more and more sectors of the society are being forced into the high school graduate and college craze. We hear reports that companies will not even interview high school dropouts, even though there is no demonstrated relationship between the job task and academic achievement. A local chain of stores insists that their carry-out boys take a *written* test to get this job, even though the only reading required is occasionally setting a price on a stamp which is then used to stamp hundreds of cans. Carole Williams found that

> only 5 percent of the graduates of inner-city high schools are placed in colleges, jobs, or job-training programs by fall, while 50 percent of the dropouts

scheduled to be graduated with the same class have found employment . . . . Inner-city schools don't teach these youngsters job skills, so they seek jobs as unskilled workers—jobs that have already been grabbed by the dropouts. In effect, they have been betrayed by the myth that they should stay in school.

Do these young people need an academic education, or do the personnel managers need an education into the types of skills needed for these jobs?

One example of the frustration encountered because of this thinking is a ninth-grade, 15-year-old boy recently evaluated at the Kenny Institute. He had academic potential within the average range, but, despite years of remedial help, he was still reading at about beginning fourth-grade level and was, of course, flunking most of his courses. He did not make friends easily, so it was not too surprising that when his family moved he refused to attend the new school. He could not bear to demonstrate his "dumbness" to the other students who, not atypically for their age, teased him. He was artistically gifted and good at working with things. What could we do for him? There were no vocational schools where he lived, and even if there had been, most such schools insist on passing grades in academic courses before admission. He was too young for the Department of Vocational Rehabilitation, which also usually encourages high school graduation or else sends the client back for additional course work in books. We could not locate a place where he might study art below a college level. Apprenticeship programs were not available for a high school dropout, as this boy was soon to become. Thus, we had a child who logically could contribute to society, but, because of his reading, was barred from education for an occupation—or rather was barred because the agencies that could help him would not because of their insistence on academic competence.

No one is attempting realistically to assess the wide variations in abilities and talents that exist among young children. Elitists claim that IQ differences among children are not only quantitative, they also represent qualitative differences: a child with a higher IQ is "smarter" than a child with a lower IQ. The trouble with this view is that it expects too much of IQ tests, which do only what they are supposed to do: predict success within an academic curriculum. In addition, it does not recognize the fact that academic curricula were developed for a small portion of the society and cannot be expected to be appropriate for everyone. Elitists regard children with low IQs as deadwood; one influential government official was recently quoted as saying, "Let's teach them to turn a lathe and leave it at that."

On the other side, we find equalitarians whose philosophy is diametrically opposed to that of the elitists. They seem to view people as having equal potential. Thus, we can teach anyone anything, if our teaching techniques are appropriate and if the reward system is appropriate.

We feel the truth lies somewhere between these two points of view. Unquestionably, there are innate differences between individuals. It is also true that most people learn to survive quite well in this society, independent of their success in school. The problems come, however, because society places hierarchical values upon these differences. Higher IQ does not mean "better," it only means "different." Children with lower IQs can learn to do many things that are possibly more important and appropriate to a modern society than the tasks performed by college professors.

Most agencies and professionals exist to satisfy the parents or the school. Most also accept the narrow limits of behavior considered appropriate for children, and then try to fit the individual child into these narrow limits. But who is to speak for the child? What is needed is an advocate for the child.

The function of the advocate is not to attempt to satisfy unrealistic demands by parent or school or government. Rather, the advocate should interpret the child realistically to all concerned and attempt to help the child make it through childhood with the least possible stress. He should focus on the strengths of the child, rather than attempting to remake his weaknesses. Children are not clay; they have their own personalities, traits and talents, as do adults. Parents and the school must begin to recognize these individual differences, and appreciate them, rather than attempt to change them. Options must be made available for those children who are unable to conform, whatever the reason. To view those children who read poorly as defective and requiring a "cure" only increases the frustrations and unhappiness of these children, many of whom are already suffering from the pressure of overzealous parents and educators. A child's advocate would try to relieve this pressure and bring reality into planning for the individual.

If one is willing to accept this point of view, one can then reassess the child. Does the child truly have a learning disability, or, alternatively, do we as a society have a teaching disability? Most of the children we see in clinics or private practice are not incapable of learning. Many of them are incapable of reading comfortably, and many of them, often because of this inefficiency in reading, are unable to behave in a conforming manner. The relationship of poor school achievement to antisocial behavior is well documented. The question is, should we be devoting so much effort to changing the children, or should we be channeling some of our efforts into changing how and what we teach them? Does a child have a right to read, or does he have a right to learn?

As we have pointed out earlier, many children can be taught by other means. One can easily imagine a bookless curriculum which teaches through media other than the printed word, while the teaching of reading takes place much as other skills, such as lathe work, are taught. Art is taught as a skill, but nobody thinks of a child's proficiency in this medium as important to his education. Nevertheless, one should keep in mind that reading is only one skill in a vast repertoire of skills possessed by most children. If we could find ways to teach children by presenting them with more curricular options, we might reduce the stress on them and possibly reduce their rejection of the learning situation as well.

Alternative Skills

John Dewey, decrying the fetish of reading, recommended that books be thrown out of the elementary grades while we get on with the business of educating children. We are not advocating the burning of books or the elimination of reading instruction. Rather, reading should be taught as is any other specific skill, while other available resources are used to ensure that children are not excluded from education. The use of experience units, films, field trips, records, tapes, observation, readers (good readers can put books on tape), verbal interaction between children, and verbal interaction with teachers can be learning experiences.

Education need not be an either-or situation, where a child either learns by the narrow methods traditionally used in schools (book learning) or is shunted off to something called "job training." In a democracy, it is exceedingly important that each citizen be afforded the opportunity to be educated in the fullest sense of the word. Different responses to one skill such as reading should not bar children from a serious education in the name of training. The assumption that the inefficient reader and/or verbally less proficient child is unable to learn or cannot be educated is specious and cruel.

To rid ourselves of this assumption requires not only the restructuring of education but the restructuring of society with its artificial literary requirements. Let us look at some examples of how this could be done. The United States Department of Health, Education, and Welfare, in its request for research proposals relating to "The Right to Read" Program (RFP 70-6), describes a "reading task" in the following way:

> Reading task: A real-life incident which creates an internally or externally imposed requirement for an individual to perform a discrete, observable operation which is highly dependent upon his having satisfactorily read a specific passage of written material. Examples of reading tasks are: (a) looking up a telephone number; (b) following written directions which tell how to assemble a toy or appliance; (c) responding to a written social invitation; and (d) completing a written job application.

Now, seldom, if ever, does one encounter a truly word-blind person. Even inefficient readers can look up telephone numbers, and for those who cannot, there is always "Information" (if you can get it) through the telephone itself. Following written instructions is a stickier matter. Many of us who read well are totally unable to comprehend the written instructions that come with appliances. And there are many other people, good at working with things, though not talented in the use of language, who can assemble appliances with minimal instruction in language. If records can be produced cheaply enough to put them on the backs of breakfast cereal boxes, it would seem logical that recorded instructions could be included *with* the written directions as an option. As for written social invitations, we will let Tiffany's worry about that.

The problem of the written job application is most critical. Current practice screens out people who want to work on assembly or other non-language-based tasks—tasks that can be and usually are demonstrated by the foreman without benefit of text, without determining if there is a relationship between filling out an application blank and the skill required for that job. Application blanks could be mailed out on telephone requests so that the inefficient reader can get help from friends or family in filling it out, with options provided on the job (records, demonstrations and the like) to eliminate the need to read print. The current unemployment or underemployment of many Ph.D.s raises the question of whether higher education guarantees financial security. Despite the fact that close to 50 percent of high school graduates attend college, less than 20 percent graduate. Vocational school is now becoming more and more a college level program, which means that persons who want to work in nonacademic vocations must first achieve academically for 12 years before they are even permitted access to training. For the first time, society is demanding that schools instruct today's total population of children as successfully as when less than ten out of 100 children entered high school.

Unfortunately, "the right to read" suggests that we educate our masses *in the same way* as we used to educate a small number of children who were talented in reading.

We therefore propose that people who are concerned about the academically underachieving child switch their focus. Rather than functioning as agents of changing the child, we need more people to stand up for these children. We must advocate change so that these children can be included in society as they are, so that they can be valued for persons as they are and so that they can be proud of what they are. If parent groups and professionals become advocates for the child, demanding that schools and industry focus on ways of including these children rather than developing more requirements to exclude them, some change might be achieved.

The "that's not his bag" approach is not a pessimistic one. The focus switches to defining the limits in expected variations of specific behaviors within the population. It then becomes the responsibility of the schools to alter their curricula to fit the characteristics of the entire population, rather than attempt to restructure the population to fit society's descriptions of how children *should* perform. In this technological age, it is difficult to understand why literacy has maintained such importance. With education focusing almost solely on a curriculum based on literacy, we are excluding a sizable number of potentially capable citizens from an opportunity to be educated, informed and employed in meaningful jobs.

Educators must decide what it is they want to teach children. Must education continue to emphasize the value of traditional academic education to the exclusion of all else? Couldn't we reorder our priorities so that the teaching of reading requires less of the educator's time and energies? Can't we teach children about the world around them, their own and other cultures, the similarities and differences of other people, the social and ecological needs of people, past, present and future? The child's right to learn these things should outweigh his right to read.

July/August 1971

FURTHER READING

The Psychology and Pedagogy of Reading by E.B. Huey (Cambridge: MIT Press, 1908, reprinted in 1968).

"The Bookless Curriculum" by Norman E. Silberberg and Margaret C. Silberberg in *Journal of Learning Disabilities*, 1969, Volume 2, Number 6, pages 302-307.

PRESCHOOLS
AND DAY CARE CENTERS

Taking Young Children Seriously

CAROLE JOFFE

Although a Children's Liberation Front does not yet exist, the idea is not totally whimsical. In some respects, one can speak of children as an oppressed group sharing certain characteristics with other groups which have already organized around the fact of their oppression. The two most prominent contemporary liberation movements—those of blacks and women—accuse their perceived oppressors of paternalism, a phenomenon that has linguistic roots in the relationship between adults and children. Another term borrowed from the women's movement is useful in describing children as an oppressed group—chauvinism—in this case, "adult" instead of "male."

I am grateful to Sheldon Messinger and to Norman K. Denzin for their help in formulating this essay. I am indebted also to the teachers, parents and children who permitted me to make these observations.

Adult chauvinism appears to take two basic forms. On one level is a tendency toward mystification, in which childhood is portrayed as a time of great bliss and/or children are viewed as better and wiser than adults. A second manifestation of adult chauvinism—one with great implication for social scientists—is simply to deny that children are people. Children are, to use Erving Goffman's term, "non-persons." In this respect the problem of children as an oppressed group is somewhat different from that of other groups. Both blacks and women complain that they have been subjected to unfavorable definitions which were imposed by their oppressors. Blacks have historically been given such labels as "shiftless," "sensual" (as opposed to "intellectual") and "biologically inferior"; more recently, women have come to realize the implications of such definitions as "emotional," "irrational," "earth mothers" and so forth. Children, however, have not been saddled with such stereotypes but, more fundamentally, have been denied *any* kind of social selves: they have not been taken seriously as persons. With few exceptions, the idea that very young children are "presocial" is the dominant one in the social science literature on children.

The Preschool as an Orderly Social World

A common view of early childhood is that until the age of seven, when language is mastered, children are presocial and do not have fully developed selves. A related assumption, perhaps most clearly articulated by Piaget in his use of the term "egocentric" to describe children before the age of seven, is that children of this age cannot take the role of others and thus cannot engage in cooperative enterprises. This implies that young children are incapable of abstract thinking and, while lacking a "real" self, are nonetheless "self-centered."

In this chapter, I shall argue that standard conceptions of childhood need to be reformulated. Mastery of language—on adult terms—does not necessarily mark the beginning of the possibility of a social life among children. The data I have collected in a preschool suggest that children are actors in an orderly social world consisting of similar types of social arrangements that are normally attributed to "real" people. Perhaps the best statement of the spirit in which this study was carried out can be made by quoting from Goffman's remarks in the preface to *Asylums*:

> It was then and still is my belief that any group of persons—prisoners, primitives, pilots, or patients—develop a life of their own that becomes meaningful and normal once you get close to it, and that a good way to learn about any of these worlds is to submit oneself in the company of the members to the daily round of petty contingencies to which they are subject.

The Research Setting

The data for this study were collected during two months of participant observation in a parent-participating nursery school in the San Francisco Bay area. In addition to the weekly participation of each child's parent, there were also two full-time professional teachers. The group observed consisted of 22 students, (nine male, 13 female), ranging in age from about three and one half to four and one half. The school was racially mixed, consisting of about an equal number of children of white professionals and graduate students who paid a moderate fee and black children from low-income families who received scholarships.

The schedule of the typical school day was as follows: the children arrived at nine, took part in several available activities of their choice (either in the yard or indoors), had juice at mid-morning, went to one of two music sessions, then gathered together for a very brief "quiet time" immediately before having lunch and stories in groups of about six. They went home at noon. The only "structured" activity of the session, except for lunch, was music: each child was in one of two music groups, according to the color of his nametag which he put on immediately after arriving at school. But even in the required activity of music, if the child was very preoccupied with something else when his group was meeting, or if he simply did not feel like going, little pressure was brought to make him attend. Essentially the school program provided several simultaneous possibilities and left the child free to schedule his day as he wished.

The school's overall educational philosophy in many ways reflected the same freedom that was accorded the children in scheduling their day. A certain amount of teaching, as opposed to free play activity, was part of the program, but this teaching most often was on a one-to-one basis and appeared to happen when the time was mutually convenient for teacher and student rather than at scheduled intervals. Teaching was, however, an important school goal. Records were kept of each child's mastery of various skills, and systematic efforts were made to help each child in his weakest areas.

Perhaps the most striking indicator of the school's willingness to "take children seriously" is the handling of discipline, particularly in the case of conflicts between children. The school's attitude is that the child is someone to be negotiated with: if he commits an individual transgression, such as disrupting music time, he is told why he is being reproached and, in turn, he is asked to explain his actions. In cases of conflict, especially physical ones, the school separates the fighters, but then, if possible, lets the fighting parties resolve the issue without outside interference. After a fight, the teacher immediately asks the two (or more) children to explain why they were fighting each other and continues to mediate the discussion if necessary. Neither my own observations nor conversations with teachers suggest that this policy always works. Some children respond to this method, while others do not. But significantly, in several critical areas—schedule, curriculum and discipline—the school makes assumptions about early childhood autonomy and abilities that are not found in similar institutions for children or in professional writings.

The observer's role in this preschool was that of any participating parent; each day, I was in charge of a different area of the school—the yard, the art room and so forth. Over the two-month period, I worked in all of the areas and observed virtually all aspects of school activity.

Exclusivity, Territoriality and Behavior Control

Three modes of behavior are connected to the children's attempts to establish social selves. These modes of behavior are hardly exhaustive but they are dramatically suggestive of the *negotiated* character of social life in the preschool. If, in fact, the world of children is not unlike that of adults, then one should expect to find that children, like adults, find some personal relations contaminating and others enhancing;

that they see property as well as personal relations as an attribute of self; and that, generally speaking, they operate in the context of a normative system and attempt to see that others comply to it. The data on "exclusivity," "territoriality" and "behavior control" enable us to test these hypotheses.

Exclusivity is the most immediately intriguing aspect of the children's peer behavior. It refers to the child's verbal acceptance or endorsement of some students as friends or allies and his rejection or "denouncement" of others as suitable playmates. This verbal utilization of exclusivity categories, which involved more than half the children, took several basic forms, ranging from the seemingly simple acceptance-rejection of someone as a playmate for the moment to the more complex acceptance-rejection of someone with whom one did or did not wish to be allied in the "eyes of the community."

The simplest form of the exclusivity phenomenon is typified in the following incident:

> D, upon arrival at school, enters the art room and says to R: "I'm playing with you today, right?" R answers, "No, I'm playing with M."

While the above incident had some practical consequences, in terms of the ongoing reality—R *was* playing with M—in other cases, exclusivity seems to occur when immediate consequences are not at stake, and in these circumstances, exclusivity may convey a variety of more subtle ideas.

> M enters the art room a little later than the others who are already working. She says to P, "I'm going to play with you today, OK?" P answers, "No, I'm playing with B."

These remarks had no immediate significance; each child was working individually on her own collage, and their meaning has to be understood on a more symbolic level.

For example, M conceivably wanted to receive an affirmation of friendship or perhaps, some assurance about companionship for the rest of the day.

A second incident shows an even more abstract use of exclusivity:

> I am talking to P alone in the yard. D has just arrived in the yard and calls out a greeting of "Hi" to P. P answers, "I'm playing with R now." (R is nowhere around; it is clear that "R" is being used as an euphenism for P's wish to remain for the moment, unaffiliated.)

Still another more complex form of exclusivity behavior occurs in incidents like the following in which the vocabulary of exclusivity is used to establish one's public identity as an "upright citizen."

> At the lunch table, B spills something. A sees her and says, "I am not B's friend, she spilled her milk." F immediately asks, "Are you my friend," to which A answers, "Yes."

Finally, exclusivity is closely related to other forms of social behavior in the school. It takes place in the context of clique formation; it is frequently part of a putdown attempt; it can be used by two persons wishing to strengthen their friendship by joining in collusion against a third. All these forms of exclusivity behavior seem to reveal the participants' recognition of a fundamental social principle: one's "self" is inextricably bound up with one's social ties.

The children also engage in *territoriality*, a tendency to stake out geographical spaces, objects and people as one's own. The simplest form of territoriality, and the most common, is the fight for limited supplies, for example, the struggle to maintain or acquire control of a tricycle or a shovel when there are only a few in the whole school. But sometimes territorial battles are fought on less utilitarian grounds and the territory is valued for its prestige as much as for its practicality.

>A group of about ten children are in the front room. M and K have commandeered a puppet stand and are giving shows to some of the mothers and the children. There is much applause and laughter. E trys to enter into the activity but is gruffly told to leave. S hangs around on the fringes, seemingly hopeful of being invited to join in, but is ignored by the puppeteers.

It would probably be a mistake to conclude that all the territorial incidents simply reflect the children's unwillingness to share, or failure to have mastered the idea of sharing. In some instances not sharing *does* make sense, and the school personnel seem to realize this, as is shown in the settling of the following conflict:

>P, B, and M are playing in the Doll Room, a small room set up with old clothes and furniture and other materials in which the children can play house. Their play has been underway for a few minutes when T, L, and D attempt to enter the room and join in. Such a loud outcry is made by those already there, that the teacher comes to arbitrate. The settlement agreed upon is that the first group can retain exclusive rights for ten more minutes and then the second group can replace them.

The above case is most interesting because of its subtlety. Unlike taking a turn on a tricycle or a swing, in the Doll Room there is some question about how many persons can share it at once. Often, groups of up to seven or eight children play there happily. In this case, however, a mood was already established among the first three in the room, and intrusion of others would have substantially altered the quality of their play. In terms we usually reserve for adults, their privacy would have been invaded. The point is that all forms of territoriality must not be judged on the same basis. It is a most intriguing—and difficult—task to try to determine which instances represent sheer "egoism" on the part of the child—the unwillingness to share when he "should"—and which represent, as does the Doll Room case, justifiable strivings for privacy.

The children attempt to control the behavior of their peers in various other ways, and this has implications for the social system of the school. We should, perhaps, first note the various ways in which the life of the nursery school calls for *behavior control*. A vast majority of the experiences at the school involve turn-taking: turns with play equipment, with the teacher's exclusive attention, with the juice pitcher, with private play with one's favorite companion. Not only does one have to wait for what he wants, but once he has it, he is pressured by all around him to relinquish his turn for the waiting others. This omnipresence of the turn-ethos is not the sole reason for incidents of behavior control, but it is important to note that it sets a tone of constant social negotiations that spreads to almost all play activities that involve others.

The most basic form of behavior control of one child by another is physical domination. If one child has a toy that another wants, the latter can take it way just by grabbing; if one child is quarreling with another, he may settle the quarrel by striking. Most of the physical encounters I saw involved arguments over pieces of school equipment, and the vast majority of these fights involved only two persons. When first stuck, the children would react in one of several ways: they would hit back, or they would rush to the teacher, or they would just cry in outrage until they were noticed. Some would try to ignore the attack and continue with the controversial activity. Most fights, whether or not the children actually called for the teacher, were noted and subsequently mediated by the teacher or by one of the parents and, as has been mentioned earlier, the school's policy was to have the children "talk out" the argument with both usually accepting the adult's final suggestion of reconciliation.

But the greatest number of behavior control incidents were verbal rather than physical in character. A number of strategies were used to make the other person submit to one's will without resorting to physical control. A frequent means was appealing to an adult for adjudication: if someone was not relinquishing a turn, if someone was taking someone else's possession, if someone was annoying someone who was trying to concentrate on an individual project, the teachers or the mothers would be called upon to "make him stop it," or "tell him to give it to me." The language chosen by the children suggests an implicit belief in the powers of adults to be able to "make things happen." In most cases, of course, the children were correct: nearly all the children shared a similar orientation about the powers and rights of adults, and when an adult told someone to do something, the request was usually complied with. But the relatively few occasions when adult arbitrations were not complied with also reveal the children's sense of "due process." Mediation efforts were ignored and the children took matters in their own hands when "proper satisfaction" had not been received by an injured party. This did not necessarily mean unreciprocated physical injury, but rather the sense that one's opponent had not been properly chastened. One can see this type of situation in the following conflict:

F comes up to the observer in the yard and asks if

> she has seen N. The observer says no and asks F
> why he is carrying a shovel. "I want to hit N. He
> hit me and I tried to tell his mother but she is
> making pancakes now."

It seems, therefore, that F sought his own revenge
because the usual channels for the settlement of such
problems did not work.

The form of behavior control that perhaps most
strongly indicates the normative system of the school is
the occasional appeal to a code of regulations in
interactions with others, and not just to an authority
figure. This seems even more significant because in this
school there are practically no stated rules, except for
the censure one gets for physical attacks. The children
in this institution, unlike those in others, are *not*
constantly bombarded by "don'ts." Yet, in seeking to
control one another, the children did refer to the few
elements of structure the school did have, as the
following incident about "music time" demonstrates:

> The first music group has finished. K has been
> there illegally as she belongs to the second group.
> When the first group filters out of the room, she
> leaves and then immediately re-enters with the
> second. M, in the second group, sees her and
> screams, "She can't come, she already had a
> turn." A comes over and arbitrates by saying,
> "Let her go in, it's her turn." M again screams,
> "No, she already had a turn."

Sometimes the children would try to control each
other's behavior by invoking categories that had never
been used by the adults, at least not in the context of
the school. The use of sex differences is a case in point.
The use of such categories seemed to have no relation
whatsoever to the matter at hand, or even to the
traditionally accepted notions of what is appropriate for

boys and girls, and seemed to be used as a last-ditch effort when no other good reason for control could be thought of.

> K and two other girls are playing on top of a large structure in the yard. A (male) comes over and K screams, "Girls only!" to which A screams back, "No, boys only!"

The use the children made of sex categories is a telling parody of the meaning that sex roles have in the adult world. Like adults, they seize upon an activity and then label it as appropriate for one sex and forbidden to the other. The main difference seems to be that these particular children did such labelling randomly and spontaneously, while adults have a more patterned system. (One might argue that, as in the incident mentioned above, adult definitions of certain activities as sex-specific may actually have little to do with intrinsic sexual differences.)

The three modes of behavior that have been described so far are all connected to the attempt to establish a self in the school society. Exclusivity identifies one's allies and helps one to plug into the social hierarchy of the school. Territoriality, in which objects, spaces and people are at least temporarily claimed as one's own, also helps to facilitate the social definition of the person. Behavior control also seems intimately related to the process of developing a self. Imposing one's will on others necessitates a sense of differentiation from others and thus the process, as well as the end result of behavior control—having one's own way—heightens the child's emerging sense of self.

But the point is not only that children of this age are occupied with the task of establishing selves; these modes of behavior point to the existence of a social system in which the self-definition process can take place. The full significance of exclusivity, territoriality and behavior control among preschoolers is that they force us to concede the fact of a normative system in operation among young children, who share assumptions about status, property and personal conduct.

Involvement in the Community

Two additional modes of behavior directly challenge the conception of children as "egocentric." The image of young children suggested by Piaget's use of this term is that of individuals concerned with events only of immediate significance to themselves. My observations suggest that this is not always true. Some of the children frequently choose the role of "interested observer" and participate in ongoing interactions in which they are not central parties. This most often occurs in arbitration. Sometimes, the interested citizen will try to settle directly the case for the contesting parties, as in the case concerning music time, and sometimes his role will be to make verbal observations to the concerned parties and the group at large, a phenomenon which seems strangely reminiscent of the role of the announcer in *Our Town*. The following incident shows this second form of arbitration:

> A group of children are sitting at the art table working on collages. C and D are having periodic arguments about the allocation of the various materials and C several times accuses D of hoarding. After one of C's loudest outbursts, R who has been totally uninvolved and who has been using another set of materials lifts up her head from her collage and remarks to D, "She's *really* mad now."

A Sense of Appropriateness

Another dimension of the children's abilities to engage in non-egocentric behavior is their recognition of differing standards of appropriateness for different classes of people (most notably, adults and children). Although this differentiation is somewhat related to the behavior control efforts we have spoken of, such as invoking sex differences, our interest here is not so much with control as with what such efforts reveal about the children's sense of decorum. When mild forms of propriety are violated, the child's main response is to comment with surprise. In relation to myself, this first occurred when I came to school wearing old clothes and not a dress and received M's surprised comment, "Hey, you're wearing *play* clothes!". When I sat down on a tricycle I was told with amusement, "Those are for *kids*." Perhaps most interesting is the following incident:

> P comes up to me and putting her hand in the shape of an animal's paw, pretends to claw the area near my face. I immediately shape my hand in the same way and repeat the gesture. P appears both amused and astonished and I hear her say, a short while later, "When I made a paw to Carole, she made one back to me!"

On several counts, the notion of children as egocentric before they master language must be called into question. The last two behavioral modes I have described show that children of this age most definitely are capable of taking the role of the other. An additional assumption of Piaget's connected with egocentricity, namely that children of this age play side-by-side rather than together, also does not hold. The three modes of behavior described earlier showed instances of collusion against individuals and groups, of joint efforts of territoriality and of behavior control.

Toward a Sociology of Agism

We cannot adequately examine here the question of why certain conceptions about young children have received prominence and others have not. One explanation might be that there are few studies of children in natural social settings, such as preschools or child-care centers, which I would argue are far more suggestive of the social world of children than is the family, with its fixed tradition of hierarchical relationships. Another explanation—perhaps more to the point—is the nature of these settings themselves. The preschool I observed recognized the autonomy and social skills of the children and thus actively encouraged the "coherent social order" I have described. I suspect that establishments such as these—which recognize the existence of social capacities in children—are the fortunate exception rather than the rule. And while I believe that in *any* setting where there are several children, some form of social order will emerge, sometimes this order will of necessity have to be subterranean and less fully developed—as well as less visible to the sympathetic observer. An important line of future inquiry is the ideologies of schools and other institutions which serve young children. Such an investigation might note, on a comparative basis, the consequences—in terms of the actual quality of the social life of the children—of the different assumptions about children that are held by different adult caretakers.

Although there are parallels in the situation of children and of other minorities, I do not want to leave the reader with the impression that I consider the phenomenon of agism to be similar in all respects to sexism and racism. Beyond the obvious fact that children outgrow their status, there are additional critical differences between children and other oppressed groups. While the alleged differences in competencies between blacks and whites, women and men are a matter of social definition, children are in fact quite different from adults. Three-year-olds can't drive cars or fix telephone wires or do many other things that adults can do with ease. But in face-to-face interaction, they can do much more than is normally credited to them. For this reason we should reexamine our currently accepted notions about the nature of most institutions for children.

September 1971

FURTHER READING

Six Psychological Studies by Jean Piaget (New York: Random House, 1968).

Behavior in Public Places by Erving Goffman (New York: Free Press, 1963).

Children, Society and Social Relationships by Norman K. Denzin (Chicago: Aldine-Atherton, Inc., forthcoming).

"Childhood as a Conversation of Gestures" by Norman Denzin in *Sociological Symposium*, Vol. 7, 1972.

"The Genesis of Self in Early Childhood" by Norman Denzin in *Sociological Quarterly*, Vol. 13, Summer, 1972.

The Work of Little Children

NORMAN K. DENZIN

Societies and people organize themselves into interacting moral orders: families and schools, rich people and poor people, the educated and the uneducated, the child and the adult. Relationships between them are grounded in assumptions which justify the various social evaluations. Thus, it is taken as right and proper that the rich should have more privileges than the poor, or that children cannot engage in adult activities. These assumptions are institutionalized and routinely enforced, so that those people who are judged to be less competent are kept in their place. In this chapter I want to look at

Parts of this essay are drawn from the author's forthcoming book, *Children, Society and Social Relationships* (to be published by Aldine) and from his "Developmental theories of self and childhood: some conceptions and misconceptions," a paper presented to the American Sociological Association last autumn. Reprinted with the permission of *New Society*, the weekly review of the social sciences, 128 Long Acre, London WC2, England.

some of the ideologies that surround the adult-child relationship. I shall present data from an ongoing field study of young children in "preschools," in recreational areas and in families, which challenge the view of children that is taken for granted, at least in America.

Childhood is conventionally seen as a time of carefree, disorganized bliss. Children find themselves under constant surveillance. They are rewarded and punished so that proper standards of conduct can be instilled in their emergent selves. The belief goes that they enjoy nonserious, play-directed activities. They avoid work and serious pursuits at all cost. It is the adult's assignment to make these nonserious selves over into serious actors. In America, this belief lasts at least until the child enters the world of marriage and gainful employment.

There is a paradox in these assumptions. Even if a child or adolescent wants to take part in serious concerns, he may find himself excluded. Thus, when the state of California recently passed a law, along the lines already adopted in Britain, giving the vote to 18-year-olds, members of the Assembly refused to accord them drinking privileges, and one argument held that 18-year-olds were not yet competent enough to incur debts and assume other adult responsibilities (like signing contracts).

The paradox extends beyond exclusion. Even when children go so far as to act in adult-like ways, these actions are usually defined as unique, and not likely to occur again unless an adult is there to give guidance and direction. This assumption serves to justify the position of the educator. If children could make it on their own, there would be no place for the teacher. This fact is best seen in American preschools, where instructors assume that little children have short attention or concentration spans. The belief is quite simple. If left to their own ingenuity, little children become bored. Time structures must be developed, so that the child does not become bored. In California, these timetables typically go as follows:

9-9:15: Hang up coats and say "Good morning" to other children.

9:15-10: Play inside on solitary activities (painting, puzzles, toys).

10-10:30: Go outside for group activities on swings, in sandbox, dancing, making things.

10:30-11: Juice and cookie time in small groups around tables.

11-11:20: Quiet time; small groups around instructors where instructor reads a story.

11:20-11:30: Get coats and jackets and prepare to be picked up by parents.

11:30: Session over; instructors relax and have coffee and cigarettes.

When there are clashes over timetables—if, for example, a child refuses to come in for juice and cookies—an instructor will be dispatched to inform him that it is time to come in.

These timetables are revealing and serve several functions. They tell the instructor what he will be doing at any given moment. They give instructors control over the children. They state that children, if left on their own, could not organize their own actions for two and a half hours.

Another paradox is evident. Although children are systematically informed of their incompetence, and rewarded for the quality of their nonserious conduct, adults appear to assume that something important is happening at these early ages. In fact, it is something so serious that normal, everyday adults cannot assume responsibility for what occurs. As rapidly as possible, the child is taken from the family setting and placed in any number of child-care, educational and babysitting facilities.

My interviews with, and observations of, 100 American parents, who delivered their children to a cooperative and experimental preschool, revealed two assumptions. First, the school was a cheap and effective babysitter. The parents had no fears for their child's safety when he was there. Second, if the child was an only child, or if the parents lived in a neighborhood where there were no other playmates, the preschool would expand and cultivate the child's skill at getting on with other children. These parents feared that their child would appear later in kindergarten, and not know how to interact with other children. Because preschools do not formally assess how a child is doing, the parents felt fairly safe. They transferred the function of looking after their child's sociability from themselves to a neutral party—the preschool instructor.

The school, then, gave the parents a year to get the child ready for his first encounter with formal education. The task of the preschool was to shape up the child's speech and to teach him or her how to be polite and considerate to others. A side-function was to give the child different toys and play experiences—finger painting, say, which many parents defined as too messy for their homes. Economically stable families with several children were less likely to send their child to the preschool. Brothers and sisters performed the sociability function of the preschool.

Let me now note a final paradox. Observers like Iona and Peter Opie—in their *Lore and Language of Schoolchildren* and their *Children's Games in Street and Playground*—have found that, when left on their own, children produce complex societies and social orders.

The fact that many children's games are often spontaneously produced, yet are passed on from generation to generation, and that their songs and stories are made to fit special selves, must indicate the child's ability to be a serious, accountable actor.

An example from the Opies' study of children's games reveals the serious character of play. Here the game is "playing school":

> "The most favorite game played in school is Schools," says an Edinburgh 9 year old. "Tommy is the headmaster, Robin is the schoolteacher, and I am the naughty boy. Robin asks us what are two and two. We say they are six. He gives us the belt. Sometimes we run away from school and what a commotion! Tommy and Robin run after us. When we are caught we are taken back and everyone is sorry."

In their attendant analysis of this game, the Opies observe:

> Clearly, playing Schools is a way to turn the tables on real school: a child can become a teacher, pupils can be naughty, and fun can be made of punishments. It is noticeable, too, that the most demure child in the real classroom is liable to become the most talkative when the canes are make-believe.

Urie Bronfenbrenner's recent study of child-rearing practices in the Soviet Union shows, too, that Russians take the games of their young children quite seriously. Such games are used to instill self-reliance and collective respect on the part of the child. Here is one instance:

> Kolya started to pull at the ball Mitya was holding. The action was spotted by a junior staff member who quickly scanned the room and then called out gaily: "Children, come look! See how

Vasya and Marusya are swinging their teddy bear together. They are good comrades." The two offenders quickly dropped the ball to join the others in observing the praised couple, who now swung harder than ever.

Bronfenbrenner notes that such cooperation is not left to chance. From preschool on, Soviet children are encouraged to play cooperatively. Group games and special toys are designed to heighten this side of self-development.

The point I want to make is that when they are left on their own, young children do not play; they work at constructing social orders. "Play" is a fiction from the adult world. Children's work involves such serious matters as developing languages for communication; presenting and defending their social selves in difficult situations; defining and processing deviance; and constructing rules of entry and exit into emergent social groups. Children see these as serious concerns and often make a clear distinction between their play and their work. This fact is best grasped by entering those situations where children are naturally thrown together and forced to take account of one another.

Many specialists have assumed that young children lack well-developed self-conceptions. My observations show, on the contrary, that as early as four a child can stand outside his own behavior and see himself from another's perspective. I carried out intensive interviews with 15 four-year-olds. These revealed support for the general hypothesis that a person's self-concept reflects the number of people he interacts with. The more friends a child had, or the larger his network of brothers and sisters, the more elaborate his self-conception.

Keith, who was four years seven months old at the time of the interview, described himself as follows:

1. My name is Keith —.
2. I am a boy who plays at a nursery school.
3. If I was asked, "What do you like to play best?" I would say: "I like to dance to my favorite records" [*What are your favorite records?*] "Yummy, Yummy"; "Bonnie and Clyde."
4. If someone asked me, "Where do you live?" I'd say, "[Name of street]."
5. If someone said, "Do you know how to do cartwheels?" I'd say, "No!"
6. If someone said, "What kind of picture can you draw?" I'd say, "I can draw my favorite things. I like to draw a man's head." [*Why?*] "Because so much can be added to it. I'd put hair, a chin, eyes, a forehead, a nose, a mouth and a chin on it."

Keith was a leader of the boys' group at the preschool, had nine good friends, and was one of a family that had two other children. Nancy, on the other hand, was an isolate, having only four acquaintances at the school. However, her family also had two other children. Her low integration in the social network of the school is reflected in the fact that she could only give two self-descriptions:

1. I'm at school.
2. I live in (name of city).

As extremes, Keith and Nancy point to a basic feature of life at the preschool. Insofar as a child is a member of the social life of the preschool, the more adult-like will be his, or her, behavior. The social life of the school, then, makes the child into a small adult.

Name games—which take many forms—reveal another side of the child's serious self. Children may reverse or switch names. On a Halloween afternoon, I saw three girls, all aged four, who were sitting around a table mixing pumpkin muffins, systematically assign to themselves and all newcomers the name of the child next to them. The rule was quite simple. Each child was assigned every name in the group but his own. One girl resisted and said: "That's a mistake! My name isn't Kathy, I'm Susan." Susan replied: "We know your name isn't mine, silly; we're just pretending. We don't mean it."

There was a clear separation of play, fantasy and serious activity in this episode. Each girl knew her name. The sequence merely solidified their self-identity. Martha Wolfenstein, in a study of children's humor, has observed that inevitably some child will find these games disturbing, refusing to accept the identity that goes with the new name. Probably such children are not yet firmly committed to the identity designated by their proper name.

Name calling is another game. Here, the child's proper name is dropped and replaced by either a variation on that name, or by an approving/disapproving term. Martha Wolfenstein noted names like "Heinie," "Tits," "Freeshow," "Fuckerfaster" and "None-of-your-business." In name-calling games the child's real identity is challenged. He or she is singled out of the group and made a special object of abuse or respect. (Parenthetically, it must be noted that adults also engaged in such games. Special games for sports and political figures are examples.)

A more severe game is where the child has his name taken away. The other children simply refuse to interact with him. By taking away his name, they effectively make him a nonperson, or nonself. In name-loss games the child may be referred to as a member of a social category (young child, honkie, brat, dwarf). In those moments his essential self, as a distinct person is denied.

The Opies have described another name game, which

is called "Names," "Letters in Your Name" or "Alpha-bet." Here, a child calls out letters in the alphabet, and contestants come forward every time a letter contained in their name is called.

All of these name games reflect the importance children assign to their social lives. A name is a person's most important possession simply because it serves to give a special identity.

In preschools, the children are continually construct-ing rules to designate group boundaries. In those schools where sexual lines are publicly drawn, boys and girls may go so far as to set off private territories where members of the opposite sex are excluded. One observer working with me noted boys and girls in a four-year-old group, carrying posters stating that they were "Boys" or "Girls." On another occasion I observed the creation of a "Pirate Club" which denied entry to all females and all males who did not have the proper combination of play money for paying their membership dues. This group lasted for one hour. At juice and cookie time, it was disbanded by the instructor and the boys were made to sweep out their tree house. Adult entry into the club seemed to reduce its interest for the boys.

The study of early childhood conversations reveals several similarities to adult speech. Like adults, young children build up special languages. These languages are silent and gestural. What a child says with his eyes or hands may reveal more than his broken speech. As children develop friendships, "private" terms and mean-ings will be employed. To grasp the conversations of young children, it is necessary to enter into their language communities and learn the network of social relationships that binds them together. Single words can have multiple meanings: "Baby" can cover a younger brother or sister, all small children, or contemporaries who act inappropriately. To understand what the word, "baby," means for the child, it is necessary to 1) understand his relationship to the person called a baby, 2) the situation where he uses the word and 3) the activity he is engaging in at the moment.

Neologisms are especially crucial in the development of new relationships. The involved children attempt to produce a word that outsiders cannot understand. Its use sets them off from the other children; it serves to give a special designation to the newly formed relationship. I observed two girls, aged three, who had suddenly discovered one another. Within an hour they had developed the word "Buckmanu." With smiles on their faces they came running inside the preschool, holding hands and singing their new word. After several repetitions of "Buckmanu," they came over for juice, and a mother asked them what they were saying. They ignored her and suddenly switched the word to "Manubuck." And then, with precision and correct enunciathey said, "Manuel bucked us off!" Manuel was the name of a preschool instructor. They had taken one of his actions (playing horseback) and his name, and forged the two into a new word. Once they revealed the name to the mothers, they ceased using it.

January 1970

FURTHER READINGS

Two Worlds of Childhood: US and USSR by Urie Bronfenbrenner (New York: Russell Sage, 1970).

The Lore and Language of Schoolchildren by Iona and Peter Opie (New York: Oxford University Press, 1959); *Children's Games in Street and Playground* (New York: Oxford University Press, 1969).

"Children's Humour: Sex, Names, and Double Meanings" by Martha Wolfenstein in *The World of the Child* edited by Toby Talbot (New York: Anchor Books, 1968).

Day Care Centers:
Hype or Hope?

GILBERT Y. STEINER

By the end of the 1960s it was evident that under the most prosperous of conditions, public assistance was not about to wither away. A considerable fraction of the population was still outside the sweep of social security's old age pensions, survivors' benefits or disability insurance, and also outside the sweep of the country's prosperity. "It becomes increasingly clear," the *New York Times* editorialized after the overall level of unemployment in New York City declined to 3.2 percent of the civilian labor force while at the same time the number of welfare clients in the city climbed to one million, "that the welfare rolls have a life of their own detached from the metropolitan job market."

It is detached from the national job market as well.

This article is an excerpt from *The State of Welfare* by Gilbert Y. Steiner, © 1971 The Brookings Institution, 1771 Massachusetts Ave., N.W., Washington, D.C. 20036.

In 1961, when there were 3.5 million AFDC recipients, unemployment as a percent of the civilian labor force nationally was a high 6.7 percent. By 1968 the national unemployment figure was hovering around a record low 3.4 percent, and there was serious talk among economists about the possible need for a higher rate of unemployment to counteract inflation. But the average monthly number of AFDC recipients in 1968 was up to 5.7 million, almost 4.4 million of whom were children. In 1969 the monthly recipient total averaged 6.7 million, and for the first six months of 1970 it was 7.9 million.

Public assistance also has a separate life outside the growth of the economy. The gross national product was $520 billion in 1961; in 1969 it was $932 billion. One of the things not expected to rise under those prosperous conditions was payments to relief recipients. Yet total payments in AFDC alone in 1961 were $1,149 million; in 1969 total payments were $3,546 million and rising rapidly.

To put all this another way, it is roughly accurate to say that during the 1960s the unemployment rate was halved, AFDC recipients increased by almost two-thirds, and AFDC money payments doubled. Whatever the relationship between workfare and welfare, it is not the simple one of reduced unemployment making for reduced dependency. How has government responded to this confounding news?

For the most part over the past ten years it has responded by tirelessly tinkering with the old welfare system. Special emphasis has been placed on preparing the welfare population emotionally and vocationally for participation in the labor market, thereby enjoying not only the economic security provided by employment itself, but also the unemployment insurance and survivors' insurance, if needed, which employment gives access to. The first such effort—the professional social service approach characterized by a stated plan emphasizing services over support and rehabilitation over relief—showed no progress after running its full five-year trial period from 1962 to 1967. And so, in 1967 a series of programs was invented in order to push relief clients to work. Work experience, work training, work incentives—whatever the titles and whatever the marginal differences in program content—were all designed, in the catch phrase often used, to move people off the relief rolls and onto the tax rolls. Each program assumed that the gulf between labor force participation, with accompanying economic security benefits on the one side, and relief status on the other side, was bridgeable.

It was not until 1967, however, that it came to be perfectly acceptable to think of mothers with dependent small children as proper objects of the effort to get the very poor off the relief rolls and onto the tax rolls.

Agreement on this question resulted from the confluence of two separate concerns. One concern was with costs and criticisms. Representative Wilbur Mills, powerful leader of the crucial House Ways and Means Committee, viewed with alarm the costs of an unchecked public assistance program:

> I am sure it is not generally known that about 4 or 5 years hence when we get to the fiscal year 1972, the figure will have risen by $2.2 billion to an amount of $6,731,000,000. . . . If I detect anything in the minds of the American people, it is this. They want us to be certain that when we spend the amounts of money that we do, and of necessity in many cases have to spend, that we spend it in such a way as to promote the public interest, and the public well-being of our people.

> Is it ... in the public interest for welfare to
> become a way of life?

A different concern motivated an HEW task force,
department officials and some of Mills' legislative
colleagues. The task force showed little worry over how
many billions of dollars public relief was costing, but
did concern itself with the turmoil and deprivation that
beset recipients in depressed rural areas and in urban
ghettos. Thus, to the Mills conclusion that the costs are
prohibitive, there was joined a related HEW conclusion,
shared by some members of Congress, that the quality
of life on welfare was intolerable.

One congressman with such a view is the only lady
member of the Ways and Means Committee, Martha
Griffiths. Mrs. Griffiths was especially indignant over
the conditions imposed on AFDC mothers.

> I find the hypocrisy of those who are now
> demanding freedom of choice to work or not to
> work for welfare mothers beyond belief. The truth
> is these women never have had freedom of choice.
> They have never been free to work. Their educa-
> tion has been inadequate and the market has been
> unable to absorb their talents. . . .

> Can you imagine any conditions more demoral-
> izing than those welfare mothers live under?
> Imagine being confined all day every day in a room
> with falling plaster, inadequately heated in the
> winter and sweltering in the summer, without
> enough beds for the family, and with no sheets, the
> furniture falling apart, a bare bulb in the center of
> the room as the only light, with no hot water most
> of the time, plumbing that often does not work,
> with only the companionship of small children
> who are often hungry and always inadequately
> clothed—and, of course, the ever-present rats. To

keep one's sanity under such circumstances is a major achievement, and to give children the love and discipline they need for healthy development is superhuman. If one were designing a system to produce alcoholism, crime, and illegitimacy, he could not do better.

Whatever the differing motivation, HEW's task force, Mills and Mrs. Griffiths all pointed in the direction of change from the status quo. And the change agreed upon was abandonment of the heretofore accepted idea that the only employable AFDC recipients were unemployed fathers.

In 1967 the Ways and Means Committee unveiled its social security and welfare bill at about the same time that HEW Secretary John Gardner unveiled his reorganization of the welfare agencies in his department. That reorganization merged the Welfare Administration, the Administration on Aging and the Vocational Rehabilitation Service into a new agency called the Social and Rehabilitation Service (SRS). To run it, Gardner named Mary Switzer, a veteran commissioner of vocational rehabilitation who was aptly described by a local journalist as "a diligent disciple of work." This bit of tinkering was designed to send the message through the federal welfare bureaucracy that the secretary was receptive to policy change, apparently including a new work emphasis. The great drive to employ dependent mothers and provide day care for their children thus began both in the administration and in Congress two years before President Nixon discovered it anew.

Day Care

Despite an announcement by Miss Switzer in April 1969 that a reduction in the number of people on the welfare rolls is "a top priority of the Social and Rehabilitation Service" which she asked state welfare administrators "to make yours as well," it was really beyond the power of either Miss Switzer or the state administrators to effect a big breakthrough in the AFDC problem. The key to moving some people off the rolls is employment for the AFDC employable parent. The rub is that even training for employment, a first step, requires an expensive new industry—day care—which now lacks organization, leadership, personnel and money for construction of facilities. Moreover, once the realities of work training and day care programs are examined, it becomes evident that there is not much incentive for a poorly educated AFDC mother to accept training for herself and day care service of uncertain quality for her children.

Training AFDC mothers for employment, actually finding jobs for them and providing day care facilities for their children present formidable problems. A recent survey of the AFDC population found that 43 percent of the mothers had gone no further than the eighth grade, including 10.6 percent with less than a fifth grade education. Work training that leads to employment at wages adequate to support a family is likely to be prolonged, at best, for this undereducated group.

The realities of the coming crunch in day care are even more troublesome. Day care provisions accompanying the 1967 work incentive (WIN) legislation did not extend to the creation of a federal program authorizing funds for new facilities. There are approximately 46,300 licensed facilities caring for 638,000 children. If every place in every licensed day care facility in the United States were to be reserved for an AFDC child under the age of six, there would be more than one million AFDC children in that age group with no place to go. There would also be consternation among the thousands of non-AFDC mothers with children of that age level who are already in day care centers.

In short, there are not enough facilities—good, bad or indifferent—to accomplish the day care job envisioned by the congressional and administration planners who still talk of moving parents from welfare rolls to payrolls. Representative Fernand St. Germain was undoubtedly right in stating in 1969 that "costs of new facilities are too much for the states to bear alone; centers will only be built in numbers that have any relation to the critical need if federal assistance is forthcoming." No one seems to have foreseen this in 1967, however, and the point never got into the HEW program memorandum that influenced the employable mother discussions and proposals of the House Ways and Means Committee.

But the day care problem goes beyond the matter of adequate space to an important philosophical and political question regarding the appropriate clientele for the service.

There is no political conflict over the proposition that a young mother suddenly widowed and left dependent on social security survivors' benefits should be supported with public funds so that she can stay home and take care of her children. Nor is there congressional discussion or any HEW proposal for day care for those children. If 94.5 percent of AFDC dependency were attributable to death of the father, there would be no congressional interest in day care to speak of.

But, in fact, 94.5 percent of AFDC dependency is not attributable to death of the father; only 5.5 percent is. Most of the political conflict and a good deal of the interest in day care is over whether the public should subsidize those women whom Senator Russell Long once called "brood mares" to stay home, produce more children—some of them born out of wedlock—and raise those children in an atmosphere of dependency.

While medical authorities and professional social workers are still divided philosophically over how accessible day care should be and to whom, Congress in 1967 and President Nixon in 1969 simply embraced the possibility of putting day care to work in the cause of reducing public assistance costs. In other words, political attention has focused less on the practical limits of day care and more on its apparent similarities to baby sitting.

Day care was simply not ready to assume the responsibilities thrust on it by the welfare legislation adopted in 1967, and it was not ready for President Nixon's proposal to expand it in 1969. Whether day care is a socially desirable or even an economical way of freeing low income mothers with limited skills and limited education for work or work training still has not been widely considered. In the few circles where it has been considered, there is no agreement. Both the 1967 legislation and the Nixon proposal for escalation should have been preceded by the development of publicly supported, model day care arrangements that could be copied widely; by attention to questions of recruitment and appropriate educational training for day care personnel; by an inventory of available and needed physical facilities; by the existence of a high-spirited and innovative group of specialists in government or in a private association or both; and by enough experience to expose whatever practical defects may exist in day care as a program to facilitate employment of low income mothers. Instead of meeting these reasonable conditions for escalation, public involvement in day care programs for children, a phenomenon especially of the last ten years, remains unsystematic, haphazard, patch-worky.

The Children's Bureau Approach

For many years before 1969, the HEW Children's Bureau ran the bulk of the federal day care program. It did not encourage an approach that would make day care readily available on demand. Stressing that day care can be harmful unless it is part of a broader program overseen by a trained social worker, the bureau defined day care as a child welfare service offering "care and protection." The child in need of day care was identified as one who "has a family problem which makes it impossible for his parents to fulfull their parental responsibilities without supplementary help." The social worker was seen as necessary to help determine whether the family needs day care and if so to develop an appropriate plan for the child, to place the child in a day care program, to determine the fee to be paid by the parents and to provide continuing supervision.

Change comes slowly to child welfare—as to other specialists. Those in the Children's Bureau found it difficult to adjust to the idea of day care available to all comers and especially to low-income working mothers. On the one hand, the talk from the top of the bureau has been about the need to face reality in the day care picture—"when," as one bureau chief put it as early as 1967, "thousands of infants and young children are being placed in haphazard situations because their mothers are working." On the other hand, down the line at the bureau the experts continued to emphasize the importance of the intake procedure to insure that children placed in day care "need" the service.

With this approach it might be expected that while the day care expansion movement has ground along slowly, it has ground exceedingly fine. Day care undoubtedly is a risky enterprise. Every center should have a genuinely high-quality, sympathetic environment; no center should be countenanced without clear evidence that such an environment is being created, and all centers that do not give such evidence should be discouraged. The payoff, therefore, for what might seem to be excessive caution by the Children's Bureau could have been a jewel of a limited program and no second or third rate imitations. Then, when money and will were at hand, the jewel could be reproduced.

In fact, no day care activity was discouraged, whether of low quality or not. Caution on the subject of quantity did not work to guarantee quality. Whether or not there would be any day care activity depended on the states, and the federal agency was accommodating, both because it was hard to interest the states in day care at all, and because Congress provided money in fits and starts, rather than in a steady flow. When the money did come, there was an urgent need to spend it.

Funding

Between 1962 and 1965, HEW had only $8.8 million to parcel out to the states for day care. Moreover, it was never able to count on having anything from year to year, so that it is understandable that the federal agency was in no position to threaten the states about the quality of service. The 1962 law required that federal day care money go only to facilities approved or licensed in accordance with state standards. The law said nothing about minimum federal standards. In 1962 a number of states had no day care licensing programs at all; among the states that did, the extent of licensing and the standards used varied considerably. The Children's Bureau's own guidelines were little more than advisory. To raise the quality of day care nationally, the bureau had to fall back on persuasion and consultation, weak tools compared to money.

Licensing

One certain effect of the 1962 requirement that the available federal money go only to licensed facilities was to divert a substantial part of the funds into licensing activity itself and away from actual day care services. For fiscal 1965, for example, 43 percent of the $4 million appropriated for day care was spent on personnel engaged in licensing, while only 36 percent was used to provide day care services in homes or centers. This increased licensing activity has the effect of distorting the picture of growth of day care facilities. In 1960, licensed day care facilities had a reported total capacity of 183,332; in 1965 this had increased to 310,400; in 1967 the figure was up to 473,700; in 1968 to 535,200; and in 1969 to 638,000. There is universal agreement, however, that the growth figure is mostly illusory, a consequence of formerly unlicensed facilities now being licensed.

Moreover, there is more form than substance to licensing decisions. The fact that a day care facility is licensed cannot yet be taken to mean that its physical plant and personnel necessarily satisfy some explicitly defined and universally accepted standards. Like "premium grade" automobile tires, licensed day care facilities can differ sharply in quality—and for the same reason, the absence of industry-wide standards. Licensing studies by public welfare agencies are invariably assigned to new and untrained caseworkers. The results are unpredictable and there is no monitoring body able and authorized to keep a watchful eye on who is being licensed.

Even from those who accept the simplistic assumption that only the absence of child care services and of job or training opportunities preclude AFDC recipients from becoming wage earners, there is no suggestion that just any kind of child care will do. Yet the state of the art in day care is not sufficiently advanced to make it reasonable to expect that states can meet the requirement to provide day care services other than in makeshift, low-quality programs. There is clear validity in the complaint of the National Committee for the Day Care of Children that the 1967 legislation was not designed to help children develop mentally and physically, but was "a hastily put together outline for a compulsory, custodial service which is not required to maintain even minimal standards of adequacy."

Challenge from Head Start

Only a month after taking office, President Nixon called for a "national commitment to providing all American children an opportunity for healthful and stimulating development during the first five years of life." A few weeks later Secretary of HEW Robert Finch welcomed the delegation of the Head Start program to HEW as the occasion for a new and overdue national commitment to child and parent development. Finch indicated publicly that he was not inclined to put Head Start in the Children's Bureau and instead placed it in a new HEW Office of Child Development (OCD) where the Children's Bureau was also transferred. Social planners in HEW, the Bureau of the Budget and the White House envisioned a new era: day care programs for low-income children would be modeled on Head Start: simple custodial arrangements would not be tolerated; parents would be involved. The way for this happy outcome had already been paved by issuance of the Federal Interagency Day Care Requirements, a joint product of HEW and OEO, approved in the summer of 1968.

Things have not worked out. Whatever Finch's initial intention, the day care programs operated by the Children's Bureau never made it to the OCD. In September 1969 a new Community Services Administration was created within the Social and Rehabilitation Service to house all service programs providing public assistance recipients under social security. The Head Start bureau of the OCD, according to the terms of the reorganization, was given some responsibility in Social Security Act day care programs—to participate in policy-making and to approve state welfare plans on day care. But effective control of the money and policy in the day care programs remains with the Social and Rehabilitation Service. President Nixon's "commitment to providing all American children an opportunity for healthful and stimulating development during the first five years of life" has so far produced more talk than money.

A High Cost Service

There has simply not been enough thinking about the benefits and costs of a good day care program to merit the faith political leaders now express in day care as a dependency-reducing mechanism. Federal day care program requirements are, for the most part, oriented to the idea of day care as a learning experience. They are, therefore, on a collision course with supporters of mass day care as an aspect of the struggle to reduce welfare costs. The high-quality program requirements reject simple warehousing of children, but the prospects for meeting high standards are not good. It seems inevitable that there will be disappointment both for those who think of day care as a welfare economy and for those who think of day care for AFDC children as an important social and educational advance.

Consider the situation in the District of Columbia, which is reasonably typical of the day care problem in large cities. The District Public Welfare Department (DPW) in May 1969 was purchasing child care for 1,056 children, of whom about 400 were children of women in the WIN program. Of the total 1,056 children, 865 were in day care centers, 163—primarily infants too young to be placed in centers—were in family day care homes, and 28 were in in-home care arrangements, a service considered practical only for large families. The total anticipated day care load for the end of fiscal 1969 was 1,262. District day care personnel estimated that 660 AFDC mothers to be referred to WIN during fiscal 1970 (on the basis of 55 per month) would need, on the average, day care for two children. These additional 1,320 children would bring the likely number for whom the District would be paying for care to 2,582 by July 1, 1970. Budget requests for day care for fiscal 1970 totaled $3,254,300 in local and federal funds ($1,148,000 of local funds brings $2,106,300 in federal money). Of this amount, about $3 million is for purchase of care, the remainder for administrative expenses. If budget requests were met, the purchase cost of day care in the District would thus be expected to average almost $1,200 per child. Costly as that may seem to be, it represents only a little more than half the actual cost.

It is the beginning of day care wisdom to understand

that it is an expensive mechanism and to understand that there are qualitative differences in the care provided. The elegantly stated effort of the DPW is to secure "in addition to good physical care, the kind of exceptionally enriched day care experience that is specifically designed and programmed to stimulate and promote the maximum in emotional, physical, and educational growth and development of the child." Alas, one-third of the centers with which the DPW contracts only "offer primarily custodial and protective care," a code phrase for warehousing. Fees paid day care centers by the District Welfare Department are supposed to be a function of the quality of services offered. Grade A centers are paid $4.00 a day, B centers $3.00 a day, and C centers $2.50 a day. The department's Standards for Day Care Centers say that it uses a fee schedule for two reasons: "to assure that proper value is received for each dollar spent and, secondly, to provide a monetary stimulus to contract day care facilities to upgrade the quality of their services to meet the Department's maximum expectations." Each center's "rating," known only to it and to the Welfare Department, is for "internal use" and is not revealed to the welfare mother because, according to department officials, it would not be fair to the center to do so. A more pertinent question is whether it is fair to the mother, since 25 of the 55 centers from which day care is purchased are graded B or C, and since half of all placements are in B or C centers.

All centers—whether A, B or C—must meet the Health Department's licensing requirements, as well as additional specific standards set down by the Welfare Department in the areas of educational qualifications of personnel, program content, and equipment and furnishings. Yet there are two problems with this seemingly tidy picture. The first is the insistence of close observers that while the Welfare Department's standards for centers look satisfactory on paper, they have not been put into practice very consistently. The second is that even the paper standards will not do when the federal interagency standards become effective July 1, 1971. Spokesmen for the National Capital Area Child Day Care Association (NCACDCA) and District Health Department licensing personnel are critical of the Welfare Department's day care operation. Both suggest there is a lack of awareness in the Welfare Day Care Unit of what constitutes good day care. That high ranking is reserved, in the judgment of these people, for the centers operated by NCACDCA. The critics complain that only the NCACDCA centers can legitimately meet the Welfare Department's own A standards and maintain that the other A centers simply do not meet them. They claim, for example, that one way these latter centers "meet" the educational qualifications for personnel is to list as a director an "absentee"—perhaps a kindergarten teacher in the District of Columbia school system or that of a neighboring county.

No one disputes that most centers in the District cannot meet the Federal Interagency Day Care Requirements—particularly the child-adult ratios and the educational qualifications for staff. Even a good number of the A centers do not meet the child-adult ratio requirements, and the B and C centers meet neither the staff educational qualifications nor the child-adult ratios of the federal requirements. If the day care centers have not met the federal standards by July 1, 1971, DPW cannot continue making payments on behalf of children for whom it receives federal matching funds. But in the District Welfare Department the view is that the requirements are unrealistic and that widespread complaints from private users who cannot afford the costs involved may result in a lowering of standards.

All the evidence suggests that day care is expensive whether the auspices are public, private or mixed. In a curiously chosen experiment, the Department of Labor decided in 1969 to fund an experimental day care program for its own employees at a time when emphasis was presumably being placed on supporting day care for the welfare poor. Its estimated budget for the first full year of care for 30 children was $100,000, one-third of which was for nonrecurring development costs, including renovation for code compliance, equipment and evaluation. Tuition from the group of working mothers involved amounted to only $7,300, leaving $59,600 of public funds necessary to provide care for 30 children—a subsidy of almost $2,000 per child without considering nonrecurring cost items. Doubling the number of children served the second year would require a budget of $100,000, resulting in an average annual per child cost over the two years of $1,850, or of $2,225, if the renovation and equipment items are not dismissed as readily as the department sought to dismiss them in its official explanation.

The National Capital Area Child Day Care Association estimates costs at almost $2,400 per child per 50-week year. Its standard budget for a 30-child center exceeds $71,000. Tight-fisted budget examiners might effect reductions, but they cannot be consequential unless the pupil teacher ratio is drastically revised. Morever, NCACDCA salary figures are unrealistically low. Head teachers for a 30-child center are hard to come by at $7,300 (see table).

If these per child costs of desirable day care are

projected nationally, the annual bill for all preschool AFDC children must be figured conservatively at $3 billion.

Client Arithmetic

Most women in the District of Columbia WIN program are being trained in clerical skills in anticipation that they will take jobs with the federal government as GS-2s. This is an optimistic view since most trainees have ninth to eleventh grade educations while a GS-2 needs a high school diploma or equivalency or six months' experience and the ability to pass a typing test. That problem aside, the District AFDC mother who completes work incentive training and is placed in a GS-2 job will be better off financially than the mother who stays on welfare. Her gain will be greater the smaller the size of her family. She will have fewer children to support on her fixed earnings, whereas the larger the family on AFDC, the larger the grant.

For many a female head of a family of four in the spring of 1970, however, the work and day care

Standard Day Care Center Budget for Thirty Children for One Year

A. Personnel

3 full-time teachers (head teachers, $7,300; teacher, $7,000; teacher assistant, $4,700)	$19,000
2 full-time aides ($4,140 each)	8,280
1 half-time clerk	2,400
Part-time maintenance help (cook, $2,610; janitor, $2,024)	4,634
Substitute (teacher aide, $4,300) and part-time student aide ($1,214)	5,514
Subtotal	$39,828
Fringe benefits (11 percent)	4,381
Total	$44,209

B. Consultant and Contract Services
Part-time social worker ($2,500), psychiatric
   consultant ($5,000), and educational
   consultant ($1,000) $8,500
Dietitian   500
Dental and Emergency medical service   450
    Total $9,450

C. Space
Rent ($1,800); custodial supplies and minor
   repairs ($1,800) $3,600

D. Consumable Supplies
Office, postage, and miscellaneous
   (blankets, towels, etc.) $450
Educational ($400) and health supplies ($30)   430
Food and utensils   4,674
    Total $5,554

E. Rental, Lease, or Purchase of Equipment
Children's furniture ($3,000) and office
   equipment ($200) $3,200
Equipment: basic (easels, blocks, etc., $1,500);
   expendable (dolls, puzzles, books, etc., $700);
   outdoor, with storage ($1,000)   3,200
    Total $6,400

F. Travel
Staff ($240) and children's trips $720) $960

G. Other
Telephone ($36 a month; installation $50) $482
Insurance (liability, property, and
   transportation liability) $700

    Total $1,182
    Total project cost $71,355
    Child cost per year $2,378

Source: Derived from budget of National Capital Area Day Care Association, Inc., Washington, D.C., August 1968.

arithmetic was not encouraging as the following illustration shows. If the GS-2 mother has three children and
claims four exemptions, about $39 of her monthly
salary of $385 is deducted for retirement ($18.50) and
for federal ($17) and local ($3.50) taxes, leaving a take
home pay of about $346 a month. If two of the three
children are in Welfare Department child care arrangements, placed there when the mother entered the WIN
program, the mother would pay the department about
$6.00 a week toward their care; if the mother had only
one child in care, she would pay $5.50. Assuming two
children in care, the mother's monthly cost would be
about $26, lowering her net earnings to $320.

Suppose, however, that the woman stayed on AFDC.
The average benefit for a four-person family on AFDC
in the District would bring her $217 monthly. Both the
welfare mother and the working mother would be
eligible for Medicaid, but only the welfare mother
would be eligible for food stamps. For $60 a month she
could receive $106 in food stamps, a gain of $46. The
welfare mother's child could also receive free lunches at
school while the working mother's could not. (The
working mother is considerably above the income scale
used to determine eligibility for free lunches, although
in cases where it is felt children are going hungry,
exceptions to the income scale can be made.) A school
lunch costs 25 cents in the District's elementary schools.
If the welfare child took advantage of the free lunch the
mother would save about $5 a month. Thus, the welfare
mother would end up with a total of about $268 in
welfare, food stamps and school lunches while the
working mother would have about $320 a month. In
addition, the 1967 welfare amendments allow a welfare
mother to earn $30 per month without loss of benefits.
The net gain for working full time compared to working

only 19 hours a month at the minimum wage is thus reduced to $22. From this, the working mother would have expenses to cover such items as transportation and extra clothes for herself and might have to make some after school care arrangement for her third (school-aged) child.

City Arithmetic

How much work training and day care can save the District of Columbia will depend on how many trainees complete training successfully, get a job and keep it, and on how many children of trainees need child care. The Welfare Department will benefit financially by the AFDC mother's entering a training program and becoming employed as a GS-2 unless the mother has four or more children in day care—which would be most unusual. While it might give the AFDC mother of three $217 each month, the department would pay only part of her day care cost once she begins working (the department pays all costs for the first three months). With an average cost to the department for day care of $17.50 per child per week, using our hypothetical GS-2 mother with two children in day care and one in elementary school, the mother would pay $6 a week and the Welfare Department $29 a week for day care. This working mother thus represents a monthly saving to the department of about $56. If, however, the AFDC mother had four children in day care centers and one in elementary school, the mother would pay $6.50 a week toward their care (this figure is the same for three or more children) and the department $63.50. The department would thus spend $273 a month for child care—and save nothing compared to what it would have given her on AFDC to care for her own children at home.

Prospects

What are the prospects for success in turning day care into a program that will reduce the costs of AFDC? They hinge, first, on large numbers of AFDC mothers actually turning out to be trainable and able to be placed in jobs under any conditions and, second, on finding some cheaper substitute for traditional day care centers.

The difficulty in securing the physical facilities and staff needed to develop the traditional centers looked overwhelming to state welfare administrators examining the day care problem in 1967. They did, however, see some hopes for neighborhood day care, a kind of glorified, low-income equivalent of the middle-class babysitting pool. Stimulated by OEO's success in involving poor people in poverty programs, HEW early in 1967 started pushing neighborhood day care demonstration projects using welfare mothers to help care for other welfare mothers' children. This seemingly ideal solution has its own problems. One of them is sanitary and health requirements that, if enforced, disqualify the substandard housing used by many recipients. The unknown emotional condition of the AFDC mother is an equally important problem in this use of the neighborhood care idea. A spokesman for the Welfare Rights Organization warns:

> Do not force mothers to take care of other children. You do not know what kind of problem that parent might have. You do not know whether she gets tired of her own children or not but you are trying to force her to take care of other people's children and forcing the parents to go out in the field and work when you know there is no job.
>
> This is why we have had the disturbance in New

York City and across the country. We, the welfare
recipients, have tried to keep down that disturbance among our people but the unrest is steadily
growing. The welfare recipients are tired. They are
tired of people dictating to them telling them how
they must live.

Not surprisingly, day care and work training through
WIN are lagging as the hoped-for saving graces of public
assistance. New York City's experience is instructive. In
1967 the City Council's finance committee concluded
that an additional expenditure of $5 million for 50
additional day care centers to accommodate 3,000
additional children was warranted. "The Committee on
Finance is informed," said its report, "that many
(welfare) mothers would seek employment if they could
be assured of proper care of their children while at
work. We feel that expansion . . . on a massive scale is
called for." The mayor's executive expense budget for
day care was thereupon increased by about 60 percent
and appropriations in subsequent years have continued
at the higher level. But the New York City Department
of Social Services—like the U.S. Department of Health,
Education, and Welfare—lacks a program for such a
rapid expansion of day care. Actual expenditures have
lagged. In contrast to the anticipated 50 new centers
caring for 3,000 additional children, it was reported in
June 1969 that 19 new centers accommodating 790
children had been established.

The national figures resulting from the 1967 amendments are no more encouraging. Like New York City,
the federal government has not been able to shovel out
the available money. Consider the situation around the
time of the Nixon family assistance message. Of a
projected June 1969 goal of 102,000 WIN enrollees,
only 61,847 were in fact enrolled by the end of that
month. Of a projected 100,000 child care arrangements,

only about 49,000 children were receiving care at the end of June 1969, and 50 percent of them were receiving care in their own homes. Thus, when President Nixon proposed 150,000 new training slots and 450,000 new day care places in his August 1969 welfare message, the Labor Department and HEW had already found that 18 months after enactment of the 1967 legislation they were unable to meet more than 60 percent of their modest work and training goals or more than 50 percent of their even more modest day care goals.

WIN Loses

The gap between original projections and depressing realities held constant into 1970. The Labor Department first estimated a WIN enrollment level at 150,000 at the close of fiscal 1970, later scaled the figure down to 100,000. And as of February 1970 the cumulative WIN data took the shape of a funnel:

Welfare recipients screened by local agencies for possible referral	1,478,000
Found appropriate for referral to WIN	301,000
Actually referred to WIN	225,000
Enrolled in WIN program	129,000
Employed	22,000

As for day care, 188,000 children were initially expected to be receiving "child care"—which includes care in their own homes by grandmothers or other relatives—on June 30, 1970. The target later was dropped to a more modest 78,000. In May 1970 there were just 61,000 reported in child care, and only about one-fifth of these children were really cared for in a day care facility. Approximately one-half were cared for in their own homes, one-tenth in a relative's home, and the last one-fifth were reported to have "other" arrangements—a category that actually includes "child looks after self."

By July 1970 the House Labor-HEW appropriations subcommittee was discouraged about the progress of work training-day care activity. "It doesn't sound too good," said Chairman Dan Flood (Democrat of Pennsylvania) after hearing the WIN program statistics. The committee proposed a reduction of $50 million from the administration's request for $170 million in 1971 work incentive funds. There was no confusion about either the purpose of the program or its lack of accomplishment:

> The objective of the work incentives program is to help people get off the welfare rolls and to place them in productive jobs. While the committee supports the program, it has just not been getting off the ground for several reasons, such as poor day care standards for children.

Unfortunately, the sorry history and the limitations of day care and work training as solutions to the welfare problem could not be faced by the administration's welfare specialists in 1970 because all of their energies were directed toward support for the Nixon family assistance plan. But after a few years it will inevitably be discovered that work training and day care have had little effect on the number of welfare dependents and no depressing effect on public relief costs. Some new solution will then be proposed, but the more realistic approach would be to accept the need for more welfare and to reject continued fantasizing about day care and "workfare" as miracle cures.

July/August 1971

Domestic Pacification

GEORGE D. COREY and RICHARD A. COHEN

Although the bus wouldn't pick them up until 8:30, many of them were there by 6:00 AM. There was the normal quota of noisy playfulness that comes with any large group of pre-teens and young teenagers. But beyond that there was an air of tingling excitement—these kids were going to summer camp, many of them for the first time. The bus would eat away the 40 miles to the camp in no time. Then there would be swimming, fishing, softball, basketball, volleyball, boxing, cookouts. And talks on moral leadership, character guidance and citizenship; arms demonstrations, police demonstrations, military training films, marching instruction, patriotism and military discipline lectures. And maybe even a session or two on "The Communist Conspiracy."

No, this is not a privately funded camp, a church-affiliated camp, a YMCA camp or even a camp run by a right-wing political group. It is a composite picture that would easily fit any of the thousands of summer camps for "disadvantaged" children run by the Department of Defense (DoD) under its rapidly expanding Domestic Action Program (DAP). The DoD claims its motives are altruistic, but a careful examination of the program and a close reading of its readily available literature indicate otherwise. The key idea that recurs in a majority of the reports, pamphlets and brochures is that this program "will enhance [DoD's] ability to provide total national security." And while this somewhat vague concept is never clearly defined, it appears to translate into control or pacification of ghetto populations. Each year since 1968, the federal government has taken an increasingly large number (2.7 million in 1971) of impressionable ghetto children (primarily male and largely black) and attempted to mold them into right-thinking individuals —as defined by the Department of Defense with the blessings of President Richard Nixon:

The White House
Washington

April 11, 1969

Honorable Melvin R. Laird
Secretary of Defense
Washington, D.C.

Dear Mr. Secretary:

At a recent meeting of the Urban Affairs Council, I reviewed a presentation by Deputy Secretary of Defense David Packard and a member of his staff concerning ways in which the Department of Defense can participate in the alleviation of our Nation's serious domestic problems.

I concur with Secretary Packard's conclusion that the Department of Defense can make a meaningful contribution to our Administration's efforts in these areas without detracting from its primary mission of national security. I feel that the Department's traditional dedication to service and great talent for solving complex problems can and should be directed toward our domestic goals through coordination with the Urban Affairs Council.

I believe that your creation of the Department's Domestic Goals Action Council is an effective means of insuring continued emphasis on this subject. I know that your successful implementation of this concept will demonstrate to the public the Department of Defense's continued service to the Nation.

Sincerely yours,
(signed) Richard Nixon

With that letter President Nixon officially authorized the creation of a Domestic Action Program and a Domestic Action Council to direct an already ongoing effort. According to Colonel William Earl Brown, Jr., USAF, Special Assistant for the DAP:

April 1969 [was not] the initiation of domestic action activities by the Military Departments. . . . The history of our Armed Forces is one of military-civilian cooperation. . . . The establishments of the Domestic Action Program simply brought together, at DoD level, a body of men (the Domestic Action Council) to coordinate and organize such efforts.

Back in 1965, the Department of Labor in its publication *The Negro Family* (also known as *The Moynihan Report*) argued that at least one viable goal for black males might be to join the military. In fact, Daniel P. Moynihan reasoned that the military satisfies many of their psychological needs.

There is [a] special quality about military service for Negro men; it is an utterly masculine world. Given the strains of the disorganized and matri-focal family life in which so many Negro youth come of age, the Armed Forces are a dramatic and desperately needed change: a world away from women, a world run by strong men of unquestioned authority, where discipline, if harsh, is nonetheless orderly and predictable, and where rewards, if limited, are granted on the basis of performances. The regimentation of the military according to this line of thought offers an alternative to their volatile existence.

Moynihan portrays the family structure as the only significant determinant of a child's development. Actually, as Ulf Hannerz and other critics have shown, there is an interplay between the family and community environments; the community can and does provide the necessary male images that Moynihan contends the black family lacks.

Despite its inherent flaws, Moynihan's position filtered down into several military programs, most prominently into Jr. ROTC, which claims to offer:

> an excellent opportunity to give disadvantaged [male] children, at their option, a chance to make up for the opportunities many of them have missed because they come from broken homes, and have not had the advantages of parental attention, training, leadership and discipline.
> (1970 *Blue Ribbon Defense Report*)

The Blue Ribbon Defense Report not only suggests that Jr. ROTC had a rehabilitative effect on disadvantaged youngsters, but adds that the program should actively seek to enlist these children because this would contribute to overall community betterment. This is in line with ROTC's stated goal of insuring the "community a well-groomed male body."

The attempt to regulate potentially rebellious youngsters by grounding them in military codes and training is nothing new. Some urban social workers have generally valued the rehabilitative function of the military. It is not uncommon, for instance, to find social workers in metropolitan areas arranging with military officials to induct poor black teenagers in order to prevent judges from sentencing them to training schools or jails. In such cases social workers become the undeputized agents of the armed services and channel the children of the poor into military life.

Plans for the establishment of a volunteer army will necessitate greatly augmented enlistment rates to maintain armed services manpower at effective levels. As the draft calls are eliminated, recruiting will take on more significance. New incentives will thus become necessary to encourage more people to enter the military service. With the unemployment level for black teenagers soaring, the manpower potential of the ghetto is overwhelming. Military public relations has thus aimed its sights toward the area. But a key factor in reducing the number of ghetto recruits has been their failure to pass mental and physical examinations. Something had to be done to increase the successful induction of this group.

The government's solution was to initiate in 1966 Project 100,000, which Pentagon spokesmen claimed would "salvage the poverty-scarred youth of our society" for military service and later civilian life. Called "the greatest contribution to the war on poverty," its original objective was to successfully enlist 100,000 men each year who had formerly failed to qualify. To accomplish this, the Selective Service lowered health and educational requirements. Its discriminatory application resulted in only 16 to 20 percent of black enlistees being disqualified for medical reasons compared to the 30 percent of the objectively healthier whites. With the phasing out of the draft, defense officials indicate that Project 100,000 quotas will be reduced but adds that when the volunteer army becomes a reality, "100,000" will merely take a different form.

From the government's point of view, channeling young blacks and other racial minorities into the military has a number of side benefits:

1. It will reduce unemployment figures. Moynihan suggested this in his 1965 report when he noted that "if 100,000 unemployed Negro men were to have gone into the military, the Negro male unemployment rate would have been 7.0 percent in 1964 instead of 9.1 percent."

2. Removing young blacks from the inner cities of the country will reduce juvenile delinquency rates. As the Katzenbach Commission on Law Enforcement and Administration of Justice (1967) reported, in ghettos considered to be "high delinquency rate" areas, well over half the boys under 18 appear in court. Consequently, indiscriminate mass relocation of ghetto youth could greatly reduce urban delinquency levels.

3. Ghetto activism can be restrained. As juvenile gangs like the Young Lords begin to organize around political issues such as police relations, food programs or housing conditions, attempts to break up these gangs will become political actions designed to defuse minority political power.

Military programs such as Project 100,000 and Jr. ROTC deal only indirectly with the effects of poverty. DAP, on the other hand, is designed to deal directly with the problems—to provide welfare services to civilian populations, a role historically beyond the scope of DoD's responsibility. The largest of the welfare services is the Youth Opportunity Program (YOP). But DAP-YOP is significant for more than its size. While the DoD has previously concerned itself with civilian adults through the Selective Service, with the DAP it is becoming extensively involved in the welfare of children, that segment of the American population least capable of recognizing, articulating and defending its rights.

DAP's officially stated mission is to use the extensive resources of the Defense Department in cooperation with other governmental and private organizations in a national effort to overcome serious domestic problems and contribute to the constructive development of our society. In addition Domestic Action does satisfy a number of immediate military needs. Drastic troop reductions resulting from changes in our Vietnam War strategy are causing the military to look for new ways to maintain its dominant position in American society. The prospect of a volunteer army forces the armed forces to develop a positive image in order to secure enlistments. Two objectives are thus served by the military's entrance into the civilian sector via Domestic Action. While assuming its dominance in American life, the Defense Department can cultivate favorable attitudes towards the military among the young.

The DoD publicly claims that Domestic Action is an attempt to eradicate poverty. But privately it phrases its objectives in different terms. One Air Force report puts it this way:

> In military campaigns, it is important to know the enemy, define the objectives, form the strategy and tactics, and launch the offensive. So it is in the Domestic Action campaign. The "enemy" has been well defined by many people. He is the evil rampant in our society—and his offspring are the multifarious outgrowths of poverty, ignorance, and discrimination. It is difficult to separate these three villains and the evils they spawn—crime, hate, fear, and destroyed lives.

The military imagines itself to be allied with the poor—primarily those urban nonwhite poor—in fighting their common enemy to achieve a better life. But the real objective is internal security against the dangerous consequences of an unrehabilitated poor. "For in the end," as Robert McNamara said in *The Essence of Security*, "poverty and social injustice may endanger our national security as much as any military threat."

David Packard, former Deputy Secretary of Defense has said, "The activities of the Defense Department's Domestic Action Program make a real contribution to the Nation's security. Of such activities, none are more important than those which give disadvantaged youth a chance to learn and work." Other DoD officials have found DAP's work vital to the "total national security." The reason is straightforward: national security is defined to include protection from internal as well as external threats. And Colonel James A. Donavan, author of *Militarism USA*, has stated that DAP demonstrates the concern of the defense establishment "about the security of its rear, the Zone of the Interior."

Much of the DoD's official literature reflects this concern for security. The "First Six-Month Report on Domestic Action" (May-November, 1969), lists "Guidelines for Domestic Action" on the first page. The initial paragraph discusses the DoD's efforts to overcome "serious domestic problems" and adds, "By meeting this challenge, the Department will enhance its ability to provide total national security." DoD Directive 5030.37 (May 21, 1970) "provides guidelines and establishes policy" for DAP. Five major objectives are listed; number one reads: "Enhance DoD's ability to promote national security."

As of 1970, the total number of DAP activities involved 5,000 military institutions in all 50 states. Over 75 percent of the children in the summer programs were from "disadvantaged" families in poverty-stricken ghetto target areas. Since the council's formal inception of the Youth Programs in 1969, there has been more than a 300 percent increase in attendance each year. According to DoD statistics, DAP took 225,000 "disadvantaged youths" out of the ghetto in 1969. The number increased to 775,000 in 1970 (a 300 percent jump) and to 2,700,000 in 1971 (an increase of 347 percent).

Most of those attending are between the ages of ten to 21. This indicates a substantial overlap with the Kerner Commission's profile which describes a typical rioter as a "Negro, unmarried male between 15 and 24," although many studies, such as those of Robert M. Fogelson and others have subsequently challenged the validity of such profiles. Domestic Action, by reaching out to those children ages ten to 15, is attempting to divert them from becoming potential rioters by removing them from the frustrating and potentially explosive ghetto environment. It thus will curb ghetto riots rather than attacking their roots, the actual problems of poverty.

Evidently, while mouthing concern for individuals, the DoD is actually concerned with control of ghetto masses. In an article on DAP, *Commanders Digest* (A DoD publication) of July 12, 1969, stated, "wherever possible, activities should be structured to provide measurable benefits within specific time limits." In light of Directive 5030.37, it is clear that while a quantity like cultural enrichment may be somewhat difficult to measure, the decreasing incidence of ghetto violence is easily measured.

DAP Linked to Riots

The inception of Camp Concern at Bainbridge,

Maryland, is directly linked to the riots that followed the assassination of Martin Luther King, Jr.—by admission of the DoD. An official Naval press release reads:

> To fully understand the situation, it is necessary to go back to the spring of 1968. At that time the city of Baltimore was being torn by riots that left hundreds of inner city business establishments in smoking ruins. Something had to be done to direct the energies of the city's disadvantaged youth into constructive channels.

The Navy and the city of Baltimore concluded that a Domestic Action Camp could help solve the problem. During Concern's nine-week summer schedule, 500 to 600 disadvantaged children were bussed 80 miles daily from Baltimore to Bainbridge in order to "prevent the scars [of riots] from being reopened during the hot summer months." During the first two years of Concern's operation, almost 11,000 youngsters were channeled out of Baltimore in the summer. Similarly, the Strategic Air Command Report on the Offut Air Force Base program in Omaha, Nebraska, credited the removal of children from Omaha with that city's peaceful summer.

A nationwide mobilization program using community agencies and groups to identify and recommend children for consideration such as that employed by DAP can isolate and segregate potentially rebellious members of society. Domestic Action's rate of growth over the last three years attests to the efficiency and speed with which this method of social control can be and has been effectuated. The negative aspects, of course, are that such a mechanism is tantamount to establishing preventive detention centers for children. When the risk of riot becomes the greatest during the summer months, the program is activated, effectively maintaining an artificial tranquility in the ghetto.

Concerning DAP-YOP, Dr. Curtis Tarr, Director of the Selective Service System, said:

> The quality of the organization was impressive particularly on the part of the young people who acted as counselors. The experience is an exhilarating one, and I hope that we are somehow finding a way to influence the youngsters.

But in Boston, a Model Cities administrator who has worked with a local Domestic Action Project feels that the program influences the children adversely. Recalling last year's experience, he said:

> Military camps are not designed for kids. It's too spread out. You have bused them from here to there and the kids in this neighborhood have been bused to hell. They're bused to school—to the countryside—everywhere. And just to take them out of the city is not enough. It's what you do with them that counts. In this program the welfare of the children is secondary. White counselors were hired from around the base. They told the white kids (at the camp) to keep away from the others (the black and Spanish children). The white counselors fostered racial tension. It spread to the kids—some riots broke out—some theft. Then it hit the newspapers.

Program Planning

One of the first military summer camps for children is located at Offut Air Force Base in Omaha, Nebraska. The camp's curriculum includes extensive tours of the installation, various military demonstrations, competitive sports, intermittent talks by military officers and officials on subjects like citizenship, patriotism and moral development, a counseling program and job placement. This camp served as a model for others.

At Offut, each Friday is devoted to learning how to be a patriot. A patriot is defined as one who "zealously fights" for his country and his country's interest. Police demonstrations, Defense Department films and proper flag care are used as teaching activities. These efforts to involve children in political indoctrination programs are, however, outside the officially stated scope of DAP-YOP, which is to provide counseling, vocational and remedial services to ghetto youths.

According to Captain E.P. Flynn, Jr., who initiated "Operation Shipmate" at the Charleston, South Carolina, naval station, that program includes neither remedial education nor arts and crafts. While probably helpful to ghetto children and listed as an objective of DAP in Directive 5030.37, remedial education is not necessarily considered part of a typical summer camp program—but arts and crafts are. Instead, the program includes military fire-fighting demonstrations, tours of ships and fleet support units (including a tour of a mobile mine assembly unit) and flag-appreciation lectures. In addition, military films are shown, including "missions of Navy and various type ships" and "patriotism topic films."

Another typical program is the Summer Youth Activity Program of Fort Carson, Colorado. Serving 150 to 200 "disadvantaged youths" for the latter half of the summer of 1970, "Fort Carson sought to expose these youths to educational and recreational activities which would otherwise have been unavailable." Education is interpreted to mean vocational activities which include instruction in subjects like auto servicing. Recreational activities seek to take advantage of the Fort Carson environment, in terms of tours to Pike's Peak, Bust Rodeo and the Will Rogers Shrine. Organized athletics are supervised by Fort Carson soldiers, who also serve as guides, counselors, instructors and medics.

Although program content varies somewhat from base to base, it typically includes talks on moral guidance and patriotism. Some camps venture into politically controversial areas by adding sessions on "The Communist Conspiracy" and military discipline. Operation REAP of Fort McClellan, Alabama, includes "an arms demonstration . . . given by the Chemical Corps School." But virtually every program includes a heavy emphasis on athletics. And the highly competitive sporting event is one very effective method of controlling group violence. Through sports, camp counselors manage the children's aggressions. Physical combat is unbridled under strict rules, a practice common to both competitive games and military training. According to Willard Waller, all sports perform this function, but the military is one of the few environments which rewards planned physical aggressiveness. The even more disciplined format of military drills is also a major means of keeping order within the ranks of the youngsters. One DAP-YOP summer camp had a Marine instructor whose mission was stated as "the marching indoctrination of youth."

Military exercises are attuned to do more than develop merely physical discipline. Daily exposure to officers and soldiers creates ideal types for the children to emulate. After visiting a local DAP-YOP camp in 1970, a sportswriter from the *Baltimore News American* recounted:

> Little boys and girls look up at the captain, whose handsome features and military bearing make him look like the perfect Naval officer Hollywood would cast in the role.

The captain added:

> You can see how shy and withdrawn they are the first morning but they loosen up and relax. It's

usually by the end of the week that they are giving me those playful salutes and calling me "Sergeant" and "Lieutenant."

At Domestic Action camps children actively seek to imitate their adult supervisors. A particularly striking example of this behavior is depicted in the Columbia Broadcasting System documentary "The Selling of the Pentagon" which appeared on national television in 1971. One segment shows children mimicking a military demonstration of hand-to-hand combat. Shortly after the airing of the film Vice-President Spiro Agnew commented:

I watched the films of the children romping around, playing at war. I didn't lose the obvious overtones that the Department of Defense was some sort of ogre for allowing encouragement of this type of play even though it's existed traditionally in history of all countries and will probably exist just as the western movie and the villain and the hero exist there.

In spite of the vice-president's rationalization, there is little justification for the DoD to actively expose children to institutional violence. The military, however, has deemed such conditioning to be in the interest of our national security.

Many of the DAP camps also include counseling programs which contribute to DAP-YOP job-placement services by identifying the aptitudes and impediments of each child, essential knowledge for job-placement functions. DAP-YOP employment placement is determined by the guidelines in Directive 5030.37, which requires that job placement or training be coordinated with local school systems and the nearest state employment office "to insure training compatible with expressed need of the local labor market." But such policy is repressive, for it is an institutionalized equivalent of the ghetto labor market, simply training youths in skills that confine them to the restrictive opportunities already available to ghetto residents. For example, the 1969 Tinker Air Force Base program trained 703 disadvantaged youths, two-thirds of whom were black, for clerical work (40 percent), typing (20 percent) and manual labor (30 percent). All of these are socially immobile labor roles. Only the 10 percent who were trained as skilled assistants in the Tinker program will have some chance of escaping the lower echelons of the labor market. Domestic Action policy implemented in this manner fails to ensure that participating youngsters get an equal opportunity through training in skills or by otherwise expanding their employment horizons.

Through talks on moral guidance, counseling and job placement, Domestic Action emphasizes that success is personally achieved. Poverty is described as the result of the individual's failure. Poverty becomes a state of mind rather than a condition of society. As William Ryan has charged, the victim is blamed for his circumstances. In promoting this philosophy, the military is stressing that individual motivation rather than institutional reform is the solution to poverty. The effect of this is the manipulation of individuals as directed by the military establishment toward illusory ameliorative goals.

The military camp in a very real sense is a symbolic representation of the ghetto. In neither environment can one expect to significantly improve one's life chances. Overt authority figures manifest themselves either as police or military officers. And in both the camp and the ghetto, gang or troop violence is a way of life.

Goal Assessment

There is a considerable discrepancy between what

Domestic Action claims as its objectives and the methods employed to measure its success. The public mission of Domestic Action is, as characterized by Secretary Laird, "solving some of the problems that afflict our urban area." Yet the youth programs under the council are not evaluated as to their impact upon any particular community's development. Required reports more or less give body counts of participants plus some commentary on how the program affected their attitudes towards the military. Under Defense Department Directive 5030.37, the only service-wide data that would lend itself to evaluation are "summaries of significant achievements or problems encountered within the program." Yet even this information is geared for increasing the efficiency of management rather than improving the community. Other reports are only suggested for submission: narrative summaries of youth activities accompanied by photographs, movies or slides intended for public relations. Since no service-wide evaluation of the program is made, nothing is known of the overall impact of Domestic Action.

The Domestic Action Council is thus unable to examine critically DAP's performance because it lacks evaluative data. It has not even planned effective mechanisms for evaluation. Apparently the Council does not want to know any more than whatever it needs for public relations. Moreover, information about the content of the children's programs is disseminated on a camp-to-camp basis, prohibiting the public from viewing the impact DAP-YOP has nationally. The structure of DAP's public relations promotes public acceptance but prevents public scrutiny.

Funding

The funding structure further frustrates public inquiry into the workings of Domestic Action. Each program generates its own unique funding after arrangements have been made with the local military post. The council simply authors directives, formulates policy and seeks departmental assistance from other federal agencies. In this fashion the council relieves itself from much of the paperwork involved in financing. At the same time, monitoring the funding becomes impossible to control or review because it is so diverse.

Most funding comes from a variety of government sources. Participating departments include Labor, Transportation, Agriculture, Commerce and Health, Education and Welfare. Agencies which also assist range from the Civil Service Commission to the Office of Economic Opportunity. Moreover, the military by law is not permitted to expend funds to support these programs. If military facilities and resources are used, the military is not reimbursed for these costs. Unenumerated military costs include men released from service to work in the programs, extra manpower assistance totaling in the hundreds of thousands of man-weeks per year, military hardware demonstration costs and public relations expenditures.

These hidden costs violate the Budget and Accounting Act Amendment of 1950, which explicitly requires full public disclosure of all government financial and management operations. Nowhere in the federal budget are the expenses for services rendered to DAP by the Department of Defense explicitly audited. What in fact occurs, with the diffusion of DAP funding and accountability, is a circumvention of the public's right to know. Congressional investigative committees are triply hamstrung in any congressional review of the Domestic Action Program; they lack evaluative data on 1) program results, 2) financial allocations and expenditures, and 3) administrative responsibility.

But an even more insidious by-product of the diffusion of the Domestic Action Program is the encroachment of the Department of Defense into nonmilitary federal functions. Under the Domestic Action Program, nonmilitary funds from HEW, Labor and Agriculture for example, are administered within military contexts. The substantive result of this is an increasing tendency toward military usurpation and direction of nonmilitary programs and functions. And other governmental agencies are ignoring this encroachment, or at least tacitly approving it by their silence. For example, the Office of Economic Opportunity, in Guidance Memorandum 6011-1 to its Community Action Agencies (CAAs), states its approval of DAP: "The objectives of the Department of Defense Domestic Action Program are consistent with the goals of the CAA's." It goes on to list, word for word, four of the five objectives stated in DoD 5030.37. But there is no mention of DoD's primary objective of national security.

The consequenses of welfare services administered by military authorities could be nightmarish, recalling Kenneth Keniston's fantasy about the expansion of the DoD into "community mental health" maintenance. Military usurption of civilian welfare functions is particularly serious in light of the relatively secretive way in which it has been carried out. Domestic Action must therefore be seen within the context of growing secrecy in the military.

The danger is clear and present. Who or what policies govern the governing? Without such checks in government, programs of social control such as Domestic Action are free to proliferate. From the discovery of Project Camelot—the Army's counterrevolutionary task force during the early 1960s—to the recent revelation that anthropological data is being used to manipulate primitive tribal groups for military purposes in Southeast Asia, it has been clear that coercive social research programs on the part of the armed forces are forging ahead. In a real sense, we may legitimately ask: What will check the expansion of the DoD's Domestic Action social welfare bureaucracy?

Even more alarming, from a social policy point of view, is why and how such a program came into existence. Domestic Action seems to have emerged out of a program vacuum. Those parts of the federal government which are responsible for the health and welfare of the civilian population—principally HEW—have failed to supply the country and specifically ghetto areas with the resources its young people need—resources like sufficient educational opportunity or adequate job training. At the same time the government has not been able to reduce the number of the poor. As their numbers and the consciousness of the need for some type of ameliorative programs grew, the problem became a crisis. Riots increased and delinquency escalated. The Department of Defense stepped in.

It was able to do so for a number of reasons. First, the armed services command a powerful and highly disciplined organization. If nothing else, they can manage the problem until some alternative arrangements can be made. In 1970 they were even encouraged in the Blue Ribbon Defense Panel Report to use pacification techniques developed in Vietnam with minority groups and ghetto areas.

As a public program, DAP-YOP is insidious. It is apparently in violation of significant statutes involving public accountability of executive programs. Its design ignores or subverts all regulations that require congressional investigation and public disclosure of data.

DAP-YOP is a disturbing example of the creation of public policy by a bureaucratic structure outside the checks of elected representatives. It is a serious challenge to the efficacy of open democratic government.

And the YOP is only part of the total Domestic Action Program. DAP also includes Summer Hire, employing nearly 50,000 young people per year since 1969, over 75 percent of them considered "disadvantaged"; Assistance to Minority Business Enterprise, wherein DoD counsels "minority businessmen in the policies and procedures associated with doing business with DoD" and provides "technical management and other guidance;" and Project Value which trains "disadvantaged and hardcore unemployed persons for alternate employment within DoD or other agencies." These are just a few programs—there are many others.

Even more frightening, DoD think tanks may even now be involved in domestic areas. In a letter dated March 4, 1969, presumably addressed to the Secretary of HEW, Secretary of Defense Melvin Laird offered the use of "Federal Contract Research Centers (FCRC's), organizations such as RAND, Mitre Corporation and the Lincoln Laboratory of MIT" for "efforts to overcome our domestic problems." According to Laird, "the FCRC's have skills which might be used quite fruitfully by other departments of the Federal Government, as well as state and city governments."

Finally, DAP threatens the very basis of the distinction between the military and civilian sectors of American society. As the military gradually absorbs the functions of other executive departments, unnoticed by the public, the specter of an American society even more responsive to militarily defined priorities becomes frighteningly immediate.

July/August 1972

SCHOOLS
AND FINDING YOUR PLACE

Children and Their Caretakers

NORMAN K. DENZIN

Schools are held together by intersecting moral, political and social orders. What occurs inside their walls must be viewed as a product of what the participants in this arena bring to it, be they children, parents, instructors, administrators, psychologists, social workers, counselors or politicians. A tangled web of interactions—based on competing ideologies, rhetorics, intents and purposes— characterizes everyday life in the school. Cliques, factions, pressure groups and circles of enemies daily compete for power and fate in these social worlds.

Children and their caretakers are not passive organisms. Their conduct reflects more than responses to the pressures of social systems, roles, value structures or

An earlier version of this essay was commissioned by the Work Group on self-concept of the Social Science Research Council Subcommittee on Learning and the Educational Process, January 1970.

political ideologies. Nor is their behavior the sole product of internal needs, drives, impulses or wishes. The human actively constructs lines of conduct in the face of these forces and as such stands over and against the external world. The human is self-conscious. Such variables as role prescription, value configurations or hierarchies of needs have relevance only when they are acted on by the humans. Observers of human behavior are obliged to enter the subject's world and grasp the shifting definitions that give rise to orderly social behavior. Failing to do so justifies the fallacy of objectivism: the imputing of motive from observer to subject. Too many architects of schools and education programs have stood outside the interactional worlds of children and adults and attempted to legislate their interpretation of right and proper conduct.

Such objectivistic stances have given schools a basic characteristic that constitutes a major theme of this essay. Schools are presently organized so as to effectively remove fate control from those persons whose fate is at issue—that is, students. This loss of fate control, coupled with a conception of the child which is based on the "underestimation fallacy" gives rise to an ideology that judges the child as incompetent and places in the hands of the adult primary responsibility for child-caretaking.

Schools as Moral Agencies

Schools are best seen, not as educational settings, but as places where fate, morality and personal careers are created and shaped. Schools are moral institutions. They have assumed the responsibility of shaping children, of whatever race or income level, into right and proper participants in American society, pursuing with equal vigor the abstract goals of that society.

At one level schools function, as Willard Waller argued in 1937, to Americanize the young. At the everyday level, however, abstract goals disappear, whether they be beliefs in democracy and equal opportunity or myths concerning the value of education for upward mobility. In their place appears a massive normative order that judges the child's development along such dimensions as poise, character, integrity, politeness, deference, demeanor, emotional control, respect for authority and serious commitment to class-room protocol. Good students are those who reaffirm through their daily actions the moral order of home, school and community.

To the extent that schools assume moral responsibil-ity for producing social beings, they can be seen as agencies of fate or career control. In a variety of ways schools remind students who they are and where they stand in the school's hierarchy. The school institutional-izes ritual turning points to fill this function: gradua-tions, promotions, tests, meetings with parents, open-houses, rallies and sessions with counselors. These significant encounters serve to keep students in place. Schools function to sort and filter social selves and to set these selves on the proper moral track, which may include recycling to a lower grade, busing to an integrated school or informing a student that he has no chance to pursue a college preparatory program. In many respects schools give students their major sense of moral worth—they shape vocabularies, images of self, reward certain actions and not others, set the stage for students to be thrown together as friends or enemies.

Any institution that assumes control over the fate of others might be expected to be accountable for its actions toward those who are shaped and manipulated.

Within the cultures of fate-controlling institutions, however, there appears a vocabulary, a rhetoric, a set of workable excuses and a division of labor to remove and reassign responsibility. For example, we might expect that the division of labor typically parallels the moral hierarchy of the people within the institution; that is, the people assigned the greatest moral worth are ultimately most blameworthy, or most accountable. Usually, however, moral responsibility is reversed. When a teacher in a Head Start program fails to raise the verbal skills of her class to the appropriate level she and the project director might blame each other. But it is more likely that the children, the families of the children or the culture from which the children come will be held responsible. Such is the typical rhetorical device employed in compensatory education programs where the low performances of black children on white middle-class tests are explained by assigning blame to black family culture and family arrangements. Research on the alleged genetic deficiences of black and brown children is another example of this strategy. Here the scientist acts as a moral entrepreneur, presenting his findings under the guise of objectivity.

What is a Child?

Any analysis of the education and socialization process must begin with the basic question, What is a child? My focus is on the contemporary meanings assigned children, especially as these meanings are revealed in preschool and compensatory education programs.

In addressing this question it must be recognized that social objects (such as children) carry no intrinsic meaning. Rather, meaning is conferred by processes of social interaction—by people.

Such is the case with children. Each generation, each social group, every family and each individual develops different interpretations of what a child is. Children find themselves defined in shifting, often contradictory ways. But as a sense of self is acquired, the child learns to transport from situation to situation a relatively stable set of definitions concerning his personal and social identity. Indeed most of the struggles he will encounter in the educational arena fundamentally derive from conflicting definitions of selfhood and childhood.

Child Production as Status Passage

The movement of an infant to the status of child is a socially constructed event that for most middle-class Americans is seen as desirable, inevitable, irreversible, permanent, long term in effect and accomplished in the presence of "experts" and significant others such as teachers, parents, peers and siblings.

For the white middle-income American the child is seen as an extension of the adult's self, usually the family's collective self. Parents are continually reminded that the way their child turns out is a direct reflection of their competence as socializing agents. These reminders have been made for some time; consider this exhortation of 1849:

> Yes, mothers, in a certain sense, the destiny of a redeemed world is put into your hands; it is for you to say whether your children shall be respectable and happy here, and prepared for a glorious immortality, or whether they shall dishonor you, and perhaps bring you grey hairs in sorrow to the grave, and sink down themselves at last to eternal despair!

If the child's conduct reflects upon the parent's moral worth, new parents are told by Benjamin Spock that this job of producing a child is hard work, a serious enterprise. He remarks in *Baby and Child Care*:

> There is an enormous amount of hard work in child care—preparing the proper diet, washing diapers and clothes, cleaning up messes that an infant makes with his food . . . stopping fights and drying tears, listening to stories that are hard to understand, joining in games and reading stories that aren't very exciting to an adult, trudging around zoos and museums and carnivals . . . being slowed down in housework. . . . Children keep parents from parties, trips, theaters, meetings, games, friends. . . . Of course, parents don't have children because they want to be martyrs, or at least they shouldn't. They have them because they love children and want some of their very own. . . . Taking care of their children, seeing them grow and develop into fine people, gives most parents—despite the hard work—their greatest satisfaction in life. This is creation. This is our visible immortality. Pride in other worldly accomplishments is usually weak in comparison.

Spock's account of the parent-child relationship reveals several interrelated definitions that together serve to set off the contemporary view of children. The child is a possession of the adult, an extension of self, an incompetent object that must be cared for at great cost and is a necessary obligation one must incur if he or she desires visible immortality.

These several definitions of childhood are obviously at work in current educational programs. More importantly, they are grounded in a theory of development and learning that reinforces the view that children are incompetent selves. Like Spock's theory of growth, which is not unlike the earlier proposals of Gesell, contemporary psychological theories see the child in organic terms. The child grows like a stalk of corn. The strength of the stalk is a function of its environment. If that environment is healthy, if the plant is properly cared for, a suitable product will be produced. This is a "container" theory of development: "What you put in determines what comes out." At the same time, however, conventional wisdom holds that the child is an unreliable product. It cannot be trusted with its own moral development. Nor can parents. This business of producing a child is serious and it must be placed in the hands of experts who are skilled in child production. Mortal mothers and fathers lack these skills. Pressures are quickly set in force to move the child out of the family into a more "professional" setting—the preschool, the Head Start program.

Caretaking for the Middle Classes

Preschools, whether based on "free school" principles, the Montessori theory, or modern findings in child development, display one basic feature. They are moral caretaking agencies that undertake the fine task of shaping social beings.

Recently, after the enormous publicity attendant to the Head Start program for the poor, middle-income Americans have been aroused to the importance of preschool education for their children. "Discovery Centers" are appearing in various sections of the country and several competing national franchises have been established. Given names such as We Sit Better, Mary Moppit, Pied Piper Schools, Les Petites Academies, Kinder Care Nursery and American Child Centers, these schools remind parents (as did the Universal Education Corporation in the *New York Times*) that:

Evaluating children in the 43 basic skills is part of

what the Discovery Center can do for your child. The 43 skills embrace all the hundreds of things your child has to learn before he reaches school age. Fortunately preschoolers have a special genius for learning. But it disappears at the age of seven. During this short-lived period of genius, the Discovery Center helps your child develop his skills to the Advanced Level.

Caretaking for the middle classes is a moral test. The parent's self is judged by the quality of the product. If the product is faulty, the producer is judged inadequate, also faulty. This feature of the socialization process best explains why middle-class parents are so concerned about the moral, spiritual, psychological and social development of their children. It also explains (if only partially) why schools have assumed so much fate control over children; educators are the socially defined experts on children.

The children of lower-income families are often assumed to be deprived, depressed and emotionally handicapped. To offset these effects, current theory holds that the child must be "educated and treated" before entrance into kindergarten. If middle-income groups have the luxury of withholding preschool from their children, low-income, third-world parents are quickly learning they have no such right. Whether they like it or not, their children are going to be educated. When formal education begins, the culturally deprived child will be ready to compete with his white peers.

What is Cultural Deprivation?

The term "culturally deprived" is still the catchall phrase which at once explains and describes the inability (failure, refusal) of the child in question to display appropriate conduct on I.Q. tests, street corners, play-grounds and classrooms. There are a number of prob-lems with this formulation. The first is conceptual and involves the meanings one gives to the terms *culture* and *deprived*. Contemporary politicians and educators have ignored the controversy surrounding what the word *culture* means and have apparently assumed that every-one knows what a culture is. Be that as it may, the critical empirical indicator seems to be contained in the term *deprived*. People who are deprived, that is, people who fail to act like white, middle-income groups, belong to a culture characterized by such features as divorce, deviance, premarital pregnancies, extended families, drug addiction and alcoholism. Such persons are easily identified: they tend to live in ghettos or public housing units, and they tend to occupy the lower rungs of the occupation ladder. They are there because they are deprived. Their culture keeps them deprived. It is difficult to tell whether these theorists feel that depriva-tion precedes or follows being in a deprived culture. The causal links are neither logically nor empirically analyzed.

The second problem with this formulation is moral and ideological. The children and adults who are labeled culturally deprived are those people in American society who embarrass and cause trouble for middle-income moralists, scientists, teachers, politicians and social workers. They fail to display proper social behavior. The fact that people in low-income groups are under continual surveillance by police and social workers seems to go unnoticed. The result is that members of the middle class keep their indelicacies behind closed doors, inside the private worlds of home, office, club and neighborhood. Low-income people lack such privi-leges. Their misconduct is everybody's business.

The notion of cultural deprivation is class based. Its

recurrent invocation, and its contemporary institutionalization in compensatory education programs reveals an
inability or refusal to look seriously at the problems of
the middle and upper classes, and it directs attention
away from schools which are at the heart of the
problem.

Herbert Gans has noted another flaw in these
programs. This is the failure of social scientists to take
seriously the fact that many lower-income people
simply do not share the same aspirations as the middle
class. Despite this fact antipoverty programs and experiments in compensatory education proceed as if such
were the case.

Schools are morally bounded units of social organization. Within and from them students, parents, teachers
and administrators derive their fundamental sense of
self. Any career through a school is necessarily moral;
one's self-image is continually being evaluated, shaped
and molded. These careers are interactionally inter-
dependent. What a teacher does affects what a child
does and vice versa. To the extent that schools have
become the dominant socializing institution in Western
society it can be argued that experiences in them furnish
everyday interactants with their basic vocabularies for
evaluating self and others. Persons can mask, hide or
fabricate their educational biography, but at some point
they will be obliged to paint a picture of how well
educated they are. They will also be obliged to explain
why they are not better educated (or why they are too
well educated), and why their present circumstances do
not better reflect their capabilities (e.g., unemployed
space engineers). One's educational experiences furnish
the rhetorical devices necessary to get off the hook and
supply the basic clues that will shore up a sad or happy
tale.

The School's Functions

I have already noted two broad functions served by the schools: they Americanize students, and they sort, filter and accredit social selves. To these basic functions must be added the following. Ostensibly, instruction or teaching should take precedence over political socialization. And indeed teaching becomes the dominant activity through which the school is presented to the child. But if schools function to instruct, they also function to entertain and divert students into "worthwhile" ends. Trips to zoos, beaches, operas, neighboring towns, ice cream parlors and athletic fields reveal an attempt on the part of the school to teach the child what range of entertaining activities he or she can engage in. Moreover, these trips place the school directly in the public's eye and at least on these excursions teachers are truly held accountable for their class's conduct.

Caretaking and babysitting constitute another basic function of schools. This babysitting function is quite evident in church-oriented summer programs where preschools and day-care centers are explicitly oriented so as to sell themselves as competent babysitters. Such schools compete for scarce resources (parents who can afford their services), and the federal government has elaborated this service through grants-in-aid to low-income children.

Formal instruction in the classroom is filtered through a series of interconnected acts that involve teacher and student presenting different social selves to one another. Instruction cannot be separated from social interaction, and teachers spend a large amount of time teaching students how to be proper social participants. Coaching in the rules and rituals of polite etiquette thus constitutes another basic function of the school. Students must be taught how to take turns, how to drink out of cups and clean up messes, how to say please and thank you, how to take leave of a teacher's presence, how to handle mood, how to dress for appropriate occasions, how to be rude, polite, attentive, evasive, docile, aggressive, deceitful; in short, they must learn to act like adults. Teachers share this responsibility with parents, often having to take over where parents fail or abdicate, though, again, parents are held accountable for not producing polite children. Because a child's progress through the school's social structure is contingent on how his or her self is formally defined, parents stand to lose much if their children do not conform to the school's version of good conduct. When teachers and parents both fail, an explanation will be sought to relieve each party of responsibility. The child may be diagnosed as hyperactive, or his culture may have been so repressive in its effects that nothing better can be accomplished. Career tracks for these students often lead to the trade school or the reformatory.

Another function of the schools is socialization into age-sex roles. Girls must be taught how to be girls and boys must learn what a boy is. In preschool and day-care centers this is often difficult to accomplish because bathrooms are not sex segregated. But while they are open territories, many preschools make an effort to hire at least one male instructor who can serve as male caretaker and entertainer of boys. He handles their toilet problems among other things. Preschool instructors can often be observed to reinterpret stories to fit their conception of the male or female role, usually attempting to place the female on an equal footing with the male. In these ways the sexual component of self-identity is transmitted and presented to the young child. Problem children become those who switch sex roles or accentuate to an unacceptable degree maleness or femaleness.

Age-grading is accomplished through the organization of classes on a biological age basis. Three-year-olds quickly learn that they cannot do the same things as four-year-olds do, and so on. High schools are deliberately organized so as to convey to freshmen and sophomores how important it is to be a junior or senior. Homecoming queens, student body presidents and athletic leaders come from the two top classes. The message is direct: work hard, be a good student and you too can be a leader and enjoy the fruits of age.

It has been suggested by many that most schools centrally function to socialize children into racial roles, stressing skin color as the dominant variable in social relationships. Depictions of American history and favored symbolic leaders stress the three variables of age, sex and race. The favored role model becomes the 20- to 25-year-old, white, university-educated male who has had an outstanding career in athletics. Implicitly and explicitly students are taught that Western culture is a male-oriented, white-based enterprise.

Shifting from the school as a collectivity to the classroom, we find that teachers attempt to construct their own versions of appropriate conduct. Students are likely to find great discrepancies between a school's formal codes of conduct and the specific rules they encounter in each of their courses and classes. They will find some teachers who are openly critical of the school's formal policies, while at the same time they are forced to interact with teachers who take harsh lines toward misconduct. They will encounter some teachers who enforce dress standards and some who do not. Some teachers use first names, others do not, and so on. The variations are endless.

The importance of these variations for the student's

career and self-conception should be clear. It is difficult managing self in a social world that continually changes its demands, rewards and rules of conduct. But students are obliged to do just that. Consequently the self-conception of the student emerges as a complex and variegated object. He or she is tied into competing and complementary worlds of influence and experience. Depending on where students stand with respect to the school's dominant moral order, they will find their self-conception complemented or derogated and sometimes both. But for the most part schools are organized so as to complement the self-conception of the child most like the teacher and to derogate those most unlike him or her. And, needless to say, the moral career of the nonwhite, low-income student is quite different from the career of his white peer.

I have spelled out the dimensions around which a student comes to evaluate himself in school. Classrooms, however, are the most vivid stage on which students confront the school, and it is here that the teacher at some level must emerge as a negative or positive force on his career. While the underlife of schools reflects attempts to "beat" or "make-out" in the school, in large degree the student learns to submit to the system. The ultimate fact of life is that unless he gets through school with some diploma he is doomed to failure. Not only is he doomed to failure, but he is socially defined as a failure. His career opportunities and self-conceptions are immediately tied to his success in school.

Schools, then, inevitably turn some amount of their attention to the problem of socializing students for failure. Indeed, the school's success as a socializing agent in part depends on its ability to teach students to accept failure. A complex rhetoric and set of beliefs must be instilled in the students. Children must come to see themselves as the school defines them. They are taught that certain classes of selves do better than other classes, but the classes referred to are not sociological but moral. A variation of the Protestant ethic is communicated and the fiction of equality in education and politics is stressed. Students must grasp the fact that all that separates them from a classmate who goes to Harvard (when they are admitted to a junior college) are grades and hard work, not class, race, money or prestige. Schools, then, function as complex, cooling-out agencies.

Two problems are created. School officials must communicate their judgments, usually cast as diagnoses, prescriptions, treatments and prognoses, to students and parents. And second, they must establish social arrangements that maximize the likelihood that their judgments will be accepted, that is, submission to fate control is maximized, and scenes between parents and students are minimized.

Fate Control

The most obvious cooling-out agents in schools are teachers and counselors. It is they who administer and evaluate tests. It is they who see the student most frequently. In concert these two classes of functionaries fulfill the schools' functions of sorting out and cooling out children. Their basic assignment is to take imperfect selves and fit those selves to the best possible moral career. They are, then, moral entrepreneurs. They design career programs and define the basic contours around which a student's self will be shaped.

A basic strategy of the moral entrepreneur in schools is co-optation. He attempts to win a child's peers and parents over to his side. If this can be accomplished, the job is relatively easy. For now everyone significant in the child's world agrees that he is a failure or a partial success. They agree that a trade school or a junior college is the best career track to be followed.

Another strategy is to select exemplary students who epitomize the various tracks open to a student. Former graduates may be brought back and asked to reflect on their careers. In selecting types of students to follow these various paths, schools conduct talent searches and develop operating perspectives that classify good and bad prospects. Like the academic theorist of social stratification, these officials work with an implicit image of qualified beings. They know that students from middle- and upper-income groups perform better than those from lesser backgrounds. They know that students who have college-educated parents do better than those whose parents dropped out of high school. They learn to mistrust nonwhites. In these respects schools differ only slightly from medical practitioners, especially the psychiatrist who has learned that his trade works best on persons like him in background. Teachers, too, perpetuate the system of stratification found in the outside world.

Student Types

Schools can cool out the failures in their midst. They have more difficulty with another type of student, the troublemakers or militants. Troublemakers, as would be predicted, typically come from low-income white and nonwhite ethnic groups. Forced to process these children, school systems developed their own system of stratification, making low-status schools teach troublemakers. This has become the fate of the trade school or the continuation high school. Here those who have high truancy or arrest records, are pregnant, hyperactive or on probation are thrown together. And here they are presented with white middle-class curricula.

Militants and troublemakers refuse to accept the school's operating perspective. To the extent that they can band together and form a common world view, they challenge the school's legitimacy as a socializing agent. They make trouble. They represent, from the middle-class point of view, failures of the socializing system.

In response to this, schools tend to adopt a strategy of denial. Denial can take several forms, each revealing a separate attempt to avoid accountability. Denial of responsibility takes the form of a claim that "we recognize your problem, but the solution is outside our province." The need for alternative educational arrangements is recognized, but denied because of reasons beyond control. Private and public guilt is neutralized by denying responsibility and placing blame on some external force or variable such as the state of the economy.

When some resource is denied to a social group, explanations will be developed to justify that denial. My earlier discussion has suggested that one explanation places blame on the shoulders of the denied victim. Thus the theory of cultural deprivation removes blame, by blaming the victim. Scientific theory thus operates as one paradigm of responsibility.

Another form of the strategy is to deny the challengers' essential moral worth. Here the victim is shown to be socially unworthy and thereby not deserving of special attention. This has been the classic argument for segregation in the South, but it works only so long as the victim can be kept in place, which has lately in that part of the world involved insuring that the challenger or victim is not presented with alternative self-models. Shipping black instructors out of the South into northern urban ghettos represents an attempt to remove alternative self-models for the southern black child.

The Victim's Response

Insofar as they can organize themselves socially, victims and challengers may assume one of three interrelated stances. They may condemn the condemner, make appeals to higher authorities or deny the perspective that has brought injury. In so doing they will seek and develop alternative scientific doctrines that support their stance.

Condemning the condemner reverses the condemner's denial of moral worth. Here the school or political and economic system is judged hypocritical, corrupt, stupid, brutal and racist. These evaluations attempt to reveal the underlying moral vulnerability of the institution in question. The victim and his cohort reverse the victimizer's vocabulary and hold him accountable for the failures they were originally charged with (for example, poor grades or attendance records).

These condemnations reveal a basic commitment to the present system. They are claims for a just place. They are a petition to higher authority. Democratic ideology is proclaimed as a worthy pursuit. The school is charged with failure to offer proper and acceptable means to reach those goals. Here the victims' perspective corresponds with dominant cultural ideologies.

Denial of perspective is another stance. Best seen in the Nation of Islam schools, the victim now states that he wants nothing the larger system can offer. He leaves the system and constructs his own educational arrangements. He develops his own standards of evaluation. He paints his own version of right and proper conduct.

(Private educational academies in the South, partly a function of the Nixon administration, serve a similar function for whites.)

Denials of perspective thus lead to the substitution of a new point of view. If successfully executed, as in the case of the Nation of Islam, the victims build their own walls of protection and shut off the outside world. In such a setting, one's self-conception is neither daily denied nor derided. It is affirmed and defined in positive terms.

Lower self-conceptions would be predicted in those settings where the black or brown child is taught to normalize his deficiencies and to compensate for them. This is the setting offered by Head Start and Follow-Through. The victim accepts the victimizers' judgments and attempts to compensate for socially defined flaws.

Americans of all income levels and from all racial groups, including white, are troubled over the current educational system. They are demanding a greater say in the social organization of schools, they are challenging the tenure system now given teachers; they feel that schools should accept greater responsibilities for the failures of the system. (A Gallup Poll in late 1970 showed that 67 percent of those surveyed favor holding teachers and administrators more accountable for the progress of students.) Accordingly it is necessary to consider a series of proposals that would bring education more in line with cultural and social expectations.

From this perspective education must be grounded in principles that recognize the role of the self in everyday conduct. The child possesses multiple selves, each grounded in special situations and special circles of significant others. Possessing a self, the child is an active organism, not a passive object into which learning can be poured.

Conventional theories of learning define the child as

a passive organism. An alternative view of the social act of learning must be developed. George Herbert Mead's analysis provides a good beginning. Creativity or learning occurred, Mead argued, when the individual was forced to act in a situation where conventional lines of conduct were no longer relevant. Following Dewey's discussion of the blocked act, Mead contended that schools and curricula must be organized in ways that challenge the child's view of the world. Standard curricula are based on an opposite view of the human. Redundancy, constant rewards and punishments, piecemeal presentation of materials, and defining the child as incompetent or unable to provoke his own acts best characterizes these programs. Course work is planned carefully in advance and study programs are assiduously followed. The teacher, not the child, is defined as the ultimate educational resource. Parents and local community groups, because they tend to challenge the school's operating perspective, are treated only ritualistically at PTA meetings, open houses, school plays, athletic contests. Their point of view, like the child's, is seldom taken seriously. They are too incompetent. Taking them seriously would force a shift in existing power arrangements in the school.

Mead's perspective proposes just the opposite view of parents, children and education. Education, he argued, is an unfolding, social process wherein the child comes to see himself in increasingly more complex ways. Education leads to self-understanding and to the acquisition of the basic skills. This principle suggests that schools must be socially relevant. They must incorporate the social world of child and community into curriculum arrangements. Cultural diversity must be stressed. Alternative symbolic leaders must be presented, and these must come from realistic worlds of experience. (Setting an astronaut as a preferred "self-model" for seven-year-old males as a present text book does, can hardly be defined as realistic.) Problematic situations from the child's everyday world must be brought into the classroom. Mead, for example, proposed as early as 1908 that schools teach sex education to children.

Children and parents, then, must be seen as resources around which education is developed and presented. They must be taken seriously. This presupposes a close working relationship between home and school. Parents must take responsibility for their children's education. They can no longer afford to shift accountability to the schools. This simple principle suggests that ethnic studies programs should have been central features of schools at least 50 years ago. Schools exist to serve their surrounding communities, not bend those communities to their perspective.

Redefining Schools

If this reciprocal service function is stressed, an important implication follows. Schools should educate children in ways that permit them to be contributing members in their chosen worlds. Such basics as reading, writing and counting will never be avoided. But their instruction can be made relevant within the worlds the child most directly experiences. This suggests, initially at least, that black and brown children be taught to respect their separate cultural heritages. Second, it suggests that they will probably learn best with materials drawn from those cultures. Third, it suggests that they must be presented with self-models who know, respect and come from those cultures—black teachers must not be removed from southern schools.

To the extent that schools and teachers serve as referent points for the child's self-conception it can be argued that it is not the minority student who must change, but instead it is the white middle-class child who must be exposed to alternative cultural perspectives. Minority teachers must be made integral components of all phases of the educational act.

Mead's perspective suggests, as I have attempted to elaborate, that the classroom is an interactive world. Research by Roger G. Barker and Paul V. Gump on big schools and little schools supports this position and findings suggest an additional set of proposals. Briefly, they learned that as class and school size increases student satisfaction decreases. Teaching becomes more mechanized, students become more irrelevant and activities not related to learning attain greater importance— social clubs, for example. In short, in big schools students are redundant.

Classroom size and school size must be evaluated from this perspective. If schools exist to serve children and their parents, then large schools are dysfunctional. They are knowledge factories, not places of learning or self-development. Culturally heterogeneous, small-sized classes must be experimented with. Students must have opportunities to know their teachers in personal, not institutional terms. Students must be taught to take one another seriously, not competitively. Small, ecologically intimate surroundings have a greater likelihood of promoting these arrangements than do large-scale, bureaucratically organized classes.

At present, standardized, state and nationally certified tests are given students to assess their psychological, emotional, intellectual and social development. Two problems restrict the effectiveness of these methods, however. With few exceptions they have been standardized on white middle-class populations. Second, they are the only measurement techniques routinely employed.

A number of proposals follow from these problems. First, open-ended tests which permit the child to express his or her perspective must be developed. These tests, such as the "Who Am I?" question, would be given to students to determine the major contours of their self-conceptions. With this information in hand teachers would be in a better position to tailor teaching programs to a child's specific needs, definitions, intentions and goals.

Second, tests such as "Who is Important to You?" could be given students on a regular basis to determine who their significant others are. It is near axiomatic that derogation of the people most important to one leads to alienation from the setting and spokesman doing the derogation. Teachers must learn to respect and present in respectful terms those persons most important to the child.

A third methodological proposal directs observers to link a student's utterances, wishes and self-images to his or her day-to-day conduct. Written test scores often fail to reflect what persons really take into account and value. In many social settings verbal ability, athletic skill, hustling aptitudes, money and even physical attractiveness serve as significant status locators. IQ tests often do not. Furthermore, a person's score on a test may not accurately reflect his ability to handle problematic situations, which is surely a goal of education. Observations of conduct (behavior) in concrete settings can provide the needed leads in this direction.

Methodological Implications

A critic of these proposals might remark that such measures are not standardized, that their validity is

questionable, that they cannot be administered nationally, and that they have questionable degrees of
reliability. In response I would cite the ability of Roger
Barker and colleagues to execute such observations over
time with high reliability (.80-.98 for many measures).
But more to the point I would argue that conventional
tests are simply not working and it is time to
experiment with alternative techniques, perspectives and
theories.

This defense suggests that schools of education must
begin to consider teaching their students the methodologies of participant observation, unobtrusive analysis and
life history construction. These softer methods have
been the traditional province of sociologists and
anthropologists. Members of these disciplines must
consider offering cross-disciplinary courses in methodology, especially aimed for everyday practitioners in
school settings. Graduate requirements for teaching
credentials must also be reexamined and greater efforts
must be made to recruit and train minority students in
these different approaches.

These proposals reflect a basic commitment. Schools
should be organized so as to maximize a child's
self-development and they should permit maximum
child-parent participation. It is evident that my
discussion has not been limited to an analysis of
compensatory education programs. This has been
deliberate. It is my conviction that education, wherever
it occurs, involves interactions between social selves.
Taking the self as a point of departure I have attempted
to show that what happens to a preschool child is not
unlike the moral experiences of a black or brown
17-year-old senior. But most importantly, both should
find themselves in schools that take them seriously and

treat them with respect. Schools exist to serve children and the public. This charge must be also taken seriously.

July/August 1971

FURTHER READING

Centuries of Childhood by Phillipe Ariés (New York: Random House, 1962) convincingly documents the conclusion that children are both social and historical productions.

Big School and Small School by Roger Barker and Paul V. Gump (Stanford, California: Stanford University Press, 1964) presents a convenient review of Barker's and Herbert Wright's perspective on schools and education. Their work challenges current positivistic methodologies and theories of children and education.

The Sociology of Teaching by Willard Waller (New York: John Wiley, 1967, originally published in 1937) is the best analysis of life in schools as seen by teachers and students. It anticipates and goes beyond more recent critiques offered by Paul Goodman, Herb Kohl, John Holt and others.

Programmed for Social Class: Tracking in American High Schools

WALTER E. SCHAFER, CAROL OLEXA
and KENNETH POLK

If, as folklore would have it, America is the land of opportunity, offering anyone the chance to raise himself purely on the basis of his or her ability, then education is the key to self-betterment. The spectacular increase in those of us who attend school is often cited as proof of the great scope of opportunity that our society offers: 94 percent of the high school age population was attending school in 1967, as compared to 7 percent in 1890.

Similarly, our educational system is frequently called more democratic than European systems, for instance, which rigidly segregate students by ability early in their lives, often on the basis of nationally administered examinations such as England's "11-plus." The United States, of course, has no official national policy of educational segregation. Our students, too, are tested and retested throughout their lives and put into faster or slower classes or programs on the basis of their presumed ability, but this procedure is carried out in a decentralized fashion that varies between each city or state.

However, many critics of the American practice claim that, no matter how it is carried out, it does not meet the needs of the brighter and duller groups, so much as it solidifies and widens the differences between them. One such critic, the eminent educator Kenneth B. Clark, speculates: "It is conceivable that the detrimental effects of segregation based upon intellect are similar to the known detrimental effects of schools segregated on the basis of class, nationality or race."

Patricia Cayo Sexton notes that school grouping based on presumed ability often reinforces already existing social divisions:

> Children from higher social strata usually enter the "higher quality" groups and those from lower strata the "lower" ones. School decisions about a child's ability will greatly influence the kind and quality of education he receives, as well as his future life, including whether he goes to college, the job he will get, and his feelings about himself and others.

And Arthur Pearl puts it bluntly:

> ... "special ability classes," "basic track," or "slow learner classes" are various names for another means of systematically denying the poor adequate access to education.

In this article we will examine some evidence bearing on this vital question of whether current educational practices tend to reinforce existing social class divisions. We will also offer an alternative aimed at making our public schools more effective institutions for keeping open the opportunities for social mobility.

Education Explosion

Since the turn of the century, a number of trends have converged to increase enormously the pressure on American adolescents to graduate from high school: declining opportunity in jobs, the upgrading of educational requirements for job entry, and the diminishing need for teenagers to contribute to family income. While some school systems, especially in the large cities, have adapted to this vast increase in enrollment by creating separate high schools for students with different interests, abilities or occupational goals, most communities have developed comprehensive high schools serving all the youngsters within a neighborhood community.

In about half the high schools in the United States today, the method for handling these large and varied student populations is through some form of tracking system. Under this arrangement, the entire student body is divided into two or more relatively distinct career lines, or tracks, with such titles as college preparatory, vocational, technical, industrial, business, general, basic and remedial. While students on different tracks may take some courses together in the same classroom, they are usually separated into entirely different courses or different sections of the same course.

School men offer several different justifications for tracking systems. Common to most, however, is the notion that college-bound students are academically more able, learn more rapidly, should not be deterred in their progress by slower, non-college-bound students, and need courses for college preparation which non-college-bound students do not need. By the same token, it is thought that non-college-bound students are less bright, learn more slowly, should not be expected to progress as fast or learn as much as college-bound students, and need only a general education or work-oriented training to prepare themselves for immediate entry into the world of work or a business or vocational school.

In reply, the numerous critics of tracking usually contend that while the college-bound are often encouraged by the tracking system to improve their performance, non-college-bound students, largely as a result of being placed in a lower-rated track, are discouraged from living up to their potential or from showing an interest in academic values. What makes the system especially pernicious, these critics say, is that non-college-bound students more often come from low-income and minority group families. As a result, high schools, through the tracking system, inadvertently close off opportunities for large numbers of students from lower social strata, and thereby contribute to the low achievement, lack of interest, delinquency and rebellion which school men frequently deplore in their non-college track students.

If these critics are correct, the American comprehensive high school, which is popularly assumed to be the very model of an open and democratic institution, may not really be open and democratic at all. In fact, rather than facilitating equality of educational opportunity, our schools may be subtly denying it, and in the process widening and hardening existing social divisions.

Tracks and Who Gets Put on Them

During the summer of 1964, we collected data from official school transcripts of the recently graduated senior classes of two midwestern three-year high schools. The larger school, located in a predominantly middle-class, academic community of about 70,000, had a graduating class that year of 753 students. The smaller school, with a graduating class of 404, was located nearby in a predominantly working-class, industrial community of about 20,000.

Both schools placed their students into either a college prep or general track. We determined the positions of every student in our sample by whether he took tenth grade English in the college prep or the general section. If he was enrolled in the college prep section, he almost always took other college prep sections or courses, such as advanced mathematics or foreign languages, in which almost all enrollees were also college prep.

Just how students in the two schools were assigned to—or chose—tracks is somewhat of a mystery. When we interviewed people both in the high schools and in their feeder junior highs, we were told that whether a student went into one track or another depended on various factors, such as his own desires and aspirations, teacher advice, achievement test scores, grades, pressure from parents and counselor assessment of academic promise. One is hard put to say which of these weighs most heavily, but we must note that one team of researchers, Cicourel and Kitsuse, showed in their study of *The Educational Decision-Makers* that assumptions made by counselors about the character, adjustment and potential of incoming students are vitally important in track assignment.

Whatever the precise dynamics of this decision, the outcome was clear in the schools we studied: socioeconomic and racial background had an effect on which track a student took, quite apart from either his achievement in junior high or his ability as measured by IQ scores. In the smaller, working-class school, 58 percent of the incoming students were assigned to the college prep track; in the larger, middle-class school, 71 percent were placed in the college prep track. And, taking the two schools together, whereas 83 percent of students from white-collar homes were assigned to the college prep track, this was the case with only 48 percent of students from blue-collar homes. The relationship of race to track assignment was even stronger: 71 percent of the whites and only 30 percent of the blacks were assigned to the college prep track. In the two schools studied, the evidence is plain: children from low-income and minority group families more often found themselves in low-ability groups and non-college-bound tracks than in high ability groups or college-bound tracks.

Furthermore, this decision-point early in the students' high school careers was of great significance for their futures, since it was virtually irreversible. Only 7 percent of those who began on the college prep track moved down to the non-college prep track, while only 7 percent of those assigned to the lower, non-college track, moved up. Clearly, these small figures indicate a high degree of rigid segregation within each of the two schools. In fact, greater mobility between levels has been reported in English secondary modern schools, where streaming—the British term for tracking—is usually thought to be more rigid and fixed than tracking in this country. (It must be remembered, of course, that in England the more rigid break is between secondary modern and grammar schools.)

Differences Between Tracks

As might be expected from the school men's justification for placing students in separate tracks in the first place, track position is noticeably related to academic performance. Thirty-seven percent of the college prep students graduated in the top quarter of their class (measured by grade point average throughout high school), while a mere 2 percent of the non-college group achieved the top quarter. By contrast, half the non-college prep students fell in the lowest quarter, as opposed to only 12 percent of the college prep.

Track position is also strikingly related to whether a student's academic performance improves or deteriorates during high school. The grade point average of all sample students in their ninth year—that is, prior to their being assigned to tracks—was compared with their grade point averages over the next three years. While there was a slight difference in the ninth year between those who would subsequently enter the college and non-college tracks, this difference had increased by the senior year. This widening gap in academic performance resulted from the fact that a higher percentage of students subsequently placed in the college prep track improved their grade point average by the senior year, while a higher percentage of non-college prep experienced a decline in grade point average by the time they reached the senior year.

Track position is also related strongly to dropout rate. Four percent of the college prep students dropped out of high school prior to graduation, as opposed to 36 percent of the non-college group.

Track position is also a good indication of how deeply involved a student will be in school, as measured by participation in extracurricular activities. Out of the 753 seniors in the larger school, a comparatively small number of college prep students—21 percent—did not participate in any activities, while 44 percent took part in three or more such activities. By contrast, 58 percent, or more than half of the non-college group took part in no extracurricular activities at all, and only 11 percent of this group took part in three or more activities.

Finally, track position is strikingly related to delinquency, both in and out of school. Out of the entire school body of the larger school during the 1963-1964 school year—that is, out of 2,565 boys and girls—just over one-third of the college-bound, as opposed to more than half of the non-college-bound committed one or more violations of school rules. Nineteen percent of the college-bound, compared with 70 percent of the non-college-bound, committed three or more such violations. During this year, just over one-third of all the college-bound students were suspended for infractions of school rules, while more than half of all the non-college-bound group were suspended.

Furthermore, using juvenile court records, we find that out of the 1964 graduating class in the larger school, 6 percent of the college prep, and 16 percent of the non-college-bound groups, were delinquent while in high school. Even though 5 percent of those on the non-college track had already entered high school with court records, opposed to only 1 percent of the college prep track, still more non-college-bound students became delinquent during high school than did college prep students (11 percent compared with 5 percent). So the relation between track position and delinquency is further supported.

We have seen, then, that when compared with college prep students, non-college prep students show lower achievement, greater deterioration of achievement, less participation in extracurricular activities, a greater tendency to drop out, more misbehavior in school, and more delinquency outside of school. Since students are assigned to different tracks largely on the basis of

presumed differences in intellectual ability and inclination for further study, the crucial question is whether
assignment to different tracks helped to meet the needs
of groups of students who were already different, as
many educators would claim, or actually contributed to
and reinforced such differences, as critics like Sexton
and Pearl contend.

The simplest way to explain the differences we have
just seen is to attribute them to characteristics already
inherent in the individual students, or—at a more
sophisticated level—to students' cultural and educational
backgrounds.

It can be argued, for example, that the difference in
academic achievement between the college and non-
college groups can be explained by the fact that college
prep students are simply brighter; after all, this is one of
the reasons they were taken into college prep courses.
Others would argue that non-college-bound students do
less well in school work because of family background:
they more often come from blue-collar homes where
less value is placed on grades and college, where books
and help in schoolwork are less readily available, and
verbal expression limited. Still others would contend
that lower-track students get lower grades because they
performed less well in elementary and junior high, have
fallen behind, and probably try less hard.

Fortunately, it was possible with our data to separate
out the influence of track position from the other
suggested factors of social class background (measured
by father's occupation), intelligence (measured by
IQ—admittedly not a perfectly acceptable measure) and
previous academic performance (measured by grade
point average for the last semester of the ninth year).
Through use of a weighted percentage technique known
as test factor standardization, we found that even when

the effects of IQ, social class and previous performance are ruled out, there is still a sizable difference in grade point average between the two tracks. With the influence of the first three factors eliminated we nevertheless find that 30 percent of the college prep, as opposed to a mere 4 percent of the non-college group attained the top quarter of their class; and that only 12 percent of the college prep, as opposed to 35 percent of the non-college group, fell into the bottom quarter. These figures, which are similar for boys and girls, further show that track position has an independent effect on academic achievement which is greater than the effect of each of the other three factors—social class, IQ and past performance. In particular, assignment to the non-college track has a strong negative influence on a student's grades.

Looking at dropout rate, and again controlling for social class background, IQ and past performance, we find that track position in itself has an independent influence which is higher than the effect of any of the other three factors. In other words, even when we rule out the effect of these three factors, non-college-bound students still dropped out in considerably greater proportion than college-bound-students (19 percent vs. 4 percent).

When the Forecasters Make the Weather

So our evidence points to the conclusion that the superior academic performance of the college-bound students, and the inferior performance of the non-college students is partly caused by the tracking system. Our data do not explain how this happens, but several studies of similar educational arrangements, as well as basic principles of social psychology do provide a number of probable explanations. The first point has to do with the pupil's self-image.

Stigma. Assignment to the lower track in the schools we studied carried with it a strong stigma. As David Mallory was told by an American boy, "Around here you are *nothing* if you're not college prep." A non-college prep girl in one of the schools we studied told me that she always carried her "general" track books upside down because of the humiliation she felt at being seen with them as she walked through the halls.

The corroding effect of such stigmatizing is well known. As Patricia Sexton has put it, "He [the low track student] is bright enough to catch on very quickly to the fact that he is not considered very bright. He comes to accept this unflattering appraisal because, after all, the school should know."

One ex-delinquent in Washington, D.C. told one of us how the stigma from this low track affected him.

> It really don't have to be the tests, but after the tests, there shouldn't be no separation in the classes. Because, as I say again, I felt good when I was with my class, but when they went and separated us—that changed us. That changed our ideas, our thinking, the way we thought about each other and turned us to enemies toward each other—because they said I was dumb and they were smart.

> When you first go to junior high school you do feel something inside—it's like ego. You have been from elementary to junior high, you feel great inside. You say, well daggone, I'm going to deal with the *people* here now, I am in junior high school. You get this shirt that says Brown Junior High or whatever the name is and you are proud of that shirt. But then you go up there and the teachers says—"Well, so and so, you're in the basic

section, you can't go with the other kids." The devil with the whole thing—you lose—something in you—like it just goes out of you.

Did you think the other guys were smarter than you? Not at first—I used to think I was just as smart as anybody in the school—I knew I was smart. I knew some people were smarter, and I *wanted* to go to school, I wanted to get a diploma and go to college and help people and everything. I stepped into there in junior high—I felt like a fool going to school—I really felt like a fool. *Why?* Because I felt like I wasn't a part of the school. I couldn't get on special patrols, because I wasn't qualified. *What happened between the seventh and ninth grades?* I started losing faith in myself—after the teachers kept downing me. You hear "a guy's in basic section, he's dumb" and all this. Each year—"you're ignorant—you're stupid."

Considerable research shows that such erosion of self-esteem greatly increases the chances of academic failure, as well as dropping out and causing "trouble" both inside and outside of school.

Moreover, this lowered self-image is reinforced by the expectations that others have toward a person in the non-college group.

The Self-fulfilling Prophecy. A related explanation rich in implications comes from David Hargreaves' *Social Relations in a Secondary School*, a study of the psychological, behavioral and educational consequences of the student's position in the streaming system of an English secondary modern school. In "Lumley School," the students (all boys) were assigned to one of five streams on the basis of ability and achievement, with the score on the "11-plus" examination playing the major role.

Like the schools we studied, students in the different

streams were publicly recognized as high or low in status and were fairly rigidly segregated, both formally in different classes and informally in friendship groups. It is quite probable, then, that Hargreaves' explanations for the greater antischool attitudes, animosity toward teachers, academic failure, disruptive behavior and delinquency among the low-stream boys apply to the non-college prep students we studied as well. In fact, the negative effects of the tracking system on non-college-bound students may be even stronger in our two high schools, since the Lumley streaming system was much more open and flexible, with students moving from one stream to another several times during their four-year careers.

Streamed Schools

As we noted, a popular explanation for the greater failure and misbehavior among low-stream or non-college-bound students is that they come from homes that fail to provide the same skills, ambition or conforming attitude as higher stream or college-bound students. Hargreaves demonstrates that there is some validity to this position: in his study, low-stream boys more often came from homes that provided less encouragement for academic achievement and higher level occupations, and that were less oriented to the other values of the school and teachers. Similar differences may have existed among the students we studied, although their effects have been markedly reduced by our control for father's occupation, IQ and previous achievement.

But Hargreaves provides a convincing case for the position that whatever the differences in skills, ambition, self-esteem or educational commitment that the students brought to school, they were magnified by what happened to them in school, largely because low-stream boys were the victims of a self-fulfilling prophecy in their relations with teachers, with respect to both academic performance and classroom behavior. Teachers of higher stream boys expected higher performance and got it. Similarly, boys who wore the label of streams "C" or "D" were more likely to be seen by teachers as limited in ability and troublemakers, and were treated accordingly.

> In a streamed school the teacher categorizes the pupils not only in terms of the inferences he makes of the child's class room behavior but also from the child's stream level. It is for this reason that the teacher can rebuke an "A" stream boy for being like a "D" stream boy. The teacher has learned to *expect* certain kinds of behavior from members of different streams. . . . It would be hardly surprising if "good" pupils thus became "better" and the "bad" pupils become "worse." It is, in short, an example of a self-fulfilling prophecy. The negative expectations of the teacher reinforce the negative behavioral tendencies.

A recent study by Rosenthal and Jacobson in an American elementary school lends further evidence to the position that teacher expectations influence student's performance. In this study, the influence is a positive one. Teachers of children randomly assigned to experimental groups were told at the beginning of the year to expect "unusual intellectual" gains, while teachers of the control group children were told nothing. After eight months, and again after two years, the experimental group children, the "intellectual spurters," showed significantly greater gains in IQ and grades. Further, they were rated by the teachers as being significantly more curious, interesting, happy and more likely to succeed in the future. Such findings are consistent with theories of interpersonal influence and with the interactional or labelling view of deviant behavior.

If, as often claimed, American teachers underestimate the learning potential of low-track students and expect more negative attitudes and greater trouble from them, it may well be that they partially cause the very failure, alienation, lack of involvement, dropping out and rebellion they are seeking to prevent. As Hargreaves says of Lumley, "It is important to stress that if this effect of categorization is real, it is entirely unintended by the teachers. They do not wish to make low streams more difficult than they are!" Yet the negative self-fulfilling prophecy was probably real, if unintended and unrecognized, in our two schools as well as in Lumley.

Two further consequences of the expectation that students in the non-college group will learn less well as differences in grading policies and in teacher effectiveness follow.

Grading Policies. In the two schools we studied, our interviews strongly hint at the existence of grade ceilings for non-college prep students and grade floors for college-bound students. That is, by virtue of being located in a college preparatory section or course, college prep students could seldom receive any grade lower than "B" or "C," while students in non-college-bound sections or courses found it difficult to gain any grade higher than "C," even though their objective performance may have been equivalent to a college prep "B." Several teachers explicitly called our attention to this practice, the rationale being that non-college prep students do not deserve the same objective grade rewards as college prep students, since they "clearly" are less bright and perform less well. To the extent that grade ceilings do operate for non-college-bound students, the lower grades that result from this policy, almost by definition, can hardly have a beneficial effect on motivation and commitment.

Teaching Effectiveness. Finally, numerous investigations of ability grouping, as well as the English study by Hargreaves, have reported that teachers of higher ability groups are likely to teach in a more interesting and effective manner than teachers of lower ability groups. Such a difference is predictable from what we know about the effects of reciprocal interaction between teacher and class. Even when the same individual teaches both types of classes in the course of the day, as was the case for most teachers in the two schools in this study, he is likely to be "up" for college prep classes and "down" for non-college prep classes—and to bring out the same reaction from his students.

A final, and crucial factor that contributes to the poorer performance and lower interest in school of non-college-bound students is the relation between school work and the adult career after school.

Future Payoff. Non-college-bound students often develop progressively more negative attitudes toward school, especially formal academic work, because they see grades—and indeed school itself—as having little future relevance or payoff. This is not the case for college prep students. For them, grades are a means toward the identifiable and meaningful end of qualifying for college, while among the non-college-bound, grades are seen as far less important for entry into an occupation or a vocational school. This difference in the practical importance of grades is magnified by the perception among non-college-bound students that it is pointless to put much effort into school work, since it will be unrelated to the later world of work anyway. In a study of *Rebellion in a High School* in this country, Arthur Stinchcombe describes the alienation of non-college-bound high school students:

> The major practical conclusion of the analysis above is that rebellious behavior is largely a reaction to the school itself and to its promises, not a failure of the family or community. High school students can be motivated to conform by paying them in the realistic coin of future advantage. Except perhaps for pathological cases, any student can be motivated to conform if the school can realistically promise something valuable to him as a reward for working hard. But for a large part of the population, especially the adolescent who will enter the male working class or the female candidates for early marriage, the school has nothing to offer. . . . In order to secure conformity from students, a high school must articulate academic work with careers of students.

Being on the lower track has other negative consequences for the student which go beyond the depressing influence on his academic performance and motivation. We can use the principles just discussed to explain our findings with regard to different rates of participation in school activities and acts of misbehavior.

Tracks Conformity and Deviance

For example, the explanations having to do with self-image and the expectations of others suggest that assignment to the non-college-bound track has a dampening effect on commitment to school in general, since it is the school which originally categorized these students as inferior. Thus, assignment to the lower track may be seen as independently contributing to resentment, frustration and hostility in school, leading to lack of involvement in all school activities, and finally ending in active withdrawal. The self-exclusion of the non-college group from the mainstream of college student life is probably enhanced by intentional or unintentional exclusion by other students and teachers.

Using the same type of reasons, while we cannot prove a definite causal linkage between track position and misbehavior, it seems highly likely that assignment to the non-college prep track often leads to resentment, declining commitment to school and rebellion against it, expressed in lack of respect for the school's authority or acts of disobedience against it. As Albert Cohen argued over a decade ago in *Delinquent Boys*, delinquency may well be largely a rebellion against the school and its standards by teenagers who feel they cannot get anywhere by attempting to adhere to such standards. Our analysis suggests that a key factor in such rebellion is non-college prep status in the school's tracking system, with the vicious cycle of low achievement and inferior self-image that go along with it.

This conclusion is further supported by Hargreaves' findings on the effect of streaming at Lumley:

> There is a real sense in which the school can be regarded as a generator of delinquency. Although the aims and efforts of the teachers are directed towards deleting such tendencies, the organization of the school and its influence on subcultural development unintentionally fosters delinquent values. . . . For low stream boys . . . , school simultaneously exposes them to these values and deprives them of status in these terms. It is at this

point they may begin to reject the values because they cannot succeed in them. The school provides a mechanism through the streaming system whereby their failure is effected and institutionalized, and also provides a situation in which they can congregate together in low streams.

Hargreaves' last point suggests a very important explanation for the greater degree of deviant behavior among the non-college-bound.

The Student Subculture. Assignment to a lower stream at Lumley meant a boy was immediately immersed in a student subculture that stressed and rewarded antagonistic attitudes and behavior toward teachers and all they stood for. If a boy was assigned to the "A" stream, he was drawn toward the values of teachers, not only by the higher expectations and more positive rewards from the teachers themselves, but from other students as well. The converse was true of lower stream boys, who accorded each other high status for doing the opposite of what teachers wanted. Because of class scheduling, little opportunity developed for interaction and friendship across streams. The result was a progressive polarization and hardening of the high- and low-stream subcultures between first and fourth years and a progressively greater negative attitude across stream lines, with quite predictable consequences.

The informal pressures within the low streams tend to work directly against the assumption of the teachers that boys will regard promotion into a higher stream as a desirable goal. The boys from the low streams were very reluctant to ascend to higher streams because their stereotypes of "A" and "B" stream boys were defined in terms of values alien to their own and because promotion would involve rejection by their low stream friends. The teachers were not fully aware that this unwillingness to be promoted to a higher stream led the high informal status boys to depress their performance in examinations. This fear of promotion adds to our list of factors leading to the formation of anti-academic attitudes among low stream boys.

Observations and interviews in the two American schools we studied confirmed a similar polarization and reluctance by non-college prep students to pursue the academic goals rewarded by teachers and college prep students. Teachers, however, seldom saw the antischool attitudes of non-college prep students as arising out of the tracking system—or anything else about the school—but out of adverse home influences, limited intelligence or psychological problems.

Implications. These, then, are some of the ways the schools we studied contributed to the greater rates of failure, academic decline, uninvolvement in school activities, misbehavior and delinquency among non-college-bound students. We can only speculate, of course, about the generalization of these findings to other schools. However, there is little reason to think the two schools we studied were unusual or unrepresentative and, despite differences in size and social class composition, the findings are virtually identical in both. To the extent the findings are valid and general, they strongly suggest that, through their tracking system, the schools are partly causing many of the very problems they are trying to solve and are posing an important barrier to equal educational opportunity to lower income and black students, who are disproportionately assigned to the non-college prep track.

The notion that schools help cause low achievement, deterioration of educational commitment and involvement, the dropout problem, misbehavior and delinquency is foreign and repulsive to many teachers, administrators and parents. Yet our evidence is entirely consistent with Kai Erikson's observations that " . . . deviant forms of conduct often seem to derive nourishment from the very agencies devised to inhibit them."

What, then, are the implications of this study? Some might argue that, despite the negative side effects we have shown, tracking systems are essential for effective teaching, especially for students with high ability, as well as for adjusting students early in their careers to the status levels they will occupy in the adult occupational system. We contend that however reasonable this may sound, the negative effects demonstrated here offset and call into serious question any presumed gains from tracking.

Others might contend that the negative outcomes we have documented can be eliminated by raising teachers' expectations of non-college track students, making concerted efforts to reduce the stigma attached to non-college classes, assigning good teachers to non-college track classes, rewarding them for doing an effective job at turning on their students, and developing fair and equitable grading practices in both college prep and non-college prep classes.

Attractive as they may appear, efforts like these will be fruitless, so long as tracking systems, and indeed schools as we now know them, remain unchanged. What is needed are wholly new, experimental environments of teaching-learning-living, even outside today's public schools, if necessary. Such schools of the future must address themselves to two sets of problems highlighted by our findings: ensuring equality of opportunity for students now "locked out" by tracking, and offering—to all students—a far more fulfilling and satisfying learning process.

One approach to building greater equality of opportunity, as well as fulfillment, into existing or new secondary schools is the New Careers model. This model, which provides for fundamentally different ways of linking up educational and occupational careers, is based on the recognition that present options for entering the world of work are narrowly limited: one acquires a high school diploma and goes to work, or he first goes to college and perhaps then to a graduate or professional school. (Along the way, of course, young men must cope with the draft.)

The New Careers model provides for new options. Here the youth who does not want to attend college or would not qualify according to usual criteria, is given the opportunity to attend high school part time while working in a lower level position in an expanded professional career hierarchy (including such new positions as teacher aide and teacher associate in education). Such a person would then have the options of moving up through progressively more demanding educational and work stages; and moving back and forth between the work place, the high school and then the college. As ideally conceived, this model would allow able and aspiring persons ultimately to progress to the level of the fully certified teacher, nurse, librarian, social worker or public administrator. While the New Careers model has been developed and tried primarily in the human service sector of the economy, we have pointed out elsewhere that it is applicable to the industrial and business sector as well.

This alternative means of linking education with work has a number of advantages: students can try different occupations while still in school; they can earn while studying; they can spend more time outside the four walls of the school, learning what can best be learned in the work place; less stigma will accrue to those not immediately college bound, since they too will have a future; studying and learning will be inherently more relevant because it will relate to a career in which they are actively involved; teachers of such students will be less likely to develop lower expectations because these youth too will have an unlimited, open-ended future; and antischool subcultures will be less likely to develop, since education will not be as negative, frustrating or stigmatizing.

To ensure equality of opportunity is not enough. Merely to open the channels for lower income youth to flow into educational careers that are now turning off millions of middle class, college-bound youth is hardly doing anyone a favor. Though not reflected in our data, many middle-class students now find school even less tolerable than do low income youth. The empty grade-scrambling, teacher-pleasing and stultifying passivity such youth must endure stands in greater and greater contrast to their home and other non-school environments which usually yield much greater excitement, challenge and reward. More and more are dropping out psychologically, turning instead to drugs, apathy or political activism, often of an unthinking and self-defeating kind.

What is needed, then are entirely new and different models that will assure not only equality of opportunity but also much more in the way of an enriching and rewarding growth process. Educational environments of the future, incorporating New Careers as well as other new forms, must follow several simple guidelines.

First, successful new learning environments must be based on the recognition and acceptance of each individual's uniqueness. Each person must be allowed and stimulated to develop, learn and grow as an individual, not as a standardized occupant of any gross human category. As Kenneth Keniston stated in *The Uncommitted*, "Human diversity and variety must not only be tolerated, but rejoiced in, applauded, and encouraged."

At the beginning, we pointed out that tracking was an educational response to the increased pupil diversity created by pressure on adolescents from employers, parents and educators themselves to stay in school longer. While it may be an efficient way to screen large numbers of youth out of the educational and economic systems, and while it may be bureaucratically convenient, tracking is crude at best and destructive at worst in psychological and educational terms. Predictably, the occupants of the categories created by tracking come to be perceived, treated and taught according to what they are thought to have in common: college material or not college material, bright or not bright, motivated or not motivated, fast or not fast. Yet psychologists of individual differences and learning have told us for years what every parent already knows from common sense and experience: each child is unique in aptitudes, style of interaction, learning style and rate, energy level, interests, self-attitudes, reactions to challenge and stress, and in countless other ways. New educational environments must be adaptable to these differences.

The second guideline must be that the potential for individual growth and development is virtually unlimited and must be freed and stimulated to develop as fully as possible during each student's lifetime. We must stop assuming human potential is somehow fixed or circumscribed. Tragically, tracking—and indeed the whole structure of schooling—is founded on this premise. George Leonard puts it well in his *Education and Ecstacy*: "... the task of *preventing* the new generation from changing in any deep or significant way is precisely what most societies require of their educators." Not surprisingly, then, "The most obvious barrier between our children and the kind of education that can free their enormous potential seems to be the educational system itself: a vast, suffocating web of people, practices, and presumptions, kindly in intent, ponderous in response." In building new environments for becoming—with rich and limitless opportunities for exploration into self and others, other places, times and ideas, and the unknown—educators can play a part in seeing to it that more than today's mere fraction of potential learning and growing is unleashed.

The third guideline must be that "learning is sheer delight," to quote Leonard. For the non-college bound—indeed for the vast majority, including neat and tidy "high achievers"—"schooling" (we can hardly call it learning) is the very opposite. Tragically, Leonard may be all too right: "A visitor from another planet might conclude that our schools are hell-bent on creating—in a society that offers leisure and demands creativity—a generation of joyless drudges . . . when joy is absent, the effectiveness of the learning process falls and falls until the human being is operating hesitantly, grudgingly, fearfully at only a tiny fraction of his potential." For joy to enter learning, "cognitive learning" must be reunited with affective, physical and behavioral growth. The payoff must be now. Will learning then stop with the diploma?

If new learning-teaching-living environments follow these simple guidelines, not only will the negative effects of tracking be eliminated, but several features of the student role that alienate all types of students can also be avoided: passivity, subordination, forced separation from self, fragmented sequencing of learning, age segregation, isolation from community life with the unrealities of school that follow, an almost exclusive instrumental emphasis on future gains from schooling.

In summary, then, education must afford a chance for every student to experience an individualized, mind-expanding, joy-producing educational process, based on equity of opportunity. But it must do even more. Education must, in the final analysis, address itself to the vital issues of man and his survival. Educators then can take a long step toward preserving life itself.

"Right answers," specialization, standardization, narrow competition, eager acquisition, aggression, detachment from the self. Without them, it has seemed, the social machinery would break down. Do not call the schools cruel or unnatural for furthering what society had demanded. The reason we now need radical reform in education is that society's demands are changing radically. It is quite safe to say that the human characteristics now being inculcated will not work much longer. Already they are not only inappropriate, but destructive. If education continues along the old tack, humanity sooner or later will simply destroy itself (Leonard.)

We must start now.

October 1970

FURTHER READING

New Careers for the Poor, by Arthur Pearl and Frank Riessman (New York: Free Press, 1965) presents a thorough and insightful description of the rationale and operation of the New Careers program of job creation and training.

Social Relations in a Secondary School, David H. Hargreaves

(New York: Humanities Press, 1967) is an excellent comprehensive study of a Secondary Modern School in England which points up the pervasiveness of tracking (they call it streaming) in molding the structure of social relations in the school.

"Delinquency and the Schools," by Walter E. Schafer and Kenneth Polk, in *Task Force Report: Juvenile Delinquency and Youth Crime* (President's Commission on Law Enforcement and Administration of Justice, 1967), is a comprehensive study of the effect of the schools on delinquency.

White Rites and Indian Rights

A.D. FISHER

The lyrics of a song in the top ten last summer put the matter unequivocally. "Education's the thing," wails the lead singer of a black group called The Winstons, "if you want to compete. Without it, life just ain't very sweet." Almost everyone in North America, I suspect, would say "Amen" to that. The belief in increasing educational opportunities as the avenue to social progress has become an article of faith, and "going to school" an assurance of secular salvation akin to "good works" and "saving grace" in other times and other religions.

That for many sectors of North American society this belief flies in the face of observable facts should surprise no one. Yet it is a fact that the propitiation of the gods of learning simply isn't working for vast numbers of Americans and Canadians, especially the poor, the black and the Indian. Indeed, for those with whom I am most concerned in this essay, the Indian people of Canada, it can be demonstrated that education has been very nearly a total disaster.

Despite a considerable expansion of the number of schools and in the number of years of schooling available to Canadian Indian children, the unemployment rate among them has increased. Between the years 1959-60 and 1962-63, the welfare costs among Alberta's Indian population jumped from $294,625 to $683,080, and a sizeable portion of the latter figure went to unemployed but "educated" Indians. The incidence of unemployment among Indians with education is even more graphically illustrated by comparing the average unemployment of the total Indian population (43 percent) to that of Alberta Indian students who terminated their education in 1964-65 (64 percent).

While these figures clearly indicate that the Canadian Indian fails to use whatever education he receives once his schooling is over, other studies show that he also fails to take advantage of the schooling available to him. For example, in 1965 a study was made of junior high school dropouts at the Blackfoot Indian Reserve, Gleichen-Cluny, Alberta. It was determined that 86 of 168 students, or 51 percent, had dropped out of school in the years since 1961 and of these dropouts, 95 percent left school before they had completed grade nine. Something quite obviously happened to these children between grades five and nine.

Numerous hypotheses have been advanced to explain the phenomenon of the school dropout by persons of lower socioeconomic class; however none has been wholly satisfactory. This essay is an attempt to account for the phenomenon in a more fruitful manner, by redefining the dropout situation, and by applying this definition to the specific case of dropouts among Canadian Indians.

It will be useful to list some hypotheses used to explain dropping out, not because they are the most important or the most misleading, but because they illustrate the direction of concern among various students of education. Seymour Rubenfeld, in his 1965 study, *Family of Outcasts*, offers the hypothesis that the dropout as well as the juvenile delinquent gets that way because of an incomplete socialization that results in a self-discontent which is then externalized and "lived out" through deviant behavior, some of which is in relation to the school.

Lucius F. Cervantes' *The Dropout: Causes and Cures* presents the dropout as suffering from the failure of his primary group, his family. The result of this failure is the inability to achieve success in primary interpersonal relationships, which produces personality disorganization. This causes an end to interpersonal communication and makes personal satisfaction unattainable. For these reasons the individual leaves school.

Richard Cloward and Lloyd Ohlin, in the immensely influential *Delinquency and Opportunity*, focus on what might be called "objective status discontent." This implies that the deviant or delinquent individual is alienated from his environment and the legitimate means to success in that environment, (e.g. "education") because these institutions are, quite objectively, alienating. Because of this alienation, however, the individual turns to illegitimate means to nurture success. Another author utilizing the theme of alienation is John F. Bryde, who sees the Indian student of South Dakota as literally being outside of and between both Indian and white-man cultures. As such, he is alienated from both the goals of education and his Indian identity, which leads to his scholastic failure and "dropping out."

Finally, Murray and Rosalie Wax's study of the same

Sioux Indian students that Bryde discussed, indicates
that one of the major causes of dropping out is what can
be called "institutional intolerance." The Waxes argue
that the school situation at Pine Ridge, South Dakota, is
characterized by a lack of communication between the
school functionaries and those they serve. There is
"social distance" between students and teachers and
considerable individual isolation, even within the same
school.

The School as Ritual

These explanations appear to be suitable for the
particular cases they describe. Almost all of them,
however, concentrate upon one variable, the student or
ex-student. They fail to consider the institutional and
cultural variable, the school. It is the latter that I shall
focus on in this essay.

In Euro-Canadian society the school is a "primary
institution," in the sense that it is basic and widespread.
All Euro-Canadian children are expected to attend
school for extensive periods of time and to profit from
the experience. It is, in fact and in theory, the major
socialization device of the industrialized, urbanized
segment of the Canadian population. As such it
consumes a tremendous amount of time, substantial
amounts of money and a great deal of energy.

In this chapter, then, I define "the school," all formal
education from kindergarten to grade 12 or 13, as a rite
of passage, or rather a series of rites signifying
separation from, transition through and incorporation
into culturally recognized statuses and roles. Within the
larger chronological rite there are also numerous other
rites and ceremonials indicating partial transitions and
new role relationships.

This redefinition of the school as a rite of passage is likely to provoke some disagreement. Anthropologists and laymen alike choose to think of ritual and rites of passage as essentially magico-religious activities, and of schools as being only partially or minimally engaged in this type of activity. This is not altogether so. Not all ritual must be magico-religious, nor are schools as institutions, or what goes on in schools, completely free from magico-religious significance. It is quite difficult to categorize ritual activity clearly as to religious content. Further, ritual activity ranges from the purely magical and religious through the pseudorational to rational routine, albeit it is up to the observer to ascertain its rationality. Clearly, in any case, there are numerous calendrical and other rites and ceremonies in the public school that signify changes in the student's social life. Thus, the whole educational structure can be envisioned as a long-term ritual marking various changes in the social lives of the individuals. It is difficult for an outside observer to assess their magico-religious or secular content.

Nevertheless, it would be very hard to argue that the majority of Canadian students, parents and teachers see "education" in a wholly rational light. In a recent study, a noted American educator pointed out that despite scientific knowledge to the contrary the vast majority of public school classrooms in the United States operate on the two-thirds theory (*trans*action, 1967): two-thirds of the time someone is talking, two-thirds of the time it is the teacher who is talking, two-thirds of the time the teacher is talking she is lecturing or commenting upon the behavior of children in the classroom. If this is the case in the United States, then Canadian schools, generally, operate on the three-quarters theory, and schools catering to Indians operate on the seven-eighths

theory. The involvement of the school in teaching
moral-ethical behavior, the continuing belief in "disci-
plining the mind" through rigid curricula and repetitive
testing, the various rites of prayer and of patriotism,
indeed, the whole defensive ethos of the school point to
the pseudorational nature of the school.

Rites of Passage

More succinctly, one can look at "the school" as a
series of "ideological rituals," using "ideological" here
in Mannheim's sense, as a means to protect and perfect
the existing social system, in contrast to the "utopian"
striving for revolutionary change. In this sense the
public school in North America is indeed an ideological
rite of passage. Educators have long thought the
institution of the public school as the common ground
that allows immigrant and indigenous groups the
wherewithal for intelligent self-government, common
mores and economic perfection and advancement within
the ideological system of North American "democratic"
society.

There is little doubt that the characteristic form of
North American public education is typical of North
American society. It exemplifies and reflects the values
of that society, and prepares students for urban,
industrialized middle-class society. Finally the whole
ritual culminates in a pseudoreligious ceremonial known
as "convocation" or "commencement" in which it tells
the ex-student, "Now do it." Those who "can do it"
have been certified for that society. From kindergarten
or grade one when the child learns who his "helpers" in
the school and neighborhood are, to grade 12 to 13,
when each student is ranked and evaluated on the
formalized "external" or departmental examinations, he
passes through a multitude of statuses and plays many

roles. The result of the whole process is the development of a particular sort of individual—that is if the process is successful.

But, what would happen if we were to take this ceremonial system out of its context, North American middle-class society, and place it in a wholly or partly alien context such as an Indian reserve? The answer is that unless there were community support for it, it would fail. Let me stress this point. It would be the rite of passage, the rituals recognized and enjoined by middle-class society that would fail, *not the Indian student*.

Since 1944 there has been little doubt among scholars that students of North American Indian ancestry have intelligence adequate for most activities, exclusive of school. Robert Havighurst's well-known 1957 article demonstrates that Indian children perform "... about as well ..." as white children on performance tests of intelligence. More recently, in Charles Ray, Joan Ryan and Seymour Parker's 1962 study of Alaskan secondary-school dropouts, the authors state:

> The conclusion to be derived from the data is that intelligence *per se* cannot be considered a major contributing factor to dropouts and that achievement levels are not markedly different.

As this essay is focused primarily on dropouts with Eskimo, Aleut or Tlingit ethnic backgrounds as contrasted with white children, it appears to indicate that the cause of dropout is elsewhere than intelligence. But where are we to find it?

Thinking in Two Tongues

California Achievement Test scores in Alberta and South Dakota among Plains Cree, Blackfoot and Sioux

Indians indicate that the young Indian starts out *ahead* of his white peers, but then gradually tails off in achievement. Fourth-grade Indians who had averaged 4.3 on achievement tests while their white counterparts scored only 4.1, had by the eighth grade been surpassed by the white students who achieved an 8.1 average while Indian students had one of 7.7. Test scores consistently decline between grades five and seven. Furthermore, a parallel phenomenon in retardation of grade placement in relationship to age has been indicated in a study of Kwakiutl Indians on Gilford Island, British Columbia. The number of students at the expected grade-level decreased sharply from four at grade one to one by grade five and zero by grade six. At the same time, the number of students *below* the expected grade-level increased from two at grade one to four at grade five. Similar studies done by the Waxes on South Dakota Sioux also reveal that between the fifth and seventh grades the number of students of appropriate grade-age decreases. Thus, where the majority of fifth-grade students are in the ten- to 11-year category, the majority of sixth-grade students are in the 12- to 13-year range. From these patterns of slumping achievement-test scores and increasing age-grade level retardation, it appears that some sort of difficulty arises in the relationship between "the school" and the prepubescent/pubescent Indian. Admittedly, some Indian students drop out later than others but it would appear that in most cases of prolonged schooling it is the enforcement of the School Act that made the difference. The Blackfoot and Blood Indians of southern Alberta, for example, are under considerable compulsion to stay in school. If they do not "fit" the existing academic program, they are enrolled in "pre-employment" courses or in special programs such as "upgrading." It is therefore quite difficult for these students to leave school. The younger student often "solves" this problem by becoming a troublemaker in school (sassing teachers, being truant, refusing to work, etc.) or by becoming delinquent outside school (drinking and sexual escapades, fighting and theft). Of these Blackfoot early dropouts, ages 13 to 16 (which is the school-leaving age) 75 percent of the 15-year-olds and 70 percent of the 16-year-olds were considered delinquent. Among the older students, ages 17, 18 and 19, the amount of delinquent behavior was radically reduced. Apparently, then, when a Blackfoot student passes the school-leaving age, he can choose to stay or to go, and he generally chooses to go.

Another difference leading to local variation in the school-leaving age may be the attitudes of Indians about what is appropriate for them in the school. What the Indian expects to get out of school, what it means to him and what he believes himself to be are really the critical issues. Even though the specific answers to these questions may vary with different tribes, the result of these answers is the same: early dropout and unused education.

Indian expectations of school are conditioned by what the young Indian learns in the environment of his home community. Because what he learns at home often differs widely from what he learns at school, the Indian student is frequently forced to separate the two learning experiences. George Spindler once heard a "successful" Blood Indian say:

> I have to think about some things in my own language and some things in English. Well, for instance, if I think about horses, or about the Sun Dance, or about my brother-in-law, I have to think in my own language. If I think about buying a pickup truck or selling some beef or my son's grades in school I have to think in English.

The languages of Blackfoot and English are kept entirely apart; the former is for thinking about basic cultural elements, while the latter is used for school work. The Indian student grows up in a particular society with its own particular role transitions and in the presence of or absence of appropriate ritual recognition of these changes. Since the expectations about ritual and about role transitions held by any society and recognized as legitimate for that society are peculiar to that society, and to part-societies, at any time the school, as a rite of passage, may become inappropriate to members of a particular society that differs from North American middle-class society. This is what seems to happen to the Indian student.

Identity and Work

Young Blood Indians have certain very specific ideas about what they are and what they are going to be. Among a stratified sample of 40 young Bloods the most popular choices of a career or vocation were as follows: ranching, automechanic, carpenter, bronc rider, haying and farming. All of these occupations can be learned and practiced right on the Blood Reserve. They chose these occupations for two important reasons: knowledge and experience or, in other words, experiential knowledge that they already held. Among the Blackfoot dropouts and "stay-ins" a very similar pattern emerged. They, too, chose occupations that were familiar to them, even if they pertained little to their academic life. And this pattern emerges elsewhere in only slightly different form.

In Harry Wolcott's "Blackfish Village" Kwakiutl study he mentions in passing the response by students to the essay topic, "What I Would Like to Be Doing Ten Years from Now." Almost all the students thought they would be in and around their village. Two of the older girls guessed they would be married and in the village. Farther north, in Alaska, the Ray, Ryan and Parker study notes that the three primary reasons given for dropping out of secondary school are "needed at home," "marriage" and "wanted to work." Of the secondary reasons, to help at "home," "marriage" and "homesick" were most important. These reasons appear to indicate that the Alaskan dropout was opting out of formal education to return home to what he or she knows. As the authors indicate, "The majority of dropouts saw little relationship between what they were learning in school and jobs that were available to them."

Turning inland from British Columbia and Alaska we note the same phenomenon among the Metis of the Lac La Biche area (Kikino, Owl River, Mission), among the Blackfoot dropouts of Gleichen and Cluny and among the young Blood of southwestern Alberta. In each case the Indian student on the one hand expects to be doing what is now done in the context of his community, and on the other hand sees only a vague, if any, correlation between the demands of formal education in the context of the school and that which he expects to do.

A final point in this regard is made in the Waxes' study of the Pine Ridge Sioux. They state that education and being a good Sioux Indian are two separate processes, if becoming a good Indian is a process at all. They say that the full-bloods think that:

> ... education harms no one, but on the other hand it has almost nothing to do with being a good person... [They] do not seem to be aware that their offspring are regarded as unsocialized, amoral or backward by their teachers. That a child could be educated to the point where he would become critical of his kin or attempt to disassociate himself from them is still beyond their comprehension.

In conclusion, these studies show that the expanded educational opportunities for Canadian Indians are not really opportunities at all. For what the school offers is an irrelevant set of values and training. Moreover, the school often comes into direct conflict with certain moral and cultural values of the student. Thus, it is the educational system that fails the student and not the student who fails the system. In trying to be a good and successful Indian, the Indian student must often be a bad and unsuccessful student.

November 1969

FURTHER READING

Structure and Function in Primitive Society by A.R. Radcliffe-Brown (New York: Free Press, 1965).

The Adolescent Society by James S. Coleman (New York: Free Press, 1962).

A Kwakiutl Village and School by Harry Wolcott (New York: Holt, Rinehard and Winston, 1967).

Psychological Frontiers of Society by Abram Kardiner (New York: Columbia University Press, 1945).

Interracial Dating

FRANK A. PETRONI

Early in the still unfolding story of school desegregation, many observers were saying that what white opponents of integration were most afraid of was interracial sex. People who had been comforting themselves with such abstractions as "Negroes are OK, but I wouldn't want my daughter to marry one," now, with desegregation, had suddenly to cope (they thought) with a real possibility, not a farfetched hypothesis.

Be this as it may, I doubt there are many Americans who have not, at one time or another had to cope with the question of interracial sex, either in imagination—"what would happen if . . ."—or in fact. Interracial dating and interracial marriage are social realities, however much white racists and black nationalists may deplore it.

A few years ago, while I was with the Menninger Foundation in Topeka, Kansas, my wife and I had an opportunity to study the extent of, and students' feelings about, interracial dating at a desegregated high school. Our procedure was rather unorthodox. Instead of trying to gather a 5 percent random sample of the 3,000-member student body, we began slowly by letting our initial student contacts tell us what they considered to be the principal "types" of student in the school. They distinguished 12 such types: middle-class whites, hippies, peaceniks, white trash, "sedits" (upper-class blacks), elites, conservatives, racists, niggers, militants, athletes and hoods. Then, and again through our initial contacts, we brought in other students and roughly classified them according to "type." In this way, I believe we got a representative cross-section of the social world of this high school. We interviewed the boys and girls in groups of three or four, and in time 25 groups came to our house for these conversations. We had two refusals: a black girl canceled her appointment after Martin Luther King was killed, and a boy told us he wouldn't talk to white people.

Few topics demonstrate the multiple pressures students are subject to better than interracial dating. These pressures come from parents, teachers, counselors, school administrators and peers. However, mixed dating is emphatically not a barometer of the amount of "integration" in a desegregated school; that is not the reason we chose to study it.

Needless to say, the students did not all share the same point of view on interracial dating. Yet, most of them—independent of race—did feel that it was none of the school's business: if students wanted to date interracially, the school had no right to stop them.

White Boys and Black Girls

Not one student knew of a case of interracial dating involving a white boy and a black girl. There was considerable speculation about why. A conservative white girl said that white boys are too proud to date blacks. The two white boys with her disagreed: both said that it's because black girls aren't as pretty as white girls. One of the two also suggested that blacks and whites have little in common and so he would not consider dating a black. Note the popular stereotypes in this answer:

> Well, there are cultural differences, and their attitudes are different. I think that's what makes the difference. They're easygoing. They like to have a lot of fun. They don't think about the future, about things that are important like getting a job, or supporting a family. They don't try for grades. They're just out to have a good time.

Even when black girls met an individual's standard of physical attractiveness, however, white boys spoke of other obstacles: where to go, how to ignore community disapproval and what to do about family and friends who disapprove. These conflicts are cogently summarized in the response of a white boy who considered dating a black:

> I think if you dated a Negro, you would lose a lot of so-called friends. Buy you would probably gain some Negro friends. I contemplated asking this Negro girl for a date, but I chickened out. I thought, where would I take her? The only place where people wouldn't stare at me would be a drive-in movie, and I don't have a car. If you went to a restaurant, you would get dirty looks from people. I couldn't take her home and introduce her to my mom; she'd probably kill me.

Social obstacles apart, there is some doubt in my mind whether a black girl, in the school we studied, would go out with a white boy even if asked. Each black girl we interviewed was asked, "Suppose a white boy asked you out, how easy would it be for you to accept?" One girl answered: "Any white boy who asked me out, I would know what he wants. For a Negro boy to have a white girl is some sort of status symbol, but if a white boy asked me out, it would be a step down for him. I would think he wants something I'm not about to give him."

Other black girls spoke of the double standard between boys and girls, and how girls were less free to date interracially because their reputations would be ruined. Fear for one's reputation was also a factor among white girls. The students associated interracial dating with sex; and girls, be they black or white, stood to lose the most. Yet sex was not always associated with dating. There was no reference to sex when respondents talked about dating within one's race. Sometimes the reference to sex in interracial dating was subtle, but nonetheless it was present. A white girl's comment demonstrates this: "When you think of mixed dating, you always think of a colored boy with a white girl. And you always think it is the white girl who is low. If it was a white boy with a colored girl, then it would be the white boy who was low."

When asked for the meaning of low, another white girl said: "Well, generally the public thinks that the girl has low standards and low morals, if she's willing to go out with a Negro."

Particularly among "elite" blacks, parental disapproval of interracial dating also stood between black young women and dates with white boys. Most of the black students in this strata stated that their parents would not tolerate interracial dating. The parents expected their children to compete with white students academically, for school offices and in extracurricular activities; socially, however, they expected them to stay with blacks.

Still other respondents saw the white boys' reluctance to date blacks as essentially a matter of status considerations. If the belief that *all* whites are better than *all* blacks is general in this society (and it showed up among some of the blacks in our sample as well), then the response of an 18-year-old black girl, who was given the highest academic award the school has to offer, makes sense:

> White boys would be scared to ask us out anyway. The Negro boys will ask white girls out, but white boys will never ask Negro girls out. For a Negro boy, going out with a white girl is an accomplishment; it raises his status, even if the white girl is lower-class. All white kids are supposed to be better than Negro kids. If a white boy dated a Negro, even if the white boy was one of the "trashy" kind, and the girl was, say me, his status would drop. They would ask him if he was hard-up or something. White boys would be stepping down if they asked Negro girls for dates.

Aside from the black girl's fear of parental disapproval and loss of her reputation, we were told that few blacks would accept a date from a white boy because of pressures from black young men, who would object if black girls dated whites. However, this pressure doesn't appear to count for much with the elite, college-bound black girl; it was the athletic girl who gave us this answer. Unlike her elite counterpart, the athletic black girl was not preoccupied with achieving what the white man prized for whites: academic achievement, social popularity and a svelte figure. The reference group for these girls was the black community. A star on the girl's track team said:

> No Negro girls that I know of have ever been dated by a white guy. There are some that wish they

could. In fact, I know some white guys, myself, I wouldn't mind going out with, but the Negro girls are mostly afraid. Even if a white guy asked them out, they wouldn't go out with them. Negro boys don't like for Negro girls to date white guys. Sometimes I see white guys who look nice, and I stop and talk to them. The Negro boys get upset. They are real screwy. They can date white girls, but we can't date white guys.

The black young men in our sample at times disagreed on how they would react to dating between white boys and black girls, but in general their answers fell into one of the categories predicted by the black girls. A boy, who has dated white girls, admitted to the double standard alleged by the girl athlete. He told us:

You know, I think that Negro boys would detest having a Negro girl go out with a white boy. They don't want Negro girls to date white boys. They don't like it. I feel like that, and I think I'm a hypocrite. I've been out with white girls, but I don't like it if a Negro girl goes out with a white boy. If I see a colored girl with a white boy, I think, why didn't she date me, or another Negro? What's he got that I ain't got?

Not all blacks who date whites felt this way. The young man whom we just quoted identified positively with the black community. But another young man, with a steady white girl friend, and who prized white over black, had this to say: "I don't think most of the white boys would ask Negro girls out. Maybe I shouldn't say this, but I think any Negro girl would consider it a privilege to have a white boy ask her out. I feel if a colored girl is good enough to get a white boy, they should go out together."

It was easier for most of the students, white or black,

to talk about interracial dating in which the girl is white. This is the kind of dating most of them have seen. Some students, however, had seen black girls with white boys at the state university and in larger communities. One black spoke frankly of his reactions when he first saw a white man with a black woman:

> You see this at the colleges [white boys with Negro girls]. You know, it's a funny thing now that you mention it, you never see Negro girls with white boys here. I was in New York once. It was kind of funny; I saw this Negro girl with a white guy. I was shocked. You know, I looked, and it seemed kind of funny to me. I mean you see white girls with Negro boys, but you never see a Negro girl with a white guy; it kind of shocks you at first.

Black Males and White Girls

The pressures from parents, teachers, counselors, peers and the community are also brought to bear on the black boy and white girl who cross the barrier against interracial dating. As one student poignantly put it, "For those who violate this convention, the tuition is high." Just how high is exemplified by the white girl in the most talked-about relationship involving an inter-racial couple.

> Around Christmas time, I got to know this colored guy real well and wanted to date him. There was a big mix-up; my parents didn't like it. My parents put a lot of pressure on me not to go out with him. They are the type people, like Dad, who says he's not prejudiced. He even has *them* working in his office, but he wants them to stay in their place. At school there was a lot of talking behind my back

and snickering when I walked down the hallway. I tried to tell myself it didn't matter what people thought, but it still hurt. It hurt an awful lot. My parents made me feel so guilty. They made me feel so cheap. They were worried about what people would say. They made me feel like two pieces of dirt. You know, I never thought interracial dating was a good idea, but when I met this colored guy, it changed me. I never went with anyone I really liked before. I think this changes your outlook. It gives you hope, when you find someone you really like.

That sexual intercourse is associated with interracial dating is indicated by the fact that one reaction to such dating is to question the girl's moral standards. We heard this frequently from both white girls and boys, but particularly the latter. Prior to dating a black, however, the girl's personal conduct is rarely mentioned. It seems as if the disbelief among the white community that a white girl would date a black is softened by the rationalization that she "must be immoral." One white girl found it hard to accept this student reaction: "I got kind of sick of the kids throwing her to the dogs. There were times when you had to take a stand. You either turned the other cheek, or you fought back for her. They thought she was cheap, and they said nasty things about her. Even the guy I'm dating, he's that way, too."

However, a white girl doesn't have to date a black to have others question her morality. Just talking to a black student can result in the same labeling process. A liberal white girl, identified as a hippie, told us: "One day we were talking to some black power students in front of school. Some adults going by in cars made some filthy remarks. You can imagine what they think of white women, hanging around talking to Negroes. They shot it right out as they drove by. These are the good, white middle-class people."

A very articulate black youth described a similar incident in which he was talking to a white girl: "One time I was walking down the stairs outside school. I was standing with this white girl, and we were talking. About six white kids drove by and yelled, 'White trash, you're nothing but white trash.' I guess because she was white and I'm black, and we were talking, she was white trash."

Other blacks, aware of the white community's reaction to white girls who date or talk in public with blacks, were prevented from asking white girls out because they did not want to ruin the girls' reputations. The son of a prominent black professional, who was a football letterman, in the student government and extremely popular, refused to date a white girl for this reason.

> In general, I would say that just the fact that I was taking out a white girl, the imaginations would go wild. They think the moral standards are lower in interracial dating. There's this one white girl I goofed around with a lot. It's gone beyond the friendship stage, but we never dated. If I did go out with a white girl, it would be hard to take her anyplace. I would have to think about it for a while before I took out a white girl, because I feel she would be downgraded. I wouldn't want to ruin her reputation.

White girls who date across the color line find themselves unacceptable to white boys. Most of the students agreed that to date interracially limited a girl's field of potential dates. For many white girls, knowledge of this reaction on the part of white boys served as a deterrent to interracial dating. Nevertheless, a number of white girls told us they were attracted to certain black young men. One of the girls who did defy her society reported this also. She said, "When I was dating him, I was surprised at how many girls wanted to date colored guys. They would come up to me and ask me things. They really wanted to date colored guys, but they were afraid."

We found, too, that the white boycott (as it were) persisted after the interracial couple no longer dated, albeit only among white boys still in school. Girls who broke off their relationship with blacks were dated by older whites in the community. But to regain admission as an acceptable date among the high school boys, a girl would have to move to a new community to lose the pejorative label, which is part of the price for dating interracially.

The black male who dates a white girl does not escape criticism from his own race, particularly the black girls. Part of their disapproval is motivated, again, by the lack of reciprocity: black girls were not dated by whites. When a high-status black, generally an athlete, dated a white girl, he was replaced by neither a high-status nor low-status white. The black girls' resentment is summarized in the answer of one of our respondents, identified as a "militant."

> Well, in junior high, the Negro girls resented the fact that I went out with a white girl, and they really got onto me. They feel inferior. The white girls get all the guys. Some hostility between the Negro girls and white girls comes from this. The Negro girls kind of feel left out. She doesn't have white guys to date, and she doesn't have Negro guys to date. She says, "Hey, gal, you dating that Negro, and I can't get a date with him." This kind of builds up a resentment in her.

Pressure on the black male comes in two forms. First, his racial identification may be questioned. Often he is accused of thinking he is white. Second, retaliation by black girls can be more direct and swift. There were reports of boys physically beaten for dating a white girl. However, this response was the exception; it was more common for girls to spread the rumor that a boy is an "Uncle Tom."

Parental Pressures

The double threat of losing one's reputation and losing favor among the white boys prevented many white girls from dating blacks. Yet the pressures do not end there. Interracial dating is a test of the white liberal's commitment to civil rights—a test that few have passed. A number of white students spoke of their disappointment in their parents who gave lipservice to "liberalism" but in the final analysis were prejudiced. White girls reported this more often than white boys. However, white girls *tested* their parents more often. A white girl who sensed this in one of her parents said:

> This Negro friend of mine gets along beautifully with my mother, but not my father. He senses this, too. After meeting my father, he said my father didn't like him. This is something new for me because my father and mother have always been liberal. Now that he has been over to my house a couple of times, my father is acting strange. I guess I'm learning something about him I didn't know before.

Sometimes the parental reaction isn't as subtle as the feeling that one's father doesn't approve of interracial dating. A rather tough black girl, who admitted that at one time she was a hood, told us what happened to a white girl, who used to date her ex-boyfriend:

> For many Negro boys, dating white girls is their way of showing their superiority, their way of trying to hurt the white man. This boy I used to date went with a white girl once. She went through hell with her parents and everyone else to go out with him. But he didn't really care. He was just showing off. Her father even spit in her face. Her parents attacked her; they beat her and called her a slut.

Parental disapproval of interracial dating is not restricted to whites. The blacks reported a generation gap between themselves, their parents and their grandparents on this issue. In general, they reported that the intensity of the disapproval varied directly with age. Thus, grandparents showed more disapproval than parents. By and large, however, the black students agreed that the mixed couple that chooses to go out together should have that choice without interference from members of the adult community, be they parents, teachers, counselors, school administrators or anonymous members of the community.

The sample included few Mexican-Americans; those interviewed, however, reported the same phenomenon: Mexican parents, like white and black parents, objected to interracial dating. An outspoken Mexican-American girl related the Mexican parents' position. Her answer reveals the confusion parental inconsistencies can create for a young person.

> Mom always said have your fun as long as you're young, and as long as you marry a Mexican. I don't feel that way. If I fall in love with a Negro, I'll marry him. If I fall in love with a white, I'll marry a white. My parents would frown on us dating a Negro, even if he has higher standards than the Mexicans we date now: even if the Negro's father

was a lawyer or a doctor, and he was a better person than many of the lower-class Mexicans we date now. I don't understand it. They would rather see us go out with white people, who aren't as good, just because of skin color. They say they want the best for us; if the best meant going out with a Negro, they would say no!

The School

As if the pressures of peers, parents and community were not enough, those who try to break down the barrier against interracial dating, or who ignore it, must also cope with teachers, counselors and school administrators, who, by and large, are united on this issue. In a word, boy-girl relationships should be white-white, or black-black, but not black-white.

It became apparent to us that when we discussed the school's position on interracial dating, the students' objections to interference became more emotionally charged. This suggested to us that the students perceived the school and its functionaries as having less legitimacy than either parents or peers in attempting to control and dictate norms for their social life.

The hostility was increased by the fact that both black and white students perceived a selective interference by the school. The teachers, counselors and school administrators did not interfere with interracial dating per se. Their interference increased in direct proportion to the white girl's social status. A black girl described this selective process to us.

I think it's their business, not the school's. She was crazy about him, and he was crazy about her. They went to school to get an education, and that's what the school should be concerned with: giving them an education. Instead, they threatened him, they said he wouldn't get an athletic scholarship. I felt this was entirely wrong for the school to interfere. It's not the school's affair to concern itself with whether or not the students have companionship. It's their business to teach. These kids aren't the only couple at school. But she was somebody. With some of the other couples, the girls aren't important. In fact, one of the other girls is just white "trash." They don't say too much to these others; it's the important ones they want to save.

Another girl left little doubt of the painful slur implicit in this attitude of the school functionaries: "If you're a low white person, the administration could care less, but if you're a higher white person, they're worried that you might be dragged down by a Negro."

Although we cannot be certain, there is a possibility that the school's policy in these matters is dictated by the reality of the situation. There was little that the school could do to low-status students who dated across the color line; the school did not have an effective lever to stop them from continuing except to inform the parents, and most parents already knew. The only other course open to them was to expel the students for the slightest infraction of the rules. Among high-status students, however, the school could threaten removal from the very positions the students worked to achieve. Black athletes were called in and ordered to desist or forfeit their chances for an athletic scholarship; others were threatened with removal from the team. And white girls were told they could not run for a school office, they were not eligible to become cheerleaders and they would receive no assistance in obtaining a scholarship.

Interracial dating was one of the most emotionally charged subjects in our discussions with these young people. Although we have not cited all our respondents in this brief presentation, all of them had opinions on the issue. There was complete agreement on the type of interracial dating that occurred. In no case was the male white and the female black. Generally the black male, who dated the white girl, was a high-status athlete; however, by high status we are not referring to his father's socioeconomic position in the community. This may, or may not, have been high; in most cases it was not.

The fact that black students with prestige took up with white girls was a source of tension between black and white girls. More than her male counterpart, the black girl preached black separatism. Some students felt that this was because the girls did not share a sports experience such as that shared by black and white boys. On the surface, that may appear to be right. However, since there was little camaraderie between black and white athletes off the field or court, direct competition for high-status blacks in the dating-mating complex seems to be a more plausible explanation for the friction between the white and black girls.

While interracial dating was not commonplace, it did exist, and those who did it paid a heavy price. Payment was exacted from peers, parents, the community, teachers, counselors and other school administrators. In short, the entire social world of these teenagers was united against them. There was no citadel to protect them. When school and peers were allied against them, there was no comfort from their parents. The couple had each other, and a small enclave of "friends," but even among the latter the attrition rate was high.

Join this to the implication that their moral standards were lower if they dated interracially, and it is small wonder that few felt strongly enough to weather all these assaults.

September 1971

FURTHER READING

2, 4, 6, 8, When You Gonna Integrate? by Frank A. Petroni, Ernest A. Hirsch and C. Lillian Petroni (New York: Behavioral Publications, 1970).

Racially Separate or Together by Thomas F. Pettigrew (New York: McGraw-Hill, 1971) is an excellent account of factors—past, present and future—which have impeded and may continue to impede un-self-conscious interracial mixing.

BAD KIDS OR BAD PARENTS?

Delinquents Without Crimes: The American Approach to Juvenile Status Offenses

PAUL LERMAN

About 100 years ago, the state of New Jersey built a special correctional facility to save wayward girls from a life of crime and immorality. Over the years the ethnic and racial backgrounds of the institutionalized girls changed, the educational level of their cottage parent-custodians shifted upward, and the program of correction grew more humane. But the types of offenses that constitute the legal justification for their incarceration in the State Home for Girls have not changed appreciably.

The vast majority of the girls in the Home today, as in past years, were accused of misbehavior that would not be considered crimes if committed by adults. They

An earlier version of this chapter was commissioned by the Work Group on Self-Concept of the Social Science Research Council Subcommittee on Learning and the Educational Process, January 1970.

were formally adjudicated and institutionalized as delinquents, but most of them have not committed real criminal acts. Over 80 percent of them in 1969 were institutionalized for the following misdeeds: running away from home, being incorrigible, ungovernable and beyond the control of parents, being truant, engaging in sexual relations and becoming pregnant. Criminologists classify this mixture of noncriminal acts "juvenile status offenses," since only persons of a juvenile status can be accused, convicted and sentenced as delinquents for committing them. Juvenile status offenses apply to boys as well as girls, and they form the bases for juvenile court proceedings in all 50 states.

Historical Background

Most Americans are probably unaware that juveniles are subject to stricter laws than adults, and to more severe penalties for noncriminal acts than are many adults who commit misdemeanors and felonies. This practice, so apparently antithetical to our national image of child-centeredness, began well before the Revolution. The Puritans of the Plymouth Bay Colony initiated the practice of defining and treating as criminal children who were "rude, stubborn, and unruly," or who behaved "disobediently and disorderly towards their parents, masters, and governors." In 1824, when the House of Refuge established the first American juvenile correctional institution in New York City, the board of managers was granted explicit sanction by the state legislature to hold in custody and correct youths who were leading a "vicious or vagrant life," as well as those convicted of any crime. The first juvenile court statute, passed in Illinois in 1899, continued the tradition of treating juvenile status offenses as criminal by including this class of actions as part of the definition of "delinquency." Other states copied this legislative practice as they boarded the bandwagon of court reform.

The contention that juvenile status offenders are still handled through a *criminal* process will be disputed by many defenders of the current system who argue that the creation of the juvenile court marked a significant break with the past. They contend that juvenile courts were set up to deal with the child and his needs, rather than with his offense. In line with this benign aim, the offense was to be viewed as a symptom of a child's need for special assistance. The juvenile court was designed to save children—not punish them. Only "neglectful" parents were deemed appropriate targets of punishment.

Unfortunately, the laudable intentions of the founders of the court movement have yet to be translated into reality. The U.S. Supreme Court, in 1967, reached this conclusion; so, too, did the Task Force on Delinquency of the President's Commission on Law Enforcement and the Administration of Justice. Both governmental bodies ruled that juvenile court dispositions were, in effect, sentences that bore a remarkable resemblance to the outcomes of adult criminal proceedings. The Supreme Court was appalled at the idea that 15-year-old Gerald Gault could be deprived of his liberty for up to six years without the benefits of due process of law found in adult courts. The majority was persuaded that the consequences of judicial decisions should be considered, not just the ideals of the founders of the juvenile court.

From an historical perspective, the Supreme Court's ruling appears quite reasonable—although it was 70 years overdue. The juvenile court was grafted onto an existing schema for defining youthful misdeeds as illegal behavior. It was also grafted onto a correctional system that had begun separating youngsters from adults, and boys from girls, for many years before the first juvenile court was established. Long before there was a juvenile court, the American predilection for utilizing legal coercion to control youthful behavior had been well established. The form of the jurisdictional mandate changed with the emergence of the juvenile court—but the substantive range and scope of youthful liability for noncriminal behavior has not really changed.

Since the Supreme Court ruling in *Gault v. Arizona*, there has been increased concern and debate over the introduction of legal counsel and minimal procedural rights in the operation of the juvenile court. The preoccupation with legal rights in the courtroom has, however, obscured the fact that the sociolegal boundaries of delinquency statutes were unaffected by *Gault*. Nevertheless, some revision of the laws has been undertaken by the states, at least since 1960 when the Second United Nations Congress on the Prevention of Crime and the Treatment of Offenders recommended that juveniles should not be prosecuted as delinquents for behavior which, if exhibited by adults, would not be a matter of legal concern.

One state, New York, even approached a technical compliance with the United Nations standard. In New York, juvenile status offenders are adjudicated with a separate petition alleging a "person in need of supervision" (PINS); traditional criminal offenses use a petition that alleges "delinquency." However, true to American tradition, both types of petitioned young people are locked up in the same detention facilities and reform schools. One of the most "progressive" juvenile court laws in the country was initially enacted with restrictions on mixing, but this was soon amended to permit the change to be merely semantic, not substantive. Besides New York, six other states have amended their juvenile codes to establish a distinctive labeling procedure to distinguish criminal and non-criminal acts. Each of these states (California, Illinois, Kansas, Colorado, Oklahoma and Vermont) has banned *initial* commitment to juvenile reformatories of children within the noncriminal jurisdiction of the court. Whether this ban will be continued in practice (and in the statutes) is uncertain. Meanwhile, young people can still be mixed in detention facilities, transfers to reformatories are technically possible, and subsequent petitions permit commitments to delinquent institutions. In addition, it is doubtful whether the public (including teachers and prospective employers) distinguishes between those "in need of supervision" and delinquents.

Discretionary Decision-Making

If the letter and spirit of American juvenile statutes were rigorously enforced, our delinquency rates and facilities would be in even deeper trouble than they are today. For few American youths would reach adulthood without being liable to its stern proscriptions. However, mitigating devices are used to avoid further overcrowding court dockets and institutions, and to demonstrate that parents and enforcement officials can be humane and child-centered. Adult authorities are permitted to exercise discretionary behavior in processing actions by official petitions. The American system is notorious for its widespread use of unofficial police and judicial recording and supervision of juveniles, whether status offenders or real delinquents. As a matter of historical fact, the hallmark of the American system is the intriguing combination of limitless scope of our delinquency statutes and enormous discretion granted in their enforcement and administration. Our statutes appear to reflect the image of the stern Puritan father, but our officials are permitted to behave like Dutch uncles—if they are so inclined.

Discretionary decision-making by law enforcement officials has often been justified on the grounds that it permits an "individualization" of offenders, as well as for reasons of pragmatic efficiency. While this may be true in some cases, it is difficult to read the historical record and not conclude that many juvenile status actions could have been defined as cultural differences and childhood play fads, as well as childhood troubles with home, school and sex. Using the same broad definition of delinquency, reasonable adults have differed—and continue to differ—over the sociolegal meaning of profanity, smoking, drinking, sexual congress, exploring abandoned buildings, playing in forbidden places, idling, hitching rides on buses, trucks and cars, sneaking into shows and subways, and so forth. While many judgments about the seriousness of these offenses may appear to be based on the merits of the individual case, delinquency definitions, in practice, employ shifting cultural standards to distinguish between childhood troubles, play fads and neighborhood differences. Today, officials in many communities appear more tolerant of profanity and smoking than those of the 1920s, but there is continuing concern regarding female sexuality, male braggadocio and disrespect of adult authority. In brief, whether or not a youth is defined as delinquent may depend on the era, community and ethnic status of the official—as well as the moral guidelines of individual law enforcers.

Extent of the Problem Today

National studies of the prevalence of the problem are not readily available. However, we can piece together data that indicate that the problem is not inconsequential. A conservative estimate, based upon analysis of national juvenile court statistics compiled by the United States Children's Bureau, indicates that juvenile status crimes comprise about 25 percent of the children's cases initially appearing before juvenile courts on a formal petition. About one out of every five boys' delinquency petitions and over one-half of all girls' cases are based on charges for which an adult would not be legally liable even to appear in court.

The formal petitions have an impact on the composition of juvenile facilities, as indicated by the outcomes of legal processing. A federal review of state and local detention facilities disclosed that 40 to 50 percent of the cases in custody, pending dispositional hearings by judges, consisted of delinquents who had committed no crimes. A companion study of nearly 20 correctional institutions in various parts of the country revealed that between 25 and 30 percent of their resident delinquent population consisted of young people convicted of a juvenile status offense.

The figures cited do not, however, reveal the number of youths that are treated informally by the police and the courts. Many young people are released with their cases recorded as "station adjustments"; in a similar fashion, thousands of youths are informally dealt with at court intake or at an unofficial court hearing. Even though these cases are not formally adjudicated, unofficial records are maintained and can be used against the children if they have any future run-ins with the police or courts. The number of these official, but nonadjudicated, contacts is difficult to estimate, since our requirements for social bookkeeping are far less stringent than our demands for financial accountability.

One careful study of police contacts in a middle-sized city, cited approvingly by a task force of the President's Commission on Law Enforcement and the Administration of Justice, disclosed that the offense that ranked highest as a delinquent act was "incorrigible, runaway"; "disorderly conduct" was second; "contact suspicion, investigation, and information" ranked third; and "theft" was a poor fourth. In addition to revealing that the police spend a disproportionate amount of their time attending to noncriminal offenses, the study also provides evidence that the problem is most acute in low-income areas of the city. This kind of finding could probably be duplicated in any city—large, small or middle-sized—in the United States.

Legal Treatment of Delinquents without Crimes

A useful way of furthering our understanding of the American approach to dealing with delinquents without crimes is provided by comparing judicial decisions for different types of offenses. This can be done by reanalyzing recent data reported by the Children's Bureau, classifying offenses according to their degree of seriousness. If we use standard FBI terminology, the most serious crimes can be labeled "Part I" and are homicide, forcible rape, armed robbery, burglary, aggravated assault and theft of more than $50. All other offenses that would be crimes if committed by an adult, but are less serious, can be termed "all other adult types" and labeled "Part II." The third type of offenses, the least serious, are those acts that are "juvenile status offenses." By using these classifications, data reported to the Children's Bureau by the largest cities are reanalyzed to provide the information depicted in the table. Three types of decisions are compared in this analysis: 1) whether or not an official petition is drawn after a complaint has been made; 2) whether or not the juvenile is found guilty, if brought before the court on an official petition; and 3) whether or not the offender is placed or committed to an institution, if convicted. The rates for each decision level are computed for each of the offense classifications.

Table 1. Disposition of Juvenile Cases at
Three Stages in the Judicial Process
19 of the 30 Largest Cities, 1965

	Part I (Most Serious Adult Offenses)	Part II (All Other Adult Offenses)	Juvenile Status Offenses
% Court Petition after complaint	57% N=(37,420)	33% (52,862)	42% (33,046)
% Convicted— if brought into court	92% N=(21,386)	90% (17,319)	94% (13,857)
% Placed or Committed— if convicted	23% N=(19,667)	18% (15,524)	26% (12,989)

The table discloses a wide difference between offense classifications at the stage of deciding whether to draw up an official petition (57 percent versus 33 percent and 42 percent). Part I youth are far more likely to be brought into court on a petition, but juvenile status offenders are processed at a higher rate than all other adult types. At the conviction stage the differences are small, but the juvenile status offenders are found guilty more often. At the critical decision point, commitment to an institution, the least serious offenders are more likely to be sent away than are the two other types.

It is apparent that juvenile justice in America's large cities can mete out harsher dispositions for youth who have committed no crimes than for those who violate criminal statutes. Once the petitions are drawn up, juvenile judges appear to function as if degree of seriousness is not an important criterion of judicial decision making. If different types of offenders were sent to different types of institutions, it might be argued that the types of sentences actually varied. In fact, however, all three offender types are generally sent to the same institutions in a particular state—according to their age and sex—for an indeterminate length of time.

Length of Institutionalization and Detention

If American juvenile courts do not follow one of the basic components of justice—matching the degree of punishment with the degree of social harm—perhaps the correctional institutions themselves function differently. This outcome is unlikely, however, since the criteria for leaving institutions are not based on the nature of the offense. Length of stay is more likely to be determined by the adjustment to institutional rules and routine, the receptivity of parents or guardians to receiving the children back home, available bed space in cottages and the current treatment ideology. Juvenile status offenders tend to have more family troubles and may actually have greater difficulty in meeting the criteria for release than their delinquent peers. The result is that the delinquents without crimes probably spend more time in institutions designed for delinquent youth than "real" delinquents. Empirical support for this conclusion emerges from a special study of one juvenile jurisdiction, the Manhattan borough of New York City. In a pilot study that focused on a random sample of officially adjudicated male cases appearing in Manhattan Court in 1963, I gathered data on the range, median and average length of stay for boys sent to institutions. In New York, as noted earlier, juvenile status youth are called "PINS" (persons in need of supervision), so I use this classification in comparing this length of institutionalization with that of "delinquents."

The range of institutional stay was two to 28 months for delinquents and four to 48 months for PINS boys; the median was nine months for delinquents and 13 months for PINS; and the average length of stay was 10.7 months for delinquents and 16.3 months for PINS. Regardless of the mode of measurement, it is apparent that institutionalization was proportionately longer for boys convicted and sentenced for juvenile status offenses than for juveniles convicted for criminal-type offenses.

These results on length of stay do not include the detention period, the stage of correctional processing prior to placement in an institution. Analyses of recent detention figures for all five boroughs of New York City revealed the following patterns: 1) PINS boys and girls are more likely to be detained than are delinquents (54 to 31 percent); and 2) once PINS youth are detained they are twice as likely to be detained for more than 30 days than are regular delinquents (50 to 25 percent). It is apparent that juvenile status offenders who receive the special label of "persons in need of supervision" tend to spend more time in penal facilties at *all* stages of their correctional experience than do delinquents.

Social Characteristics of Offenses and Offenders

The offenses that delinquents without crimes are charged with do not involve a clear victim, as is the case in classical crimes of theft, robbery, burglary and assault. Rather, they involve young people who are themselves liable to be victimized for having childhood troubles or growing up differently. Three major categories appear to be of primary concern: behavior at home, behavior at school and sexual experimentation. "Running away," "incorrigibility," "ungovernability" and "beyond the control of parental supervision" refer to troubles with parents, guardians or relatives. "Growing up in idleness," "truanting" and creating "disturbances" in classrooms refer to troubles with teachers, principals, guidance counselors and school routines. Sexual relations as "minors" and out-of-wedlock pregnancy reflect adult concern with the act and consequences of precocious sexual experimentation. In brief, juvenile status offenses primarily encompass the problems of growing up.

Certain young people in American society are more likely to have these types of troubles with adults: girls, poor youth, rural migrants to the city, underachievers and the less sophisticated. Historically, as well as today, a community's more disadvantaged children are most likely to have their troubles defined as "delinquency." In the 1830s the sons and daughters of Irish immigrants were overrepresented in the House of Refuge, the nation's first juvenile correctional institution. In the 1970s the sons and daughters of black slum dwellers are disproportionately dealt with as delinquents for experiencing problems in growing up.

Unlike regular delinquents, juvenile status offenders often find a parent, guardian, relative or teacher as the chief complainant in court. Since juvenile courts have traditionally employed family functioning and stability as primary considerations in rendering dispositions, poor youth with troubles are at a distinct disadvantage compared to their delinquent peers. Mothers and fathers rarely bring their children to courts for robbing or assaulting nonfamily members; however, if their own authority is challenged, many parents are willing to use the power of the state to correct their offspring. In effect, many poor and powerless parents cooperate with the state to stigmatize and punish their children for having problems in growing up.

Recent Criticisms

At least since *Gault*, the system of juvenile justice has been undergoing sharp attacks by legal and social critics. Many of these have pertinence for the processing and handling of juvenile status offenders. The current system has been criticized for the following reasons:

1. The broad scope of delinquency statutes and juvenile court jurisdictions has permitted the coercive imposition of middle-class standards of child rearing.

2. A broad definition has enlarged the limits of discretionary authority so that virtually any child can be deemed a delinquent if officials are persuaded that he needs correction.

3. The presence of juvenile status offenses as part of the delinquency statutes provides an easier basis for convicting and incarcerating young people because it is difficult to defend against the vagueness of terms like "incorrigible" and "ungovernable."

4. The mixing together of delinquents without crimes and real delinquents in detention centers and reform schools helps to provide learning

experiences for the nondelinquents on how to become real delinquents.

5. The public is generally unaware of the differences between "persons in need of supervision" and youths who rob, steal and assault, and thereby is not sensitized to the special needs of status offenders.

6. Statistics on delinquency can be misleading because we are usually unable to differentiate how much of the volume reflects greater public and official concern regarding home, school and sex problems, and how much is actual criminal conduct by juveniles.

7. Juvenile status offenses do not constitute examples of social harm and, therefore, should not even be the subject of criminal-type sanctions.

8. Juvenile institutions that house noncriminal offenders constitute the state's human garbage dump for taking care of all kinds of problem children, especially the poor.

9. Most policemen and judges who make critical decisions about children's troubles are ill equipped to understand their problems or make sound judgments on their behalf.

10. The current correctional system does not rehabilitate these youths and is therefore a questionable approach.

Two Unintended Consequences

In addition to the reasons cited, there are two unintended consequences that have not been addressed even by critics. Analysis of the data presented earlier provides evidence that the current system is an unjust one. Youngsters convicted of committing the least serious offenses are dealt with more severely by virtue of their greater length of detention and institutionalization. Any legal system that purports to accord "justice for all" must take into account the degree of punishment that is proportionate to the degree of social harm inflicted. The current system does not meet this minimal standard of justice.

The recent ruling by the U.S. Supreme Court (*Gault v. Arizona*) found that the juvenile court of Arizona—and by implication the great majority of courts—were procedurally unfair. The court explicitly ruled out any consideration of the substantive issues of detention and incarceration. It may have chosen to do so because it sincerely believed that the soundest approach to insuring substantive justice is by making certain that juveniles are granted the constitutional safeguards of due process: the right to confront accusers and cross-examine, the right to counsel, the right to written charges and prior notice, and the right against self-incrimination. While this line of reasoning may turn out to be useful in the long run of history, adherence to this approach would involve acceptance of an undesirable system until the time that substantive justice could catch up with procedural justice. The likelihood that the injustice accorded to youth is not intentional does not change the current or future reality of the court's disposition. Nevertheless, the inclusion of juvenile status offenders as liable to arrest, prosecution, detention and incarceration probably promotes the criminalization of disadvantaged youth. Earlier critics have indicated that incorrigible boys and girls sent to reform schools learn how to behave as homosexuals, thieves, drug users and burglars. But what is the impact at the community level, where young people initially learn the operational meaning of delinquency? From the child's point of view, he learns that occurrences that may be part of his daily life—squabbles at home, truancy and sexual precocity—are just as delinquent as thieving, robbing and assaulting. It must appear that nearly anyone he or she hangs around with is not only a "bad" kid but a delinquent one as well. In fact, there are studies that yield evidence that three-quarters of a generation of slum youth, ages ten to 17, have been officially noted as "delinquent" in a police or court file. It seems reasonable to infer that many of these records contain official legal definitions of essentially noncriminal acts that are done in the family, at school and with peers of the opposite sex.

It would be strange indeed if youth did not define themselves as "bad cats"—just as the officials undoubtedly do. It would be strange, too, if both the officials and the young people (and a segment of their parents) did not build on these invidious definitions by expecting further acts of "delinquency." As children grow older, they engage in a more consistent portrayal of their projected identity—and the officials dutifully record further notations to an expected social history of delinquency. What the officials prophesy is fulfilled in a process that criminalizes the young and justifies the prior actions of the official gatekeepers of the traditional system. Our societal responses unwittingly compound the problem we ostensibly desire to prevent and control—real delinquent behavior.

In the arena of social affairs it appears that negative consequences are more likely to occur when there is a large gap in status, power and resources between the "savers" and those to be "saved." Evidently, colonial-type relationships, cultural misunderstandings and unrestrained coercion can often exacerbate problems, despite the best of intentions. Given this state of affairs, it appears likely that continual coercive intrusion by the state into the lives of youthful ghetto residents can continue to backfire on a large scale.

We have probably been compounding our juvenile problem ever since 1824 when the New York State Legislature granted the board of managers of the House of Refuge broad discretionary authority to intervene coercively in the lives of youth until they become 21 years of age—even if they had not committed any criminal acts. Generations of reformers, professionals and academics have been too eager to praise the philanthropic and rehabilitative intentions of our treatment centers toward poor kids in trouble—and insufficently sensitive to the *actual* consequences of an unjust system that aids and abets the criminalization of youth.

New Policy Perspectives

Sophisticated defenders of the traditional system are aware of many of these criticisms. They argue that the intent of all efforts in the juvenile field is to help, not to punish, the child. To extend this help they are prepared to use the authority of the state to coerce children who might otherwise be unwilling to make use of existing agencies. Not all acts of juvenile misbehavior that we currently label "status offenses" are attributable to cultural differences. Many youngsters do, in fact, experience troubles in growing up that should be of concern to a humane society. The fundamental issue revolves on how that concern can be expressed so as to yield the maximum social benefits and the minimum social costs. Thus, while the consequences of criminal-izing the young and perpetuating an unjust system of juvenile justice should be accorded greater recognition than benign intentions, it would be a serious mistake to propose an alternative policy that did not incorporate a legitimate concern for the welfare of children.

The issue is worth posing in this fashion because of a recent policy proposal advanced by the President's Commission on Law Enforcement and the Administration of Justice. The commission suggested that "serious consideration should be given complete elimination from the court's jurisdiction of conduct illegal only for a child. Abandoning the possibility of coercive power over a child who is acting in a seriously self-destructive way would mean losing the opportunity of reclamation in a few cases."

Changing delinquency statutes and the jurisdictional scope of the juvenile court to exclude conduct illegal only for a child would certainly be a useful beginning. However, the evidence suggests that the cases of serious self-destructiveness are not "few" in number, and there is reason to believe that many adjudicated and institutionalized young people do require some assistance from a concerned society. By failing to suggest additional policy guidelines for providing the necessary services in a *civil* context, the commission advanced only half a policy and provided only a limited sense of historical perspective.

Traditional American practices towards children in trouble have not been amiss because of our humanitarian concern, but because we coupled this concern with the continuation of prior practices whereby disliked behavior was defined and treated as a criminal offense (that is, delinquent). Unfortunately, our concern has often been linked to the coercive authority of the police powers of the state. The problems of homeless and runaway youths, truants, sex experimenters and others with childhood troubles could have been more consistently defined as *child welfare* problems. Many private agencies did emerge to take care of such children, but they inevitably left the more difficult cases for the state to service as "delinquent." In addition, the private sector never provided the services to match the concern that underlay the excessive demand. The problem of the troublesome juvenile status offender has been inextricably linked to: 1) our failure to broaden governmental responsibility to take care of *all* child welfare problems that were not being cared for by private social agencies; and 2) our failure to hold private agencies accountable for those they did serve with public subsidies. We permitted the police, courts and correctional institutions to function as our residual agency for caring for children in trouble. Many state correctional agencies have become, unwittingly, modern versions of a poorhouse for juveniles. Our *systems* of child welfare and juvenile justice, not just our legal codes, are faulty.

The elimination of juvenile status offenses from the jurisdiction of the juvenile court would probably create an anomalous situation in juvenile jurisprudence if dependency and neglect cases were not also removed. It would be ironic if we left two categories that were clearly noncriminal within a delinquency adjudicatory structure. If they were removed, as they should be, then the juvenile court would be streamlined to deal with a primary function: the just adjudication and disposition of young people alleged to have committed acts that would be criminal if enacted by an adult. Adherence to this limited jurisdiction would aid the court in complying with recent Supreme Court rulings, for adversary proceedings are least suited to problems involving family and childhood troubles.

If these three categories were removed from the traditional system, we would have to evolve a way of thinking about a new public organization that would engage in a variety of functions: fact finding, hearing of complaints, regulatory dispositions and provision of general child care and family services. This new public agency could be empowered to combine many of the existing functions of the court and child welfare departments, with one major prohibition: transfers of temporary custody of children would have to be voluntary on the part of parents, and all contested cases would have to be adjudicated by a civil court. This prohibition would be in harmony with the modern child welfare view of keeping natural families intact, and acting otherwise only when all remedial efforts have clearly failed.

We have regulatory commissions in many areas of social concern in America, thereby sidestepping the usual judicial structure. If there is a legitimate concern in the area of child and family welfare, and society wants to ensure the maintenance of minimum services, then legally we can build on existing systems and traditions to evolve a new kind of regulatory service commission to carry out that end. To ensure that the critical legal rights of parents and children are protected, civil family courts—as in foster and adoption cases— would be available for contest and appeal. However, to ensure that the agencies did not become bureaucratic busybodies, additional thought would have to be given to their policy-making composition, staffing and location.

Citizen Involvement

A major deficiency of many regulatory agencies in

this country is that special interests often dominate the administration and proceedings, while affected consumers are only sparsely represented. To ensure that the residents most affected by proposed family and child welfare boards have had a major voice in the administration and proceedings, they could be set up with a majority of citizen representatives (including adolescents). In addition, they could be decentralized to function within the geographical boundaries of areas the size of local elementary or junior high school districts. These local boards would be granted the legal rights to hire lay and professional staff, as well as to supervise the administration of hearings and field services.

The setting up of these local boards would require an extensive examination of city, county and state child welfare services to ensure effective cooperation and integration of effort. It is certainly conceivable that many protective family and child welfare services, which are generally administered without citizen advice, could also be incorporated into the activities of the local boards. The problems to be ironed out would of course be substantial, but the effort could force a reconceptualization of local and state responsibilities for providing acceptable, humane and effective family and child welfare services on a broad scale.

The employment of interested local citizens in the daily operation of family and child welfare services is not a totally new idea. Sweden has used local welfare boards to provide a range of services to families and children, including the handling of delinquency cases. While we do not have to copy their broad jurisdictional scope or underrepresentation of blue-collar citizens, a great deal can be learned from this operation. Other Scandinavian countries also use local citizen boards to deal with a range of delinquency offenses. Informed observers indicate that the nonlegal systems in Scandi-navia are less primitive and coercive. However, it is difficult to ascertain whether this outcome is due to cultural differences or to the social invention that excludes juvenile courts.

There exist analogues in this country for the use of local citizens in providing services to children in trouble. In recent years there has been an upsurge in the use of citizen-volunteers who function as house parents for home detention facilities, probation officers and intake workers. Besides this use of citizens, New Jersey, for example, has permitted each juvenile court jurisdiction to appoint citizens to Judicial Conference Committees, for the purpose of informally hearing and handling delinquency cases. Some New Jersey counties process up to 50 percent of their court petitions through this alternative to adjudication. All these programs, however, operate under the direct supervision and jurisdiction of the county juvenile court judges, with the cooperation of the chief probation officers. It should be possible to adapt these local innovations to a system that would be independent of the coercive aspects of even the most benign juvenile court operation.

Opposition to Innovation

Quite often it is the powerful opposition of special interest groups, rather than an inability to formulate new and viable proposals for change, that can block beneficial social change. Many judges, probation workers, correction officers, as well as religious and secular child care agencies, would strenuously oppose new social policies and alternatives for handling delinquents without crimes. Their opposition would certainly be understandable, since the proposed changes could have a profound impact on their work. In the process of limiting jurisdiction and altering traditional practices, they could lose status, influence and control over the use of existing resources. Very few interest groups suffer these kinds of losses gladly. Proponents of change should try to understand their problem and act accordingly. However, the differential benefits that might accrue to children and their families should serve as a reminder that the problems of youth and their official and unofficial adult caretakers are not always identical.

One proposal in particular can be expected to call forth the ire of these groups, and that is the use of citizens in the administration and provision of services in local boards. Many professional groups—psychiatrists, social workers, psychologists, group therapists and school guidance counselors—have staked out a claim of expertise for the treatment of any "acting out" behavior. The suggestion that citizens should play a significant role in offering assistance undermines that claim. In reply, the professionals might argue that experts—not laymen—should control, administer and staff any programs involving the remediation of child-hood troubles. On what grounds might this kind of claim be reasonably questioned?

First, there is nothing about local citizens' control of child and family welfare activities that precludes the hiring of professionals for key tasks, and entrusting them with the operation of the board's program. Many private and public boards in the fields of correction and child welfare have functioned this way in the past.

Second, any claims about an expertise that can be termed a scientific approach to correction are quite premature. There does not now exist a clear-cut body of knowledge that can be ordered in a text or verbally transmitted that will direct any trained practitioner to diagnose and treat effectively such classic problems as truancy, running away and precocious sex experimentation. Unlike the field of medicine, there are no clear-cut prescriptions for professional behavior that can provide an intellectual rationale for expecting a remission of symptoms. There exist bits and pieces of knowledge and practical wisdom, but there is no correctional technology in any acceptable scientific sense.

Third, a reasonable appraisal of evaluations of current approaches to delinquents indicates that there are, in fact, no programs that can claim superiority. The studies do indicate that we can institutionalize far fewer children in treatment centers or reform schools without increasing the risks for individuals or communities; or, if we continue to use institutional programs, young people can be held for shorter periods of time without increasing the risk. The outcome of these appraisals provides a case for an expansion of humane child care activities—not for or against any specific repertoire of intervention techniques.

Fourth, many existing correctional programs are not now controlled by professionals. Untrained juvenile court judges are administratively responsible for detention programs and probation services in more than a majority of the 50 states. Many correctional programs have been headed by political appointees or nonprofessionals. And state legislatures, often dominated by rural legislators, have exercised a very strong influence in the permissible range of program alternatives.

Fifth, the professionalization of officials dealing with delinquent youth does not always lead to happy results. There are studies that indicate that many trained policemen and judges officially process and detain more young people than untrained officials, indicating that their definition of delinquency has been broadened by psychiatric knowledge. At this point in time, there is a distinct danger that excessive professionalization can lead to overintervention in the lives of children and their families.

Sixth, there is no assurance that professionals are any more responsive to the interests and desires of local residents than are untrained judges and probation officers. Citizens, sharing a similar life style and knowledgeable about the problems of growing up in a given community, may be in a better position to enact a *parens patrie* doctrine than are professionals or judges.

Seventh, in ghetto communities, reliance on professional expertise can mean continued dependence on white authority systems. Identification of family and child welfare boards as "our own" may compensate for any lack of expertise by removing the suspicion that any change of behavior by children and parents is for the benefit of the white establishment. The additional community benefits to be gained from caring for "our own" may also outweigh any loss of professional skills. The benefits accruing from indigenous control over local child welfare services would hold for other minority groups living in a discriminatory environment: Indians, Puerto Ricans, Mexicans, hillbillies and French Canadians.

Alternative Policy Proposals in Decriminalization

The proposal to create family and child welfare boards to deal with juvenile status offenses may be appealing to many people. However, gaining political acceptance may be quite difficult, since the juvenile justice system would be giving up coercive power in an area that it has controlled for a long period of time. The proposal may appear reasonable, but it may constitute too radical a break with the past for a majority of state legislators. In addition, the interest groups that might push for it are not readily visible. Perhaps participants in the Women's Lib movement, student activists and black power groups might get interested in the issue of injustice against youth, but this is a hope more than a possibility. In the event of overwhelming opposition, there exist two policy proposals that might be more acceptable and could aid in the decriminalization of juvenile status offenses.

The two alternatives function at different ends of the traditional juvenile justice system. One proposal, suggested by the President's Task Force on Delinquency, would set up a youth service bureau that would offer local field services and be operated by civil authorities as an alternative to formal adjudication; the second proposal, suggested by William Sheridan of the Department of Health, Education, and Welfare, would prohibit the mixing of juvenile status offenders and classic delinquents in the same institutions. The youth service bureau would function between the police and the court, while the prohibition would function after judicial disposition. Both proposals, separate or in concert, could aid in the decriminalization of our current practices.

However, both proposals would still leave open the possibility of stigmatization of youth who had committed no crimes. The youth service bureau would provide an array of services at the community level, but the court and police would still have ultimate jurisdiction over its case load, and any competition over jurisdiction would probably be won by the traditional justice system. The prohibition of mixing in institutions would, of course, not change the fact that young people were still being adjudicated in the same court as delinquents, even though they had committed no crimes. In addition, the proposal, as currently conceived, does not affect mixing in detention facilities. These limitations are evident in the statutes of states that have recently changed their definitions of "delinquency" (New York, California, Illinois, Colorado, Kansas, Oklahoma and Vermont).

Both proposals deserve support, but they clearly leave the traditional system intact. It is possible that youth service bureaus could be organized with a significant role for citizen participation, thus paving the way for an eventual take-over of legal jurisdiction from the juvenile court for juvenile status offenses (and dependency and neglect cases, too). It is conceivable, too, that any prohibitions of mixing could lead to the increased placement of children in trouble in foster homes and group homes, instead of reform schools, and to the provision of homemaker services and educational programs for harried parents unable to cope with the problems of children. Both short-range proposals could, in practice, evolve a different mode of handling delinquents without crimes.

The adaptation of these two reasonable proposals into an evolutionary strategy is conceivable. But it is also likely they will just be added to the system, without altering its jurisdiction and its stigmatic practices. In the event this occurs, new reformers might entertain the radical strategy that some European countries achieved many years ago—removal of juvenile status offenders from the jurisdiction of the judicial-correctional system and their inclusion into the family and child welfare system.

New Definitions and New Responses

What is the guarantee that young people will be serviced any more effectively by their removal from the traditional correctional system? The question is valid, but perhaps it underestimates the potency of social definitions. Children, as well as adults, are liable to be treated according to the social category to which they have been assigned. Any shift in the categorization of youth that yields a more positive image can influence such authorities as teachers, employers, military recruiters and housing authority managers. For there is abundant evidence that the stigma of delinquency can have negative consequences for an individual as an adult, as well as during childhood.

It is evident, too, that our old social definitions of what constitutes delinquency have led us to construct a system of juvenile justice that is quite unjust. By failing to make reasonable distinctions and define them precisely, we not only treat juvenile status offenders more harshly but undermine any semblance of ordered justice for *all* illegal behavior committed by juveniles. Maintenance of existing jurisdictional and definitional boundaries helps to perpetuate an unjust system for treating children. That this unjust system may also be a self-defeating one that compounds the original problem should also be taken into account before prematurely concluding that a shift in social labeling procedures is but a minor reform.

We would agree, however, with the conclusion that a mere semantic shift in the social definition of children in trouble is not sufficient. The experience of New York in providing a social label of "person in need of supervision" (PINS)—without providing alternative civil modes for responding to this new distinction—indicates that reform can sometimes take the guise of "word magic." Children are often accused of believing in the intrinsic power of words and oaths; adults can play the game on an even larger scale.

We need alternative social resources for responding to our change in social definitions, if we are at all serious about dealing with the problem. Whether we are willing to pay the financial costs for these alternatives is, of course, problematic. One approach to this issue might be to identify funds currently spent for non-criminal youth in the traditional police, court, and correctional subsystems, and then reallocate the identified dollars into a new child welfare service. This reallocation strategy would not require new funding, but merely a financial shift to follow our new social definitions and intended responses. The choices would be primarily legal, political, and moral ones and not new economic decisions.

A second strategy for funding a new policy might be based on a more rational approach to the problem. We could attempt to assess the societal "need" for such services and then compute the amount of financial resources required to meet this newly assumed public responsibility. This approach could prove more costly than the reallocation strategy. Conceivably, the strategies of assessed need and reallocation could be combined at the same time or over the years. However, whether we might be willing to tax ourselves to support a more reasonable and moral social policy may turn out to be a critical issue. Perceived in this manner, the problem of defining and responding to children in trouble is as much financial as it is political, legal, and moral. But this, too, is an integral part of the American approach to delinquents without crimes.

July/August 1971

FURTHER READING

Children and Youth in America: A Documentary History edited by Robert H. Bremner (Cambridge, Mass.: Harvard University Press, 1970), 2 volumes.

Juvenile Defenders for a Thousand Years: Selected Readings from Anglo-Saxon Times to 1900 edited by Wiley B. Sanders (Chapel Hill: The University of North Carolina Press, 1970).

The Child Savers: The Invention of Delinquency by Anthony M. Platt (Chicago: University of Chicago Press, 1969).

Children in Urban Society: Juvenile Delinquency in Nineteenth-Century America by Joseph M. Hawes (New York: Oxford University Press, 1971).

Borderland of Criminal Justice: Essays in Law and Criminology by Frances A. Allen (Chicago: University of Chicago Press, 1964).

Delinquency and Social Policy edited by Paul Lerman (New York: Praeger, 1970).

Task Force Report: Juvenile Delinquency and Youth Crime, President's Commission on Law Enforcement and the Administration of Justice (Washington, D.C.: U.S.G.P.O., 1967); *Task Force Report: Corrections.*

Crime and Punishment in Early Massachusetts by Edwin Powers (Boston: Beacon Press, 1966).

Varieties of Police Behavior by James Q. Wilson (Cambridge, Mass.: Harvard University Press, 1968).

Dilemmas of Social Reform: Poverty and Community Action in the United States by Peter Marris and Martin Rein (New York: Atherton Press, 1967).

Juvenile Justice—
Quest and Reality

EDWIN M. LEMERT

The juvenile court is intended to succeed where parents have failed. But the family—even though disturbed by conflict, morally questionable, or broken by divorce or death—is the institution best suited for nurturing children into stable adults. Neither the Spartan *gymnasium*, nor the Russian *créche*, nor the kibbutz nurseries, nor American orphanages, "homes" and reformatories can successfully duplicate the complex social and psychological construction of the family. Explicit recognition of this might well replace the pious injunction now in many laws that "care, custody, and discipline of children under the control of the juvenile court shall approximate that which they would receive from their parents."

In the majority opinion delivered in May 1967 in *Gault v. Arizona*, which provided for some of the rights of criminal justice to be introduced into juvenile courts,

Justice Abe Fortas pointedly wrote of the kind of care an incarcerated delinquent can expect from the state:

> Instead of mother and father and sisters and brothers and friends and classmates, his world is peopled by guards, custodians, state employees, and "delinquents" confined with him for anything from waywardness to rape and homicide.

The harassed juvenile court judge is not a father; a halfway house is not a home; a reformatory cell is not a teenager's bedroom; a hall counselor is not an uncle; and a cottage matron is not a mother. This does not mean that the system of children's justice should not seek kindly and dedicated people, but that it is a system with its own requirements. The judges, counselors and matrons are permanent parts of the system; but their interests cannot be guaranteed to be the same as those of the children who are just passing through.

They do not pass through unmarked, however. An unwanted but unavoidable consequence to any child subjected to the system—including dependent and neglected children as well as delinquents—is the imposition of stigma. ("Dependent" refers to a residual category of nondelinquent children, such as orphans, for whom the state must take responsibility.) The necessary insight and social stamina to manage such stigma are not given to many people—least of all to the kind of children most likely to come into the juvenile court. Social rejections provoked by the stigma of wardship may convince the individual that he is "no good" or "can't make it on the outside." These beliefs may feed a brooding sense of injustice which leads to further delinquency.

Delinquency Prevention

An important rationale of state intervention is the

faith that delinquency can be prevented and that the court can prevent it. The viability of this idea can be traced to a repressive puritan psychology reinforced by the propaganda of the mental hygiene movement of the early twentieth century, which helped produce child guidance clinics, school social work and juvenile courts. The metaphor is from medicine: high blood sugar warns of diabetes and a high cholesterol count is a warning of arteriosclerosis. In the early days of children's courts the comparable signs of juvenile delinquency were thought to be smoking and drinking, shining shoes, selling newspapers or playing pool. The modern version is found in such ideas as predelinquent personality or delinquency proneness and in state laws which make truancy, running away from home or incorrigibility bases for juvenile court control.

As yet, nothing has been isolated and shown to be a sure indicator of delinquency, nor is it likely that anything will be. Furthermore, things called "delinquent tendencies" often are found on close inspection to correspond not to any particular behavior, but rather to arbitrary definitions by school authorities, parents and police. One investigation in New York found that, to a degree, truancy was simply a measure of the willingness or availability of parents to write excuses. Incorrigibility as found in juvenile court cases may mean anything from ignoring a mother's order not to see a boyfriend to assault with a deadly weapon—and often turns out to be parental neglect or unfitness.

The brave idea that the juvenile court can prevent delinquency is deflated or even reduced to absurdity by sociological studies of hidden delinquency which show that the majority of high school and college students at some time or other engage in delinquencies, not excluding serious law violations. The main difference between college students and youths who are made wards of juvenile courts is that the latter group contains more repeaters. While several interpretations are possible, these findings demand explanation. Why do youths who are made court wards commit more rather than fewer delinquencies? The conclusion that the court processing in some way helps to fix and perpetuate delinquency is hard to escape.

It must also be remembered that most youths pass through a time when they engage in delinquency. Children normally play hookey, help themselves to lumber from houses under construction, and snitch candy from dime stores; adolescent boys frequently swipe beer, get drunk, "borrow" cars, hell around, learn about sex from available females or prostitutes, or give the old man a taste of his own medicine. Transitional deviance not only is ubiquitous in our society but universal to all societies, especially among boys turning into men—even in light of Margaret Mead's droll observations on adolescence in the South Seas to the contrary.

Most youths outgrow their so-called predelinquency and law-flouting activities; they put away childish things as they become established in society by a job, marriage, further education or by the slow growth of wisdom. Maturation out of the deviance of adolescence is facilitated when troublesome behavior, even petty crime, is dealt with by parents, neighbors and policemen, and treated as a manifestation of the inevitable diversity, perversity and shortcomings of human beings—in other words, as a problem of everyday living calling for tolerable solutions, not perfection. This means avoiding, whenever possible, specialized or categorical definitions which invidiously differentiate, degrade or stigmatize persons involved in such problems. The costs of muddling through with children who become problems have multiplied with the rising number of conformities required by a high-energy society, but they must be absorbed where the alternative of not dealing with problems is even more costly.

The ideology of delinquency prevention is much more urban than rural. Handling problems of youthful disorders and petty crime in rural areas and small towns—characteristically by sheriff's deputies, town police, the district attorney and the probation officer—has been largely informal. Sharp distinctions are drawn between less consequential moral and legal infractions—"Mickey Mouse stuff"—and serious delinquencies, with no implication that one leads to the other. This is reflected in the reluctance of elective officials and those beholden to them to make records of their actions, but at the same time they want action in serious misdemeanors and felonies by youth to be swift and punitive. The juvenile court usually reserves formal action for "real problems" of families and the community; the functional context of youthful misconduct ordinarily can be realistically gauged and its consequences dealt with in a number of different situations.

A major difficulty in the bureaucratic urban juvenile court is that the functional context of child problems directed to it easily gets lost; it has to be reconstructed with bits and pieces of information obtained through investigations and inquiries conducted under highly artificial circumstances and communicated in series of stereotyped written reports. There is little or no direct community criticism or reaction that might put individual cases into a common-sense context. This, plus the rapidity with which cases are heard in large courts (three minutes per case in Los Angeles in 1959), explains why the distinction between trivia and serious child problems breaks down. A notorious illustration came to light in Orange County, California, in 1957 when a private attorney put his own investigator to work on a case of an eight-year-old boy and a nine-year-old girl accused of a "sex crime" against a seven-year-old girl. He found that the case had been presented in court by a probation officer who was only repeating without investigation what he had been told. This private inquiry pared the charge down to an imputed incident witnessed by no one and reported two days after it supposedly occurred.

Control and Detention

It would push facts too far to insist that the ideology of preventing delinquency is used by juvenile court workers and judges to justify slipshod operations. Nevertheless, it has allowed them to change the basis of jurisdiction from one "problem" to another. The practice is baldly indicated in the statement of a California judge arguing for retention under juvenile court jurisdiction of simple traffic violations by juveniles:

> Moreover it seems to have been demonstrated that the broad powers of the juvenile court can be helpfully invoked on behalf of children whose maladjustment has been brought to light through juvenile traffic violations. A girl companion of a youthful speeder may be protected from further sexual [sic] experimentation. Boys whose only amusement seems to be joyriding in family cars can be directed to other more suitable forms of entertainment before they reach the stage of

"borrowing" cars when the family car is unavailable.

The police generally are less concerned with the prevention of delinquency in individual cases than with prevention and control in the community as manifested in gang violence, disturbances of public order, a rise in crime rates or mounting property losses. The utility of specious legal categories describing delinquent tendencies is most obvious when the police seek to break up youthful gang activity, quell public disturbances such as occur at drive-ins or public parks, or seek access to witnesses or informants to solve a crime or to recover stolen property. While the arrest and detention of youth to "clear up other crimes" may be efficient police tactics, abuses may arise at the expense of individual youths if such methods can be pursued under diffuse charges. Unfortunately there have been and are judges willing to allow juvenile detention to be used for these purposes. It was for these reasons that the Juvenile Justice Commission of California, following a statewide survey, recommended in 1960 the use of citations for minor offenses by juveniles, and the requirement that detention hearings be held within specified time limits to act as a check on overzealous police action.

It is true that, in a number of areas, the police have sought to aid juveniles to avoid clashes with the law through setting up recreation programs, "big brother" assignments, systems of referral to welfare agencies, informal probation and even police social work. But such undertakings have declined in recent years and tend to be looked upon as divergent from essential police functions such as apprehension of criminals, recovery of property and maintenance of public order. This may also point to growing police disillusionment with more generalized or community delinquency prevention programs. Police in some cities sharply disagree with community organizers of such projects over the issue of maintaining the autonomy of neighborhood gangs. They take a jaundiced view of attempts to divert such groups into more compliant pursuits, preferring rather to break them up.

Research assessments of community programs to prevent delinquency—such as the Chicago Area Project, the Harlem Project and the Cambridge-Somerville Youth Study—have been disappointing; results either have been negative or inconclusive. Possible exceptions are community coordinating councils, especially in the western United States, where they originated. These councils bring police, probation officers, judges and social workers together in face-to-face discussions of local youth problems. However, they seem to work best in towns between 2,000 and 15,000 population; it remains unclear whether they can be adapted successfully to large urban areas. Significantly, they work chiefly by exchanging agency information and referrals of cases to community agencies, with full support and cooperation of the police. In effect they represent concerted action to bypass the juvenile court, and it might be said that their purpose, if not function, is prevention of delinquency by preventing, wherever possible, the adjudication of cases in the court.

Much of what has already been said about preventing delinquency through the juvenile court is equally applicable to therapeutic treatment through the court. The ideal of treatment found its way into juvenile court philosophy from social work and psychiatry. Its pervasiveness is measurable by the extent to which persons educated and trained in social work have indirectly influenced the juvenile court or moved into probation and correction. A premise of therapeutic treatment of children is that scientific knowledge and techniques make possible specific solutions to problems.

Scientific social work has come to lean heavily on Freudian theories. Updated versions of socially applied psychoanalysis conceive of delinquency as an acting out of repressed conflicts in irrational, disguised forms. The accent is on internal emotional life rather than upon external acts: the social worker or the psychiatrist is a specialist who understands the problems while the client does not; the specialist "knows best," studies, analyzes and treats—much in the manner of the authoritative medical practitioner.

A divergent, competing line of thought in social work repudiates scientific treatment in favor of a simpler task of helping, in which problems are confronted in whatever terms the child or youth presents them; responsible involvement of the client is a sine qua non of success in this process.

Generally speaking, social workers advocate assigning to other agencies many of the tasks the court has assumed. Some social workers seriously doubt whether the helping process can be carried on in an authoritarian setting, and to emphasize their stand refuse as clients children who have been wards of the court. Other social workers believe that judges should not go beyond their competence, but should use their power solely for adjudication, with determination of treatment left to social work agencies. A smaller number of social workers hold to a more sanguine view of reconciling personal help and authority within the role of the probation officer. Finally, there are some social workers who are not above using juvenile court power as a tool for getting access to clients or prolonging their contacts with them because they will "benefit from treatment."

This pattern became aggravated in Utah when juvenile courts were under the administrative control of the state department of welfare.

Referral and Rehabilitation

Actually, comparatively few juvenile court cases are referred to social workers for treatment, and many juvenile court judges and probation officers are hostile to social workers. According to a U.S. Children's Bureau study, the most frequent disposition of juvenile court cases was dismissal; next was informal or formal supervision by a probation officer. Dismissals can scarcely be called treatment, even though the associated court appearance before an admonitory judge may have a chastening effect upon some youths. At most, such cases feature a brief exchange with an investigating officer who asks some questions, issues a stern warning, and says he hopes he will not see the boy again.

The consequences of supervision of delinquents by probation officers have been little studied and the outcome, even when successful, little understood. Probation practices with juveniles have little in common across the nation, and often they consist of a meager combination of office interviews and phone or mail reports. Probation officers frequently claim that they could give more help to their charges if they had more time, but this must be regarded as an occupational complaint rather than an accurate prediction. What little experimental research there is on the subject shows that mere reduction of the size of caseloads of probation and parole officers does not in itself lower rates of recidivism. More time to deal with their client's problems is a necessary, but not a sufficient, condition of success by court workers.

If the results of probation supervision of delinquents on the whole are disappointing or inconclusive, even less can be said for the treatment of juvenile offenders in institutions. Sociological analysis and evaluations of such correctional programs tend to be negative. Some writers even say that the goals of correctional programs in prisons and reformatories are inherently self-defeating. This follows from the very fact of incarceration, which by imposing personal deprivation on inmates generates hostility to formal programs of rehabilitation. Furthermore, the population of repeaters shapes inmate socialization.

The problems of juvenile correction and rehabilitation have been highlighted in the popular press and literature as poor physical plants, meager appropriations, and underpaid, undereducated personnel, but they lie far deeper. It remains doubtful whether even the generously funded and well-staffed California Youth Authority (CYA) has neared its original purpose of providing individualized treatment for youthful offenders. This cannot be traced to lack of dedication in the leadership, but to the task of administering the institutions, where bureaucratic values and organizational inertia conspire daily to defeat the purpose of treatment. These dilemmas have led the CYA to begin establishing community treatment projects on a large scale and subsidizing probation programs with the hope of stimulating local innovation of alternatives to incarceration.

I do not mean to exclude the possibility that clinically trained and humanly wise people can help youth solve problems which have brought them athwart the law. Rather the intent is to leaven professional pretense with humility, to place the notion of treatment in a more realistic perspective, and to point out the differences between dealing with problems of human relationships and treatment as it has evolved in the practice of medicine. The treatment of delinquency is best regarded as a kind of guidance, special education and training—much more akin to midwifery than medicine—in which hopeful intervention into an ongoing process of maturation is undertaken. The judge, probation officer, correctional counselor or institutional psychiatrist can be at most a small influence among the many affecting development and emergence into adulthood. Although the juvenile court can determine that certain influences will take place in a prescribed order in the process of socialization, it cannot control the meanings and values assigned to such occurrences.

Philosophy of Nonintervention

If there is a defensible philosophy for the juvenile court, it is one of judicious nonintervention. It is properly an agency of last resort for children, holding to the analogy of appeal courts, where all other remedies must be exhausted before a case will be considered. This means that problems accepted for action by the juvenile court will be demonstrably serious. There will be a history of repeated failures at solutions by parents, relatives, schools and community agencies. The model should be the English and Canadian juvenile courts, which receive very few cases by American standards.

This statement of juvenile court philosophy rests upon the following propositions:

1. Since the powers of the juvenile court are extraordinary, properly it should deal with extraordinary cases.
2. Large numbers of cases defeat the purposes of the juvenile court by leading to bureaucratic procedures inimical to individual treatment.

3. The juvenile court is primarily a court of law and must accept limitations imposed by the inapplicability of rule and remedy to many important phases of human conduct and to some serious wrongs. Law operates by punishment, injunction against specific acts, specific redress and substitutional redress. It cannot by such means make a father good, a mother moral, a child obedient or a youth respectful of authority.

4. When the juvenile court goes beyond legal remedies, it must resort to administrative agents or become such an agency itself. This produces conflicts and confusion of values and objectives. Furthermore, whether child and parental problems can be solved by administrative means remains questionable.

It may be protested that here I am narrowing the conception of the juvenile court severely and that my model can hardly be recognized as a juvenile court at all by present standards. However, organized nonintervention by the juvenile courts can become a definite protection for youth. Children need as much or more protection from the unanticipated consequences of organized movements, programs and services on their behalf as they need from the formless "evils" which gave birth to the juvenile court. America no longer has a significant number of Fagins, exploiters of child labor, sweatships, open saloons, houses of prostitution, street trades, immoral servants, cruel immigrant fathers, traveling carnivals and circuses, unregulated race tracks, much open gambling or professional crime of the old style. The battles for compulsory education have long since been won, and technological change has eliminated child labor—perhaps too well. The forms of delinquency have changed as the nature of society has changed; social and personal problems of youth reflect the growth of affluence in one area of society and the growth of hostility and aggression in the nonaffluent sector. Current sociological theories of delinquency stress as causes drift and risk-taking, on the one hand, and dilapidated opportunity structures, on the other.

The basic life process today is one of adaptation to exigencies and pressures; individual morality has become functional rather than sacred or ethical in the older sense. To recognize this at the level of legislative and judicial policy is difficult because social action in America always has been heavily laden with moral purpose. However, if the juvenile court is to become effective, its function must be reduced to enforcement of the "ethical minimum" of youth conduct necessary to maintain social life in a high-energy, consuming, pluralistic society. It can then proceed to its secondary task of arranging the richest possible variety of assistance to those specially disadvantaged children and youth who come under its jurisdiction.

A philosophy of judicious nonintervention demands more than verbal or written exhortation for implementation. Action is needed to reshape the juvenile court. Ideally it will be so structured that it will have built-in controls, feedback mechanisms and social scanning devices which make it self-regulating and adaptive. This by no means signifies that the juvenile court should or will become "inner directed"; if anything, contacts and interaction with the community and its agencies will have more importance, if for no other reason than to protect its stance of nonintervention.

Police Juvenile Bureaus

Relationships between juvenile courts and policing agencies probably will become more critical with a shrinkage in juvenile court functions. However, it can be hoped that this will be an irritant leading more police departments to develop juvenile bureaus and to upgrade their competence for screening and adjusting cases within the department. Even now it is common practice for police departments to dismiss large numbers of juvenile arrests or "adjust" them within the department. More and better juvenile officers and rational procedures can greatly decrease referrals to juvenile courts. This does not mean that police will undertake probation or social work, but rather will work parsimoniously with relatives and community agencies, or at most will engage in brief, policemanlike counseling with youths whom they believe they can help.

Since the police will never entirely forsake their habit of using the juvenile court for their own special purpose of keeping law and order, the second line of defense for judicious nonintervention must be the intake workers of the court or probation department. Ideally, the most competent workers would be organized into a fairly autonomous division of intake, referral and adjustment, which would be oriented toward community agencies and given the prerogative of denying petitions for court jurisdiction.

As has been noted, referral of cases from juvenile courts to social work agencies is complicated because the agencies do not want to work with hostile or uncooperative clients. Juvenile courts trying to treat children with small difficulties—often indistinguishable from those being handled in large numbers by welfare agencies—lose the chance to refer them to the agencies later. For this reason, referrals should be made immediately—no detention, no confrontation with child or parent, no detailed investigation. The court intake procedure should not be turned into a fishing expedition to uncover and record "problems" to justify further court action.

Wards of the Court

In general, juvenile courts are granted control over dependent and neglected, as well as delinquent, children. Despite the early aim of the juvenile court to take stigma away from these statuses, the pall of moral questionability settles over all court wards in spite of category.

It is virtually impossible to defend the court's jurisdiction over dependent children on any grounds but convenience. Just why, for example, a child whose mother has been committed to a mental institution should be made the ward of a latently criminal court is not readily explainable. The same is true for children whose parents are troubled by unemployment or illness, and likewise for orphaned or illegitimate children. Granted that they need protection with legal sanction, there is no proof that the civil courts cannot entrust this job to the welfare agencies, assuming full protection of the rights of parents and children. Some probation officers find justification for juvenile court jurisdiction where some children in a family are delinquent and others merely dependent. But there is as much justification in such cases for allowing civil agencies jurisdiction over all but the most seriously delinquent children.

The arguments for supervision of neglected children by juvenile courts are only slightly more forceful. If the child's problem is truly the fault of his parents, why should the child be branded? The suspicion is strong that juvenile courts are used to gain control over children where the proof of parental neglect is too flimsy to stand scrutiny in an adult criminal court. It is a knotty problem, admittedly, but children should not be paying the costs of official indirection. If the parents can be shown in a general court to be at fault, let the custody of the children go to a welfare agency if necessary. If the parents cannot be shown to be at fault, let the matter end.

At the root of this desire to keep dependent and neglected children under the eye of the court is the persistent belief that crime and delinquency are caused by dependency and neglect. This idea, descended from hoary biblical notions and Victorian moralism, still turns up, as in the description of the dependency and neglect unit in the recent annual report of an urban probation department:

> Implicit in the function of this unit is the concept that it is very probable that the basis for delinquent acting has been laid in the children and that delinquency prevention is, therefore, a primary concern.

Little durable evidence has been discovered to support the contention that poverty, broken homes or parental failures—alcoholism, sexual immorality or cruelty—are in themselves causes of delinquency. Most delinquents come from intact homes, and there is little unanimity on whether broken homes produce more than their proportional share of delinquents. Furthermore, every delinquent from a broken home averages two or more brothers and sisters who are not delinquent.

If we are to have judicious nonintervention, then we cannot continue to have statutory jurisdiction defined in such subjective fashion. Given the untoward consequences of labeling, we cannot continue to work under diffuse definitions which allow almost any child, given compromising circumstances, to be caught up in the net of the court.

When such specious legal grounds as incorrigibility, truancy and running away from home are warrants for juvenile court action, they allow parents, neighbors, school officials and police—even the youths themselves—to solve their problems by passing them on to the court. Note, for instance, the lengthy conflict between juvenile court workers and school officials, in which the school people are accused of foisting off their own failures on the court. The educators reply heatedly that the court is unreceptive or does nothing about "really mean kids." Probation officers ruefully discover in some counties that sheriff's deputies expect them to settle all neighborhood quarrels in which juveniles are involved. Parents or relatives many times make it clear in court that they desire their child to be punished for highly personal reasons. A depressing sidelight is that the court itself can be a cause for incorrigibility. Failure to obey an order of the court can be an official reason for severe punishment, even though the original excuse for taking jurisdiction may have been minor.

Runaways must be understood in the same context as incorrigibles, with the added difference that they are more frequently girls. Often running away is a dramatic demonstration—a little like suicide attempts by adult women. California girls sometimes demand to be placed in detention in order to expose the "hatefulness" of their homes or to embarrass their parents. While police action often is clearly indicated for runaways, action by the court is decidedly not. If drama is needed, it should be staged under some other auspices.

Incorrigibility, truancy and running away should not be in themselves causes for court jurisdiction. The social agencies are well equipped to handle such problems. In fact, an inquiry in the District of Columbia showed that agencies were handling 98 percent of the runaways, 95 percent of the truants, 76 percent of the juvenile sex offenses and 46 percent of the incorrigibles.

Humanitarian Injustice

Much has been said of the "philosophy" of the juvenile court and little can be added, other than to note that this very preoccupation with philosophy sets it apart from other courts. In general, American courts for children have been given broad legislative grants to help and protect children, to depart from strict rules of legal procedure, and to utilize what in other courts is excluded evidence. One result has been that, under the noble guise of humanitarian concern and scientific treatment, the courts have often simply deprived the children of justice and fair play. The juvenile court originated in humanitarian concern rather than the police powers of the state, and legislators are disposed to treat it as a child welfare agency. Thus, few procedures were specified in early statutes. Later accretions in statutes and common law have proved to be extremely divergent, and little in the way of case law developed, particularly since it took until the 1960s for the first juvenile court appeal to reach the Supreme Court of the United States.

Inattention to procedure has led to the absence of hard rules on hearings, with the result that in many courts hearings are attenuated, ambiguously accusatory or even nonexistent. Thus, the least we can ask of judicious nonintervention is that a hearing be given any child whose freedom is likely to be abridged by the court. A further desirable change would be the introduction of split hearings: one devoted to factual findings rich enough to justify taking jurisdiction, and one to ascertain what should be done with the child. Both hearings should be rigorous, but the second should admit social data which might make clear the reasons for the delinquent act. This procedure will prevent the court from taking jurisdiction on the basis of impressionistic hearsay evidence, but will also allow such evidence to help the judge make the punishment fit not the crime, but the criminal. This division should be made most clear, for studies of split hearings in New York and California have showed that about two-thirds of the judges continued to read social reports before asserting jurisdiction, thus defeating the purpose of the split hearings. Appellate courts in California feel the social report is germane to adjudication; those in New York do not. Instead of more opinions, we should set about finding out whether the minority judges in these two states, as well as all English juvenile court judges, are hampered by the absence of this information in asserting jurisdiction.

Wherever the social report is admitted in the process, it should be subject to scrutiny. This implies the presence of lawyers for the prosecution and defense. In its decision in the *Gault* case this May, the Supreme Court assured the presence of defense lawyers, a practice which has been followed for several years in California, New York, Minnesota and the District of Columbia. The traditional argument against this practice, which was used by Justice Potter Steward in his dissent in *Gault*, is that the introduction of counsel may rob the juvenile court of its informal ad hoc quality and turn it into little more than a miniature criminal court. My own California studies indicate that advising parents and children of the right to counsel, as ordered by the legislature in 1961, has increased the statewide use of counsel from 3 percent of the cases to 15 percent. In some counties, the rise was from 0 to 1 or 2 percent; in others it was from 15 percent to 70 or even 90 percent. In assigning counsel, the courts have favored dependent or neglected children and those charged with serious offenses. I have found no indication of racial or social discrimination in assignments.

One problem that has emerged is that private attorneys tend to lack knowledge of the system and regularly assigned public defenders tend to get wired into it. In both instances, the client may be hurt. Mere introduction of counsel seems insufficient to guarantee judicious nonintervention if the intake of cases is not reduced.

Introduction of defense counsel has not automatically meant introduction of prosecutors. The presentation of the state's case has fallen in many instances to the probation officer, who lacks both the training and the temperament to prosecute. He knows that active prosecution will later make it difficult or impossible to help the child. Where a judge takes over the interrogation, defense attorneys may be left in the untenable position of objecting to his questions and then hearing him rule on the objections. The police are more enthusiastic about placing prosecutors in the courts than the prosecutors are, and judges are not yet disposed to permit hearings to become all-out adversary struggles. Their attitude is not ill considered. I have seen an attorney in such a situation attempt to attack the credibility of a witness—a 15-year-old girl—by bringing her juvenile record into court and referring to sexual experiences for which she received money.

Attorney Protection

My research has shown that cases with attorneys are more likely to be dismissed, less likely to result in wardship, and more likely to end in a suspended sentence than cases without an attorney. The dismissals were not evenly distributed among the delinquent, the dependent and the neglected children, however; the cases of neglected children—that is, those actions alleging unfit homes—were the ones most frequently dismissed. Attorneys were often successful in attacking imprecise charges and having them reduced. Attorneys were also able to negotiate alternative dispositions of cases, such as finding relatives to take a child rather than sending him to a foster home, proposing psychiatric help rather than commitment to a ranch school, or sometimes convincing the client that cooperation with the probation officer is preferable to resistance and ending with loss of parental control. If these findings are indicative, the adversary function is likely to be marginal in relation to the attorney's function as a negotiator and interpreter between the judge and family. Of course, the very likelihood of an attorney entering cases has a monitory value in reinforcing the new consciousness of court workers regarding the rights of juveniles. The New York concept of the attorney as a law guardian seems most fitting.

The interest in the role of attorneys in the juvenile court has brought about a concern with the sort of evidence to be accepted and the levels of proof required. The judges I have studied in California deal with the problem of hearsay evidence by admitting everything, on the assumption that they can consider only the competent evidence. This view has some support in legal opinion, where it is argued that the hearsay rule was aimed at controlling gullible juries rather than judges. But in the juvenile court much evidence is in the form of reports which are little more than compilations of professional hearsay; whether the ordinary judge is always qualified to sift this sort of evidence is questionable. Many judges seem remarkably naive about evaluating psychiatric and social science reports.

In civil courts—where only property is at stake—a preponderance of evidence is sufficient to decide the case. Considering the nature of the evidence in juvenile court, however, this may be insufficent. I would suggest that clear and convincing proof, that which admits only one conclusion, be the standard for determining guilt. For the most grievous juvenile crimes, the standard of criminal proof, guilt beyond all reasonable doubt, should prevail, as it does, for example, in English juvenile courts.

Although the justices did not discuss standards of evidence and proof explicitly in the *Gault* case, they did apply standards of adult courts in the right to counsel, the protection against self-incrimination, the right of confrontation and cross-examination, and the right to timely and explicit notice of the charges. Altogether, this is a strong indication that the extensive use of hearsay will not be viewed lightly when and if the Supreme Court is called upon to rule on standards of evidence and proof.

The words of the court in *Kent v. United States*, the first juvenile court case it ever heard, characterize the present state of affairs:

> There is evidence, in fact, that there may be grounds for concern that the child receives the worst of both worlds; that he gets neither the protections accorded to adults nor the solicitous care and regenerative treatment postulated for children.

The doctrine of judicious nonintervention is nothing more than a plea that the child in court be granted the best of both worlds. Welcome as the *Gault* decision is in granting some of the protections accorded to adults, until some attempt is made to stem the flow of cases into the juvenile courts, solicitous care and regenerative treatment may be impossible.

July/August 1967

FURTHER READING

Justice for the Child edited by Margaret K. Rosenheim (Glencoe, Illinois: Free Press, 1962). A collection of critical essays raising questions of the quality of justice in juvenile courts.

Comparative Survey of Juvenile Delinquency—Part I: North America by Paul Tappan (New York: United Nations Department of Economic and Social Affairs, 1958). A summary and overview of delinquency and juvenile court practices in Canada and the United States.

The Juvenile Courts by F.T. Gile (London: George Allen and Unwin Ltd., 1946). A highly readable discussion of the work and problems of English juvenile courts, with some tart things to say about their American counterparts.

Battered Children

SERAPIO R. ZALBA

In 1962 a group of doctors in Denver wrote a landmark paper reporting on the "alarming number" of children being admitted to hospitals for traumatic injuries for which the parents could not provide plausible explanations.

One news story in a Cleveland paper, for example, reported that a court hearing had been set "to determine the cause of injuries suffered by an eight-month-old baby hospitalized for a month . . . with two broken arms, a broken left leg, a fingernail missing from his left hand and body scars. . . . The child's mother said he fell forward from an upholstered chair and that his arms apparently caught in the sides of the chair, policewomen reported."

Generally these children are in poor health, with unsatisfactory skin hygiene, multiple soft tissue injuries, deep bruises and malnutrition. An indication of the

311

problem's gravity was provided by Dr. C. Henry Kempe, who cited one day in November 1961 when there were four battered children in Colorado General Hospital alone—two died of central nervous system traumas, and one was released to his home in satisfactory condition but subsequently died "suddenly" in an unexplained manner (a not-unusual occurrence). A new term was coined to describe such situations: "battered child syndrome."

Solving or even managing this problem is not easy. Despite evidence that serious physical assault on children is not rare, incidents are not generally brought to the attention of the authorities. And the authorities have relatively few resources to turn to for help in ameliorating the problem.

To begin with, it is often difficult for agents of societal institutions—physicians, nurses, social workers, teachers, police, prosecutors, judges—as well as concerned relatives and neighbors—to decide when the line has been crossed between severe punishment and physical assault or abuse, even though the polar extremes are fairly clear: a mild spanking on the buttocks of a two-year-old child is quite different from the case of abuse that finds its way into a protective agency, where a child may have had scalding water poured on his genitals.

The most extreme cases probably end up in hospitals (when they don't end in the death of the child), especially since the younger children typically seen there are unable to defend themselves by running away from battering or abuse. Yet some studies of nonhospital cases reveal equally serious abuse. Edgar Merrill, an official of the Massachusetts Society for the Prevention of Cruelty to Children (SPCC), gives examples of the kind of cases seen at that agency:

1. A five-year-old girl went onto her porch though told not to do so; she was kicked into the house, thrown across the room and hit on the face and head with a frying pan.
2. A nine-month-old boy's eyes were blackened, his fingers, face and neck burned, and his skull fractured by his father.
3. A 13-month-old girl was X-rayed at the hospital; revealed were multiple skull fractures—some old, some new—and marked subdural hematoma.
4. X rays on a seven-month-old boy showed healed fractures of one arm, the other one currently broken, healed fractures on both legs and multiple skull fractures.

The physical abuse of a child does not generally occur only once. In fact, in most of the cases in a study by Shirley Nurse the abuse had been going on for one to three years. Indeed, one of the medical indicators that physical injuries may have been inflicted rather than accidental is X-ray evidence of prior, often multiple, injuries, such as fractures of limbs and skull.

In the hospital studies of Elizabeth Elmer and Helen Boardman, the children were very young, over half of them being under one year of age. There was a high mortality rate among them: in 12 of the 56 cases followed up (21 percent) the children died. Of the 46 homicides of infants and preadolescents in Lester Adelson's Cleveland study, 21 were under three years old. In contrast, in the private agency protective service studies reported by Harold Bryant and Edgar Merrill in Massachusetts and James Delsordo in Philadelphia, the children were older, with half of them (in a combined sample of over 260 children) under seven years old, and with no report made of any deaths. The abusers of children were usually their own parents with whom they were currently living—mothers and fathers were identified as the abusers in equal numbers of cases. While there was a great deal of marital and family conflict found in these cases, the nonabusive parent tended to protect the abusive one, supporting his or her denial of having assaulted the child. As a way of hiding the effects of their cruelty, many parents shopped around for medical care—one child under one year of age had been hospitalized three times in three different hospitals. The grim fact is, to quote Adelson: "It is relatively simple to destroy the life of a child in almost absolute secrecy without the necessity of taking any elaborate precautions to ensure the secrecy."

Characteristics of Abusive Parents

In the child abuse cases I have seen or read about, the parents came from the complete range of socioeconomic classes. Many were middle class and self-supporting, with well-kept homes. All, however, could be characterized as highly impulsive, socially isolated and in serious difficulties, with their marriage, with money and so forth.

Irving Kaufman has taken a psychoanalytic view that the physical abuse of children implies a distortion of reality: the child as a target is perceived by the parent in a symbolic or delusional way; he stands for the psychotic portion of himself he wishes to destroy, his own abusive parent or the like. But the vast majority of abusive parents do not fall into any easy psychiatric categories, even though some of the most violent and abusive might be called schizophrenic. In Adelson's study, for example, 17 of the 41 murderers of children were patently mentally ill; that is, they had been hospitalized or had shown profound mental disturbance for some time before the eruption of violence.

The Massachusetts SPCC reported that in 50 percent of the 115 families they studied there was premarital conception. Other studies also point out the typicality of youthful marriages, unwanted pregnancies, illegitimacies and "forced" marriages. How much we can make of this is, however, questionable, since many, if not most, American families share one or another of these characteristics. More important, perhaps, is the finding that parents had themselves been abused and neglected as children. The epidemiological implications are, consequently, rather serious. While the 180 children in the Massachusetts study were generally normal physically, all of them were found to have a seriously impaired relationship with the abusive parent. These children tended to overreact to hostility, were depressive, hyperactive, destructive and fearful. The Philadelphia study characterized the children in their cases as bed wetting, truant, fire setters and withdrawn.

How Many Children Are Being Abused?

It is difficult to assess the number of children being physically abused or battered. For one thing, even the number of abuse cases that actually get reported is not known. For another, figures given by individual protective agencies or hospitals may be typical only for their geographic localities. Reported statistics on referrals to protective agencies generally include cases of both neglect and abuse; no definitive statement of how many of each are involved can be made. Eustace Chesser of England's National Society for the Prevention of Cruelty to Children concluded that between 6 and 7 percent of all children in England are at some time during their life "so neglected or ill-treated or become so maladjusted as to require the protection of community agencies." On the basis of a 1964 study in

California, it would appear that a minimum of approximately 20,000 children were in need of protective services in that state alone. The American Public Welfare Association reported that in 1958 approximately 100 cases were referred monthly to the public welfare department in Denver, Colorado, for protective services. Elizabeth Barry Philbrook cited the figure of 250,000 children living outside their own homes in 1960. She indicated that one-third of the children had been moved to at least two or three different foster homes and that protective services were needed in those cases, implying that this would serve a preventive as well as restorative function.

David Gil's reports from a nationwide study on child abuse conducted by Brandeis University for the United States Children's Bureau demonstrate once again the difficulty of determining the actual incidence of child abuse. Gil found that approximately 6,000 cases were reported in 1967. But when a sample of people were asked if they personally know of cases of abuse, their reports, if extrapolated to the total population of the United States, would have indicated an incidence of from two to three million cases *annually*. Gil charges us to be careful in interpreting the findings; it was not possible to determine whether the abuse represented only a slap on the face or something more ominous.

Extrapolation on the basis of the data from California and Colorado produces a conservative estimate of between 200,000 and 250,000 children in the United States needing protective services each year, of which 30,000 to 37,500 may have been badly hurt.

How New Is Child Abuse?

The basic problem of serious child abuse by parents and parent substitutes is not new. Indeed, as Elizabeth

Elmer has pointed out, it is only comparatively recently that there has been any community consensus and sanction for recognizing and protecting the rights of children. In much of recorded history, infanticide, child abandonment, maiming as an aid in begging and the selling of children have been common rather than exceptional. It was common to flog children without provocation in colonial times in America in order to "break them of their willfulness" and make them tractable, ostensibly for the good of their souls. Not until the last half of the nineteenth century was the first Society for the Prevention of Cruelty to Children organized in the United States. And it came about as a result of New York City's infamous Mary Ellen case in 1866 which brought out that the American Society for the Prevention of Cruelty to *Animals* was the only agency willing and able to intervene to protect a child suffering from abuse.

As Norris Class points out, early workers in the field of child welfare proceeded on the assumption that physical abuse and neglect were associated almost exclusively with poverty, slums, ignorance, industrial exploitation and immigration. Physical mistreatment was quite open in these sectors, and it was not difficult to introduce admissible and dramatic evidence into the courts in the prosecution of abusive and neglectful parents. But as the conditions they associated with physical neglect and abuse abated, so did its visibility.

During America's intensive romance with psycho-analysis and dynamic psychiatry in the 1920s and 1930s the child welfare people became concerned more with emotional factors and treatment, and greater emphasis was given to permissive, voluntarily sought services, with a consequent confusion about the role of authority and legal sanctions in social services. Acceptable legal evidence of emotional neglect or abuse was and still is more difficult to define or produce than is its physical counterpart. Interest in protective services declined, and the close working relationship between the protective agency and the court deteriorated. On the positive side, however, there was an increase in the public's awareness that prosecution of abusive and neglectful parents does not solve the problems of the victimized children or their families. As the family system came to be seen first as the diagnostic and eventually the treatment unit of reference, we began to pay greater attention to the possibility of treating the parents and attempting to maintain the structural integrity of the family. In child welfare today we still face the basic problem: at what point does the harm of leaving a child in a poor home override the negative consequences of splintering the family by use of foster homes or other placement facilities outside the parental home?

An important factor in providing protective services, and an important value in American society, has been the tradition of parental rights regarding the rearing of children. The intervention of the state in parent-child matters is for the most part invoked reluctantly and carefully. When there is a reasonable question as to parental adequacy, the tendency has been to rule in favor of the parent. This may reflect a "folk wisdom" about the child's need for enduring family ties; however, children are sometimes left in homes that are neglectful and even dangerous.

The relatively recent interest in more aggressive (that is, reaching-out) approaches in social work, greater clarification of the role of authority and accumulated experience and knowledge in work with those persons psychiatrically categorized as character-disordered have brought us to the place where we are better able to consider what we can or should do about the abuse of children.

The Child Abusers

Who are the parents that abuse their children? Are they "normal" people who have overreacted? Or are they a clearly distinguishable group?

The picture that emerges in studies done in hospitals and protective agencies is of a number of different types of abusers. One grouping can be made of abusing parents with personality problems that could be characterized in the following ways: patent psychosis, pervasive anger, depressive passive-aggressive personality and cold, compulsive disciplinarians.

A second grouping consists of parents who are impulsive but generally adequate, with marital conflicts or identity-role crises. In the first group we would expect to find a representative cross-section of American families. Findings from a national study by David Gil, however, indicate there are more cases of child abuse among the socioeconomically disadvantaged, especially in broken homes and in large families. But if there is a significantly greater proportion of abuse cases among the disadvantaged populations, it is likely to consist of cases of the second type. The reporting of such cases, and the interventions of protective services with legal sanctions, does not necessarily reflect its pattern of incidence. Police, schools, hospitals and social agencies are more likely to intervene in the lives of lower income families than they would in the lives of the more affluent. Practitioners have not tended to agree with Gil. They do not think there is a social class difference in the incidence rate. They argue that the abused child in a more affluent family will probably be taken to a private physician who will, where necessary, make arrangements to hospitalize the child. The source of injury may not be reported. If the family is poor, the child would probably be taken to the emergency room of the hospital, where the staff is likely to complete a report of suspected abuse.

It is interesting to speculate on why we tend to turn our faces away from much of the child abuse that occurs around us. Kempe and others have pointed out that physicians, teachers, social workers, nurses and others in positions where they might identify cases of abuse are reluctant to do so. They wish to avoid court appearances. They prefer not to confront or estrange patient-families (or clients). And frequently they are less than certain that they are correct in their suspicions. Thus it becomes easy not to "notice" abusive behavior.

There is still another explanation for what appears to be widespread lack of awareness of incidents of child abuse. Is there any mother or father who has not been "provoked" almost to the breaking point by the crying, wheedling, whining child? How many parents have not had moments of concern and self-recrimination after having, in anger, hit their own child much harder than they had expected they would? How many such incidents make a "child abuser" out of a normal parent? There may be a tacit agreement among us not to meddle in each other's private matters unless it is simply impossible to ignore the behavior involved.

All 50 states have attempted to counteract our "know-nothing" tendencies by passing laws regarding the reporting of suspected child abuse: some states provide protection against claims of slander and other defamatory "injuries" against persons in certain professional categories (doctors, for example).

Another interesting speculation can be made on the

societal level: why has our society provided so *little* protection for children?

Despite the historical trend toward increased children's rights and protection—the SPCC, child labor laws, the day care movement, Head Start and the *Gault* decision of the Supreme Court—it seems clear that the perception of children as property or chattels has strong roots in our society. Parental rights are still rated high on the scale of values.

Related to the issue of personal versus social control is the question about the extent to which our society is willing to invest in broad social welfare services. Our national willingness to invest heavily in public education in the past few years seems to have lost its impetus. Mental hygiene and correctional reform have likewise lost momentum. The progressive strides of the period starting with Franklin Roosevelt and ending with the first Johnson term of office have slowed almost to a standstill.

We do not seem willing to provide adequate protective services or institutional care for children in need of them. An example of our low priority for such services is the role and status of the child care worker which is quite different in the United States as compared to Scandinavian countries. In those countries the work has been professionalized through training programs that adequately prepare the worker—a preparation that is reflected in his relative income.

In the United States, in contrast, child care work is low-status work. Little is invested in professional preparation or in in-service training. And the pay is typically quite poor. The result is that few child care institutions are able to provide the quality of care and treatment that is needed.

It seems obvious that protective services *in the community*—counseling and supervision of parents and children—are called for. But it is also clear that the level of investment in community protective services is also inadequate.

Why, then, is there not *more* child abuse? Major forces work against it: 1) our society stresses the desirability of youth, the "happiness" of childhood and the reliving—with desirable modifications—of our own childhoods through our children; 2) our standard of living has increased, which attenuates the stress of physical survival—one of the sources of family stress that can lead to child abuse; and 3) for better or worse, there is a higher level of screening and surveillance in our highly organized society, where increasing amounts of information about each of us are collected and recorded at schools, hospitals, banks, license bureaus and so forth.

What, then, is to be done about child abuse? We cannot wait for all men and women to become angels to their children. One sensible, concrete proposal has been made to offer preventive mental and social hygiene services at the most obvious points of stress in the family. One such point is reached when a child is born and introduced into the family. This may be especially true for the first child, when husband and wife must now take on the additional roles of father and mother. Assistance for men and women who seem under unusual strain because of this role change might lead to fewer incidents of child abuse.

More effective remedial efforts will await our willingness to spend greater sums of money on community-based health and welfare services. Protective services are understaffed for the number of cases requiring their help and surveillance. And the alternative child care resources—whether they are institutions or paid individual or group foster homes—require additional resources if they are to be adequate either in terms of the number of children they can handle or in the quality of personnel.

What will we do about this tragic problem, apart from venting our concern for the child, and our rage and disgust toward the abuser? We could try to develop a more sensitive social monitoring network for the early identification of possible abuse cases. But our past efforts in this direction have resulted in only a slight improvement in reporting cases, and these, predictably, came primarily from lower socioeconomic classes and from racial minority groups. We are still, rightly, reluctant to invade the privacy and sanctity of most people's homes. And with the increasing encroachments on our privacy through telephone taps and recording devices, one is reluctant to propose another opportunity for the informers, however "benign" their intentions might be.

There is another part to this terrible dilemma. Neither professionals nor nonprofessionals are likely to report suspected cases of abuse when it is doubtful that such cases will subsequently receive adequate and effective service. Only when they are convinced that involving themselves in these difficult situations will result in positive benefits for the child, and his abuser, will the average citizen be willing to risk reporting cases of suspected child abuse.

July/August 1971

FURTHER READING

Violence Against Children by David G. Gil (Cambridge: Harvard University Press, 1970).

The Battered Child edited by Roy E. Helfer and C. Henry Kempe (Chicago: University of Chicago Press, 1968).

Wednesday's Children by Leontine Young (New York: McGraw-Hill, 1964).

EPILOGUE

Wednesday's Child

NORMAN K. DENZIN

Monday's child is fair of face,
Tuesday's child is full of grace,
Wednesday's child is full of woe,
Thursday's child has far to go,
Friday's child is loving and giving,
Saturday's child works hard for its living,
But the child that's born on the Sabbath day
Is bonny and blithe, and good and gay.
                    —from *The Real Mother Goose*

This *transaction/Society* volume has been directed to every person, parent, educator, politician, social scientist, social worker and physician who in some fashion enters into the process by which a child in the United States is shaped and molded into a human being. It has taken as its basic thesis the position that children, delinquents, drug users, dropouts and college students are social productions. Children are defined and acted on in diverse and contradictory ways, as can be seen in the courts, in families and in schools. Judges, parents and teachers expect children to act in ways that complement their own definitions of a good or bad child.

The moral career of every child in America today contains elements of Wednesday's child. While he or she may be fair of face and full of grace, he will at some point in his career confront frustration, hostility and woe. He will be treated as incompetent, arrogant, delinquent and childish. He will never completely satisfy his caretakers' expectations.

America's families, as the essays in this volume indicate, are painfully retarded in the stances they have taken towards children, education, the juvenile courts, the welfare systems and drug abuse programs. They have permitted large-scale bureaucratic systems of social control to take over what is their basic responsibility: seeing to it that children receive the best possible care and education. Each American, then, is in some degree accountable for the atrocities of the decaying school systems, is in some manner responsible for the plight of juveniles in the courts and jails of this country, is in some fashion obliged to ask why parents who abuse their children or physicians who knowingly prescribe tranquilizing drugs are permitted to do so. Everyone bears the burden of Wednesday's child.

These readings challenge the current systems of child socialization in the United States. The essays call for renewed citizen-parent involvement in society's educational tasks. They ask that Americans take seriously the charge that a democracy rests at root on the actions of its citizens. It is time for Americans to stop blaming the system for its failures. It is time to cease the endless debates over empty rhetorics. It is time to ask two questions. First, how can a more rational society be built? That is, how can a society such as our own bring its lofty aims, goals and ideals more in line with the everyday experiences of its members? Second, how can such a realignment of aims and experiences be accomplished? The answers have been implied. Citizens must deeply engage themselves in the political system, and, as each of the chapters in this book suggests, social science findings must be more systematically incorporated into national policy. A society that aims to be rational and just must start listening and taking seriously the one discipline in its midst that is committed to its study. Social scientists must take this charge seriously, and they must take their theories of the social world into that world. Until the findings of social scientists are grounded in the experiences of people, it can hardly be expected that people will take such findings seriously. Such is the dual challenge of this issue.

To repeat, this book will have served its purpose if it leads Americans to active involvement in their schools, courts and social welfare agencies. It will have served its end if politicians at the local, state and national level begin to question seriously what virtue there can be in legislation that never asks people what they want. It will have succeeded if it leads social scientists to concern themselves in research relevant to the lives of people. The fates of children are too important to be left in the hands of self-serving moralists. They are everyone's concern. It is time to take that charge seriously.

About the Authors

David Buckholdt ("Changing the Game from 'Get the Teacher' to 'Learn' ") is associate director of the Central Midwestern Regional Educational Laboratories. Buckholdt does experiments in the public schools with hyperaggressive and environmentally retarded ghetto children.

Donald Bushell ("Changing the Game from 'Get the Teacher' to 'Learn' ") is an assistant professor of sociology at the University of Kansas.

Richard A. Cohen ("Domestic Pacification") is a student majoring in political science at Boston University and was formerly administrative assistant with Boston Community Development, Inc., a regional OEO affiliate.

George D. Corey ("Domestic Pacification") is a student at Suffolk University Law School and was formerly on the New Hampshire Governor's Committee on Children and Youth.

Norman K. Denzin ("The Politics of Childhood," "The Work of Little Children," "Wednesday's Child") is associate professor of sociology at the University of Illinois, Urbana. For further information, see the cover.

Desmond Ellis ("Changing the Game from 'Get the Teacher' to 'Learn' ") is an assistant professor of sociology at the University of North Carolina.

Daniel Ferritor ("Changing the Game from 'Get the Teacher' to 'Learn' ") is associate director of the Central Midwestern Regional Educational Laboratories. He conducts experiments with autistic children.

A.D. Fisher ("White Rites and Indian Rights") is assistant professor of anthropology at the University of Alberta, Edmonton. He has written articles for various Canadian journals on North American Indians, and he co-edited, with Roger Owen and James J.F. Deetz, *The North American Indians: A Sourcebook*.

Estelle Fuchs ("How Teachers Learn to Help Children Fail") is a professor in the department of educational foundations, Hunter College of the City University of New York. Recent publications include studies of teachers in city schools, the Danish free schools and American Indians at school.

Robert L. Hamblin ("Changing the Game from 'Get the Teacher' to 'Learn' ") is a professor of sociology and psychology at the University of Arizona. He is completing work on *The Humanization Process: A Social Exchange Analysis of Children's Acculturation Problems* and *Foundations of a New Social Science*.

Carole Joffe ("Taking Young Children Seriously") is associated with the department of sociology and the Center for the Study of Law and Society, University of California, Berkeley.

Edwin M. Lemert ("Juvenile Justice—Quest and Reality") is an associate of the Center for the Study of Law and Society at the University of California, Berkeley, where he does research on California's juvenile court system. He served as a consultant on juvenile delinquency for the President's Commission on Law Enforcement and the Administration of Justice.

Paul Lerman ("Delinquents Without Crimes: The American Approach to Juvenile Status Offenses") is associate professor of social work at the Graduate School of Social Work, Rutgers University. He teaches courses on delinquency and social policy, social welfare policy and research. His major research interest is in understanding societal responses to youthful deviance.

Carol Olexa ("Programmed for Social Class: Tracking in American High Schools") is a faculty member at Evergreen State College, Olympia, Washington. She is co-author, with Walter Schafer, of *Tracking and Opportunity*.

Frank A. Petroni ("Teen-Age Interracial Dating") is assistant professor of sociology at the University of Arizona, Tuscon. He was formerly a research sociologist with the Meninger Foundation, Topeka, Kansas and is currently co-editing an anthology on labeling theory and social problems.

Kenneth Polk ("Programmed for Social Class: Tracking in American High Schools") is an associate professor of sociology at the University of Oregon. He is co-author, with Walter Schafer, of *Schools and Delinquency*.

Walter E. Schafer ("Programmed for Social Class: Tracking in American High Schools") is visiting associate professor at the University of Michigan. He is co-author of *Tracking and Opportunity* and *Schools and Delinquency*.

Margaret C. Silberberg ("The Right to Learn vs. the Right to Read") is the psychological consultant with the Family Health Project at Lutheran Deaconess Hospital in Minneapolis. She has done research in the areas of reading readiness and reading abilities and directed the development of a bookless program in eleventh grade humanities.

Norman E. Silberberg ("The Right to Learn vs. the Right to Read") is the director of research at Kenny Rehabilitation Institute in Minneapolis. He has worked as a school psychologist and has been lecturing and doing research in the areas of remedial reading, reading readiness, behavior problems and bookless programs.

Gilbert Y. Steiner ("Day Care Centers: Hype or Hope?") is senior fellow and director of the Governmental Studies Program at The Brookings Institution. He has written *The Congressional Conference Committee; Legislation by Collective Bargaining; Social Insecurity: The Politics of Welfare*; and *The State of Welfare*.

Charles Witter ("Drugging and Schooling") was staff director of Congressman Cornelius E. Gallagher's Special Subcommittee on

Invasion of Privacy and is now staff consultant to the House Committee on Foreign Affairs.

Serapio R. Zalba ("Battered Children") is chairman of the social services department at Cleveland State University. He is currently developing plans for a new jail in Cuyahoga County, Ohio and has written *Women Prisoners and Their Families*.